ARMED AND *Extremely* DANEROUS

THE PANORAMA OF WARFARE AND DELIVERANCE

Putting perspectives to the battles Christians face with principles for the cutting edge of life and ministry

Dr. Michael A. Frith, Ph.D

Armed And Extremely Dangerous

ISBN 10: 1-890430-38-2
ISBN 13: 978-1-890430-38-2

All Scripture quotations, unless otherwise stated, are from the King James Version of the Bible.

SECOND PRINTING

The use of short quotations or occasional extracts for personal or group study is permitted and encouraged.

Author contact:
Michael A. Frith Ministries
1448 Ferris Place
Bronx, N.Y. 10461
Bishopmfrith@aol.com
(718) 863-2363

Published by:
Triumph Publishing
P. O. Box 690158
Bronx, N.Y. 10469
www.triumphpublishing.net
(718) 652-7157

Printed in the United States of America
For Worldwide Distribution

TABLE OF CONTENTS

Acknowledgments

I would like to acknowledge and express gratitude for the following people who have had an impact on my life: My parents, Reginald F. H. Frith and Enid May Lee, for the regiment, discipline, training and godly values they instilled in me. Mom, thank you for your unwavering love, and untiring support. I will forever love you. Marcia, Annie, and Babs, my beautiful sisters, thank you for your support. Babs, your help has been invaluable to me; I love and respect you dearly. I thank God for my dearest wife, Lydia, who has been a faithful source of strength, support and encouragement to me over the past thirty five years; thank you for believing in me, and for your help in producing this book. I thank God for you. I also thank God for my children: Andre, Sean, Mike Jr., Christina and Iria; you are each a treasured gift of God to me. Thank you Chrissy for your help, ideas and encouragement in the putting together of this book; I will forever be grateful.

Dr. Audrey Barnett, the dean of Family of Christ Theological Seminary; I thank you for your support and devoted labor of love, and for your honesty and wise counsel. You have been a pillar of strength to me, and I am eternally grateful. My executive assistant, Michelle Dammar, for your tireless, labor of love, and those sacrifices that you made to make this book a reality; for the many hours of research, corrections, and godly counsel; thank you for believing in me. I will forever be grateful to the Lord for you.

Evangelist Hawthorne, thanks for the time you took in helping to edit this book, even when you were not feeling well, you pressed on. I thank God for you.

The ministerial board of Family of Christ, for your many prayers, your vote of confidence and your faithful support of me. I also want to express gratitude to the entire Family of Christ membership for your prayers and continued support; for your faith in me and for your steadfast love. May the Lord continue to bless and prosper you!

Most of all, I am eternally grateful to my Lord Jesus Christ, who has redeemed me with His own blood. Thank you Lord for your blessed and anointed hands upon me. You are truly wonderful.

PREFACE

There has never been a more demanding hour for spiritual awakening and warfare than that which exists right now. This is the climax of the age, and beginning of a new era; it is the end of the end times and the very age of which the prophets inquired about and angels desired to look into (1 Peter1:10-12).

We are living in a time of panoramic conflict, played out on the stages of our lives between the forces of good and evil. Here everyone is involved somehow at one time or another. This is not some small skirmish on the perimeters of Christian liberties, but a full-scale, all-out war. If you are a Christian then you are at war; you have been at war from the day you were saved, whether you know it or not. You are either fighting or being fought. Cosmic rebellion has brought the war to believers on every front. So, why not fight, and 'fight the good fight' effectively to win?

For too long we have been rocked by complacency in the crib of apathy by our ignorance, oblivious to battles that are raged around and against us daily. It is high time for us to awake and face the proverbial music of our age. The cost of ignorance is increasingly high and many are destroyed for lack of knowledge (Hosea 4:6). Others have gone into captivity, because they have no knowledge (Isaiah 5:13). *Armed and Extremely Dangerous* will empower and arm believers with the knowledge and principles for conducting effective spiritual warfare.

I have found two extremes in the Christian camp, one that says, "I don't mess with them, and they won't mess with me" and another which sees every situation or circumstance as an opportunity to conduct spiritual warfare, or cast out a devil. In this book I will endeavor to provide the tender balance which gives stability and spiritual stamina to the Christian walk and warfare (Isaiah 33:6).

It is not that the battlefields of life have confiscated the weapons of our fellow Christian-soldiers, but that they have voluntarily laid down their arms and have settled for a pseudo-peace. There can be no truce with the work of darkness!

There is a current revival of belief in the things of the devil, and we are seeing astonishing growth among the cult and occult groups. Have we asked ourselves why and how the devil has been able to successfully impact our world with evil? While the very source and force of God's power, being alive and at work in the believer, lays dormant to affect real change in our society? It is time to "come out and fight!" We are already in the war-zone where the *Prayerfully Militant Church* of the 21st century is arising with aggressive spiritual force to possess the promised land of this world, through intercessory prayer and spiritual warfare.

This is an exciting time of spiritual awakening. The renaissance of the *Church Age* is here—a re-birth of the power of Pentecost that makes the world take notice. The stage is being set for final conflict and world-harvest of souls. In times of war it is the generals that make the strategies and battle plans. It is also their responsibility to provide the implements and weapons of war.

When David went out to the battlefield, he deliberately chose his weapons: his staff, five smooth-stones, his bag, and his sling. The Scripture says: "*...and he drew near to the Philistine*" *(1 Samuel 17:40)*. David was armed indeed, but with unconventional weapons of his time. Nonetheless it was the armament for his battle, which proved to be a formidable and lethal weapon to his enemy (Goliath).

What is even more noteworthy about the outcome of our battle, is not the *weapons we employ* but the *tactic we deploy*. It takes a mindset, with right concepts, a working knowledge, and Biblical faith-principles to bring down the spiritual Goliaths of this millennium. The Bible says, "...that David hasted and ran toward the army to meet the Philistine" (1 Samuel 17:48). This is one of the main reasons for my writing this book. Far too often as a pastor, I have seen well meaning believers run from the battles of life, rather than towards it.

Introduction

Iam convinced that what we know and appropriate, rather than what we think we have, more often determines the outcome of our battles. Many have unfairly attributed their loss of life's battles to the sovereignty of God, and acts of the devil as God's will for their lives. Meanwhile, God desires his people to live above the mediocrity and to experience the abundant, overcoming, victorious Christian life. It is high time to know who the real enemy is and respond according to God's Word.

Armed and Extremely Dangerous is a book of Biblical Concepts for Principle-Applied Warfare. I am convinced that it is not power, wiles, knowledge or ability that liberates, but the *Truth* of God's Word that makes us free (John 8:32). My approach on the subject of spiritual warfare in this book is from a very practical viewpoint. Believers need to know how to proceed in the battles and conflicts with the enemy, and come out more than conquerors (Romans 8:37). We are often ashamed to admit the crushing blows that the work of darkness has dealt to the church and the believers.

The tragic problem of Christians being defeated by Satan and his forces are far more widespread than many of us would care to admit. Many are hurting, afraid and confused; victims, not so much of the oppression, tyranny, or victimization caused by Satan, but of the woeful lack of preaching and teaching on the subject of spiritual warfare and deliverance. The last thing we want to do is underestimate or over-estimate the enemy. It is also important that we keep a biblical balance in our warfare, and not allow ourselves to be paralyzed with fear of the Devil, or become so impracticably faith-minded, that we fail to address the realities of our Christian experiences. Even worse than these is for us to develop the mentality of seeing a 'demon around every corner, and behind every bush.' We cannot blame only the new-age, the world system, the internet, the Devil, or the occult world for the demise and destruction of the faith of many believers. God says in His Word;

> *"My people are destroyed for lack of knowledge: because thou hast rejected knowledge, I will also reject thee, that thou shalt be no priest to me..." (Hosea 4:6).*

Believers are destroyed for lack of knowledge, and rejected in their experience, because of their rejection of the knowledge of God's Word. Therefore it is quite safe to say that when they believe and receive the knowledge that God brings to them, they will be built-up, making their way prosperous, and then they shall have good success (Joshua 1:8). Without a basic knowledge of angelology, the end-time soldier and student of God's Word, in spite of his other qualifications, cannot be expected to make accurate evaluations or reach valid conclusions. His estimate of warfare, deliverance and intercession will be faulty and misleading.

This present age and stage calls for serious study on the subject of spiritual warfare and deliverance. As we see expanding supernaturalism of both good and evil, it is evident that knowledge is increasing; but only the wise will understand (Daniel 12:4; 10). Like the men of Issachar, *we must have an understanding of the times to know what ought to be done* (1 Chronicles 12:32). Let's face it, the fact is that the Holy Spirit has also come to reveal the enemy and expose his gates to the awesome power of the advancing church. Surely the gates of hell shall not prevail against it (Matthew 16:18).

After the apostle Paul had fulfilled his purpose in life and ministry, he concluded, *"I have fought a good fight, I have finished my course, I have kept the faith." (2 Timothy 4:7).* This should be the benediction of every believer. It is my sincere prayer that *Armed and*

Extremely Dangerous will bring lightning clarity and thundering understanding to your walk and warfare, equipping and enabling you to operate in the principles of spiritual might and success.

Although the market is flooded with books on warfare and deliverance, there are only few that give the how-to in obtaining victory. More than just statistics or facts, we need a working knowledge of the principles that do work.

This book is about strategic warfare principles, and how to triumph even though you may encounter set-backs and the odds may be against you.

It is my prayerful intention to revolutionize your mind-set with bulldog tenacity, and ardent stickability. The battle is not over till you triumph. Faith secrets will produce faith results when it is faithfully deployed. Fight a good fight, finish your course with excellence, and keep the Christian faith with dignity and integrity.

1

THE POWER OF INTERCESSION

A Personal Encounter

It was nine thirty in the night. The moon calmly caressed the darkness, scattering her dim light across the darkened skies, while the stars complimented the galactic heavens with her splendor on this clear summer night. The summer breeze blew serenely over the house and through the windows. I returned home earlier that evening from a full day at the office, my body was aching from the long hours of standing while at work. I felt somewhat dehydrated and a bit fatigued.

This was the third and final day of my three-day fast. At several intervals during the course of the day I was engaged quite vigorously in intercessory warfare prayers. By the close of the day I felt spiritually drained; it was as if all virtue had gone from me. I was so exhausted that evening that even though a small pot of chicken soup was prepared for me earlier to aid in breaking the fast, I was not able to sit and enjoy it.

I plopped in the bed, muttered a quick prayer, pulled up a thin sheet over my head and snuggled comfortably under it. As I laid there in the bed it occurred to me that I had not spent time with the family that evening, nor did I make inquiry of how they had spent their day; but I selfishly said to myself, 'At last, rest, sweet rest!' I quickly drifted off to sleep, and was suddenly awakened by the loud and piercing ringing of my telephone. Being anxious to silence the ringing, I quickly jumped up to answer it.

Fumbling in the dark to locate the phone, I grasped it and placed the receiver to my ear. On the other end of the line she screamed frantically, "Pastor, please help me. Let them leave me alone, let them go away, help me please!" I replied, "Who is bothering you sister?" She shouted deliriously, "Demonic spirits are all over my home!" Still a bit sleepy, with the phone now pressed up against my ear, I said, "Tell me, in what way are they bothering you?" She blurted out, "I can see dark shadows shifting back and forth, and there is an awful smell in my house, like rotten eggs."

Many thoughts flashed through my head at that moment. I was tempted to ask her, "Where have you been over the past few days, and what were your activities?" Instead, I said, "Did you pray sister?" She blurted out angrily, "Yes pastor! I prayed in my bedroom, and the smell went to the living-room." She proceeded, "I prayed binding the unclean spirits from the living-room and they went to the kitchen, I have anointed everywhere with olive oil in Jesus' name and they are still in the house, please do something!" she yelled angrily.

I realized that it was pointless to reason with her in that condition. Then I thought to myself, 'Let me just dismiss this case as quickly as possible with prayer, so both this sister and myself can get a good night's rest.' I shuffled to the edge of the bed and placed my feet on the ground. With one hand holding the phone I used my other hand to wipe my face, then I said in an authoritative voice,

'Sister, hold the phone up in the air!' I then proceeded, "By virtue of my union with Jesus Christ and seated with him in heavenly places, and by the delegated authority of Christ Jesus, I bind you prince of the power of the air, and every unclean spirit of the atmosphere. I restrict your activity and neutralize your power and authority in that home in the name of Jesus Christ of Nazareth. I command you to cease your oppression against God's child and leave that household now! I annul your work! I cancel your assignment and I challenge you to come out of her home right now in Jesus' name!"

The prayer was electrifying and fervent. The sister on the other end of the phone began to praise the Lord, thanking Him for his greatness and power of deliverance. Shortly afterwards she expressed her gratitude for my intercessory warfare prayer and for her deliverance.

Standing In the Gap

I have found that intercessory prayer has the power to ruin Satan's evil strategies. It throws a wrench in his spokes and literally shuts him down. It is not only objective, but intercession is also a subjective means of bringing healing to our nation's bitter experiences. We release healing through intercessory prayer. In Exodus 15:25, Moses cried out unto God for the bitter waters of Marah. The Lord showed him a tree. When he cast it into the bitter waters, the waters were made sweet. As I stood in the gap, I made myself the buffer between this sister and the bitter works of the enemy, and now I became their target.

*Standing in the gap for someone
can place us at times in a place
of danger and high risk.*

17

When Jesus stood in the gap for mankind, He endured all that was intended for the fallen human race, and interceded to God the Father on our account. Conversely, when we stand in the gap for someone, we place ourselves between the victim and the perpetrator, and between the need and the source, putting us at risk to endure all that is intended for the person under attack. We stand as intercessors!

The Ministry Of Intercession

"I exhort therefore, that, first of all, supplications, prayer, intercessions, and giving of thanks, be made for all men" (1 Timothy 2:1).

"And I sought for a man among them, that should make up the hedge, and stand in the gap before me for the land, that I should not destroy it: but I found none" (Ezekiel 22:30).

"And He saw that there was no man, and wondered that there was no intercessor: therefore His arm brought salvation unto him; and his righteousness, it sustained Him" (Isaiah 59:16).

True Intercession is much more than just Standing in the gap.

It is evident from the aforementioned Scripture passages, that as the watchmen in Zion, we have a serious responsibility to God, and also to our neighbor. We are called into a high tower of prayer and intercession. The law of prayer is one of the highest laws of the universe. As we move into the ministry of intercession we become the means by which God enforces His will on the earth.

There must be a uniting of His will on earth and His will in heaven. The will of God is being done in heaven through the intercessory, High-priestly ministry of Jesus. The Scripture declares: *"Wherefore he is able also to save them to the uttermost that come unto God by him, seeing he ever liveth to make intercession for them" (Hebrews 7:25).*

An intercessor is that person who fights or pleads on the behalf of another person or place through the power of prayer. Intercessors stand in the gap by waging war in the heavenlies. The English word "Intercede" is derived from a two-fold Latin word: *Inter-* between, and *cedere*, to go. Webster's dictionary defines "intercession" as to make a request on behalf of another or others, *to mediate as a go-between.* Hence, as we see the aggressive advance of evil and depravity sweep over our world, we have a moral and spiritual responsibility to enter militantly into the ministry of intercession. Intercessory prayer is said to strike the target when there is a specific crisis at hand. "Peter was therefore kept in prison, but constant prayer was offered to God for him by the church (Acts 12:5). Today, many people are kept in spiritual prisons and require intercessory warfare prayers. We must accurately strike the targets of bondage through intercession and allow these people to experience true freedom.

Abraham was a great intercessor. He interceded for Sodom and Gomorrah with its inhabitants, which included his nephew Lot and his family (Genesis 18:23-33). Moses also was certainly an undisputed intercessor. He interceded on Israel's behalf before Pharaoh and before the Lord on several occasions. However a classical case of intercession is found in Exodus chapter 17, and although this intercession was non verbal it was packed with powerful principles of the Reality of Spiritual Warfare.

When Israel came out of Egypt, one of the nations they encountered on their wilderness journey was Amalek, which means, **'warlike,'** a descendant of Esau (the twin brother of Jacob). Israel pitched their tent in a place called Rephidim, which signifies a **"proving ground."** It was here that Israel would be proven as a viable people. Israel's leadership would also be proven in symbols of intercession and warfare.

19

As leaders we have authority. Along with that authority there must be responsibility, accountability, stability, sensibility, availability, reliability, and stick-ability. The battle can be lost without the faithful discharge of these. However, do bear in mind:

The outcome of your battle is not necessarily based on your abilities but on your ability to war a good warfare.

"Then came Amalek, and fought with Israel in Rephidim. And Moses said unto Joshua, choose us out men, and go out, fight with Amalek: tomorrow I will stand on the top of the hill with the rod of God in mine hand. So Joshua did as Moses said unto him, and fought with Amalek: and Moses, Aaron, and Hur went up on the top of the hill.
And it came to pass, when Moses held up his hand, that Israel prevailed: and when he let down his hand, Amalek prevailed. But Moses' hands were heavy; and they took a stone, and put it under him, and he sat thereon; and Aaron and Hur stayed up his hands, the one on the one side, and the other on the other side; and his hands were steady until the going down of the sun. And Joshua discomfited Amalek and his people with the edge of the sword" (Exodus 17:8–13).

Moses' intercessory act was the means by which Israel won the war over Amalek. Although the people who were with Joshua did the physical fighting, their victory was predicated upon the intercession of Moses on the mountain top. **When we employ warfare strategies of intercession we will see victory in the lives of others, and ultimately victory in our own lives as well.**

PRINCIPLES TO LIVE BY

- Every ministry, whether congregational or governmental, must be proven at spiritual Rephedim   (Exodus 17:1).

- Recognize the delegated authority that God has placed over you, their intercession could determine your outcome in a given battle (Exodus 17:2-4).

- There is a transitional point in ministry, when we move from among the people to lead the people by example in going ahead of them (Exodus 17:5). There will come moments when you must rise above them (Exodus 17:9).

- Maintain your purpose, exercise your authority, and go forward as a leader; although the people may be disgruntled with your leadership, and not grasp your vision. Never reduce yourself to the level of crying to them (Exodus 17:4-5).

- It is not what is done in a congregation that determines its success in battle, but what is done with leadership in the midst of it (Exodus 17:11).

- Remember, the supportive *ministry of helps* that stands on the mountaintop with leadership largely determines the outcome among the people of God (Exodus 17:10-12; 1 Corinthians 12:28).

- We must be sensitive to leadership overload and unsteady hands. What we do for leadership can determine the prosperity of ministry (Exodus 17:12).

- Supportive ministries should always place the leader's health, comfort, peace of mind and environment as a priority. While the leader stands in the gap for the people, his intercessory team must stand in the gap for him (Exodus 17:12).

2

THE REALITY
OF OUR WARFARE

Prayer Produces Change

Rulers and nations over the years have had their laws and decrees annulled and altered through the power of prayer and intercession. A classic example is seen in the book of Daniel. We see how the evil presidents and princes of Babylonia influenced King Darius to make a decree against prayer power, which resulted in Daniel being cast into the den of lions. Through the power of prayer, Daniel emerged unscathed to declare, *"My God hath sent His angel, and hath shut the lions' mouth, that they have not hurt me" (Daniel 6:22).*

Through the power of prayer King Darius was forced to change his decree, and those evil princes were thrown instead into the lions' den. There they suffered the fate intended for Daniel, the servant of God. Prayer will reverse the decree!

The invincibility of prayer will open every servant's eyes. We are reminded of Elisha's servant, who panicked when he saw the forces of the Syrian detachment that had surrounded the place where they were (2 Kings 6:14-17). He was paralyzed with fear. This was a new servant, who had only been with him since Gehazi's dismissal and consequently had little or no experience of his master's power. His faith was greatly shaken by this unexpected alarm, he cried, *"Alas my master! How shall we do?"* (2 Kings 6:15).

An awakening to The Reality of Your Warfare could move you to either act, or react.

Elisha prayed *(intercessory prayer)*, and said, *"O Lord I pray thee, open his eyes that he may see the invisible guard of angels that encompass and defend us…. And he saw: and, behold, the mountains was full of horses and chariots of fire round about Elisha"* (2 Kings 6:17; Psalm 34:7).

The Concept of Binding

It is important to know where the teaching of binding and loosing has its genesis. The Biblical antecedent of the term and concept has its beginning in the Old Testament. Biblical Theology that examines the *"Volume of The Book"* (Psalm 40:7), finds the grounds for the doctrine of binding and loosing in the New Testament book of Matthew 18:18. We see it also in symbols of authority, rights and privileges of believers in the Old Testament book of Psalms.

"Let the saints be joyful in glory: let them sing aloud upon their beds. Let the high praise of God be in their mouth, and a two-edged

sword in their hand; To execute vengeance upon the heathen, and
punishments upon the people; To bind their kings with chains, and
their nobles with fetters of iron. To execute upon them the judgment
written: this honour have all the saints. Praise ye the Lord"
(Psalm 149:5-9).

This verse, along with Psalm 105:17-22, refers to Joseph in Egypt by providential design. He is found in a place of *authority* evidenced by his capability to bind even princes, which displays the principle of binding. A prince is a *chief one*. Therefore, when we bind principalities, we bind the chief rulers. The Scriptures says, *"To bind their kings with chains"* *(Psalm 149:8).*

We have the keys: *"And I will give unto thee the keys of the kingdom of heaven: and whatsoever thou shalt bind on earth shall be bound in heaven: and whatsoever thou shalt loose on earth shall be loosed in heaven"* *(Matthew 16:19).*

Keys are a symbol of authority and power. It gives the right of entry in allowing, and the power of forbidding in disallowance. The keys of the kingdom are the delegated authority given by Jesus Christ himself to the believer. We act as the power of attorney for Him in His physical absence. The believer has been endowed with divine inalienable rights. These rights are given to be exercised by one empowered to dominate. The keys of our rights are:

1. **The Key of Binding (Matthew 16:19; 18:18)**
2. **The Key of Loosing (Matthew 16:19;18:18)**
3. **The Key of Knowledge (Luke 11:52)**

The power to bind signifies compelling
obedience, and inexorable submission.

"Binding" also signifies restriction, restraint, prohibition, hindrance, prevention, preclusion, stoppage, interruption, retardation, constriction, blockade, interference, and obstruction.

When we say, "I Bind You Satan!" What are we actually saying?

It is to be understood, that when Christians say, "I bind you Satan," they know that he will eventually be bound for 1,000 years, but it will be an angel that binds him, not a mortal being (Revelation 20:1-2). Jesus helps us understand how one equates the work of Satan with Satan. He cast a spirit of infirmity out of a woman who had been bound for 18 years. Then later, when explaining what He had done, He said that *Satan* had kept her bound for 18 years (Luke 13:10-16). When Jesus said that, I don't think he meant that Satan himself had spent the last 18 years afflicting the woman, but that he was ultimately responsible for her affliction.

So with that in mind, when we say, *"I bind you Satan!"* What are we actually saying? Well, we are actually saying to ourselves and to others that we detest the devil and that we stand in opposition to him, his plans, his ways, and his cohorts (demons). We actually neutralize his activities and the demons that work for him.

It is appropriate for us to say, "I bind you, Satan!" as long as we understand the limitations of such an activity. While it is unlikely that we may have a direct confrontation with Satan himself, we must understand that we have a mandate to confront his demonic forces on all levels lower than himself.

There are occasions when a believer may have a confrontation directly with Satan. It is on such occasions that the Lord *Himself* steps in to engage our arch enemy on that level of spiritual warfare. Our role in such cases depends upon the battle plan of our Lord and Savior, which He will reveal as the battle ensues.

When I am binding then, what I am actually doing is placing myself by my words authoritatively in the light of *my relationship* to Christ; between the threat and the threatened, between the perpetrator and his targeted victim. Saying, *"I bind you!"* means that I am standing as a buffer and shield, to deflect, cancel, block, obstruct, or neutralize the powers of darkness aimed at the person or thing I am interceding for.

Quite often when we stand in the gap through intercessory prayer and warfare, the blows that were intended for others are dealt to us. However, when we know who we are in Christ and exercise our rights by standing on the merits of the redemptive blood and the power of Christ's atonement, the wicked one's attacks are repelled and we stand victorious.

If you remember earlier in chapter one, when I commanded the evil spirits to leave the sister's home, I told them to 'leave her home now!' However, the thing that I failed to tell them was where to go. I was taught that when you cast out devils they would go back to hell from whence they came. But I was taught wrong, and this I would learn the hard way. I was about to be rudely awakened to the reality of the warfare.

As you stand in proxy for someone, their fight becomes your fight, and your victory becomes their victory.

Standing in the gap is a kind of buffer, or insulation; it can also be seen as a vicarious way of going between two opposing parties.

The Encounter Continued Later that Night

It was approximately 11:15 pm. The children had turned in for the night and I had just finished intercessory prayer with the sister over the phone. I sat on the edge of the bed pondering on the Scripture that says:

"For though we walk in the flesh, we do not war after the flesh: For the weapons of our warfare are not carnal, but mighty through God to the pulling down of strongholds" (2 Corinthians 10:3-4).

My wife, Lydia, entered the room and joined me in prayer. We prayed together, touching and agreeing for the sister's continued freedom and peace, and also for our own family as well. After the prayer, I felt a sense of victory, as a calm peace swept over my soul. It was not long afterwards that I drifted off into a deep sleep.

They Answered the Challenge

Approximately one hour later, I was vigorously shaken by Lydia who cried urgently and repeatedly, "Mike! Warfare! Warfare!" Although I was in a deep sleep, I responded spontaneously with strong rebukes and pleading the merits of Christ's blood. Being unable to open my eyes properly, I leaped from the bed and plunged immediately into the opened doorway, with Lydia behind me fervently rebuking and binding the enemy.

I lunged forward through the opened bedroom door and into the hallway. I then opened the door that led down the stairs and outside the home. As I stood there I could sense the presence of the demonic spirits of fear, torment, and oppression. I said, 'You demons of oppression, fear and torment, I take authority over you in the name of Jesus

Christ my Lord, I bind you in the name of Jesus.' I further declared, 'Prince of the powers of the air, you cannot operate in this house, this home is committed to the Lord, and the occupants within this home are covered under the blood of Jesus Christ, you are trespassers here. I bind you and command you to leave now in Jesus' name!'

As I discharged them, I plunged down the stairs vehemently with my right hand extended outward as though gripping a sword. I opened the door leading out of the home and said, "In the authority of the name of Jesus I cancel your assignment against me and my household this night, and I expel you into outer darkness. Leave right now in Jesus name!"

When Lydia and I returned upstairs, we walked though the house praising God and affirming our victory. Soon after, as we laid in bed reminiscing over the events of the evening, I began to inquire concerning the events that led to *my frantic awakening* earlier that night. She proceeded to tell me, that about 1:00 am she was asleep, when she heard a loud "thump!" and our bedroom door flew wide open. As she laid there in a still position on her left side, and I on my right facing her, snoring mildly, she looked intently and expectantly to see who had flung the door open so violently and disrespectfully. To her surprise, no one was at the door.

It was then that she became startled, because the force that flung the door open was so intense that the door deflected against the wall, which was to the side of it. As she lay there looking towards the doorway, she was distracted by some movement in the mirror which was a part of our bed-head. As she focused her attention toward the mirror she saw a woman entering through our bedroom doorway. The bedroom was dimly lit by a baby-light, or what we call a night-light. The woman's head was wrapped with a sheet and she had a fierce look on her face. She came to the foot of the bed, the side where Lydia laid. The woman gave a glancing look at her, and then walked briskly to my side of the bed and stood over me looking. This she did apparently because she was challenged by my prayer of intercession for the sister earlier that evening. The woman appeared to be extremely agitated as she stood over me while I lay asleep on the bed. It was at this point that the woman stepped back to the entrance of the doorway and began beckoning to someone in the living room, which was across from our bedroom. Lydia thought she was calling for someone else to come into the room so she turned, looked away from the mirror directly towards the door, where the woman stood, but she did not see her. She looked again in the mirror, and to her surprise, there she was!

After looking back and forth between the mirror and the doorway a few times, Lydia ascertained that what she was seeing was real and cried out, "Mike! Warfare! Warfare!" It was her frantic cry that awakened me. After discussing the events of the night and praying together, we both drifted off to sleep.

The Next Morning

As the family awoke and prepared themselves for school, my daughter Christina, who was 15 years old at the time, entered my bedroom and asked, to my surprise, "Dad, what happened in the house last night?" I then said, trying to pacify her need to know, "Oh just a little spiritual warfare honey," to which she replied, "I don't think so!" I then said to her, "What happened, did we scare you with all that binding and rebuking?" It was then that she said, "No, that wasn't what scared me." I then said curiously, "What then?" She replied, "I heard a loud noise coming from outside, so I looked to see what had happened. I looked across the living room and saw your room door opened. I also saw people in the living room fighting but I couldn't hear any sound. There was a woman at your door calling them into your bedroom, but they couldn't go in because they were fighting furiously outside in the living-room." She continued, "Then all of a sudden, you came charging out of the bedroom like a mad man binding and rebuking. The next thing I knew is that you violently opened the door to the stairs and drove all of them down the stairs."

Now, what my wife Lydia and my daughter Christina saw were the delayed reaction and retaliation to the challenge given during the warfare prayers for the sister on the phone earlier that evening. When I told her to hold up the phone into the air, I made a direct attack against these invading forces and to the prince of the power of the air that was in the home of this oppressed sister, when I told them to 'come out now, in Jesus name!' That was an open invitation to take on my challenge, because I had disrupted their assignment of oppression and terror. When I told them to 'come out now in Jesus name!' they sure did, but they came to my house. I neglected to tell them where to go. I should have assigned them to wherever Jesus sends them; to outer darkness, or into dry places (Matthew 12:43).

Where Do We Send Them?

There are times when I hear believers sending demonic spirits into hell from whence they came. This practice is not biblical because hell was indeed prepared for them but not all of them came from hell (Matthew 25:41; Revelation 20:14-15). There was a certain class of angels that was assigned to hell, bound in chains, and reserved unto judgment (Jude vs.6).

The types of demons that Jesus encountered while he walked the earth are still operating here today. We have no account of Jesus sending demons to hell. In fact, on one occasion the demons expressed the knowledge that the final judgment and their assignment to hell had not yet come.

"And when he was come to the other side into the country of the Gergesenes, there met him two possessed with devils, coming out of the tombs, exceeding fierce, so that no man might pass by that way. And, behold, they cried out, saying, What have we to do with thee, Jesus, thou Son of God? art thou come hither to torment us before the time?"
(Matthew 8:28-29).

While we understand from scripture that it is not biblical to send demons to hell, we are told by the apostle Paul that the saints shall judge angels (1 Corinthians 6:3). However, let me remind you not to judge anything prematurely (1Corinthians 4:5). Satan and his demons will eventually receive final judgment from the Lord, but in the meanwhile let's send them wherever Jesus wills; dry places, or outer darkness. Sending them back to the pit of hell from whence they came, would not be either biblical or factual.

I want to remind you also that there are regions and territories dominated by certain spirits. When you command the evil spirit to depart from a person, place, or thing, you should address all the worker-spirits associated with the strongman or dominant spirit. If you fail to address them, it may result in them forming a cluster and you may run the risk of opening again the door for another dominant strongman to enter.

Mi throw mi corn, but mi nuh call nuh fowl!

In the early 90's, I was engaged in heavy spiritual warfare as a part of my ministry. The work of deliverance took me into many countries. As the demands grew greater at home and abroad, I thought it necessary to purchase again a book that was given to me by a man in the early 80's when a series of misfortunes took place in my life. I had since then burnt that copy of the book because of its occult contents. However, years later I purchased a new copy to investigate the inner workings of the underworld. The book was called, *"The Sixth and Seventh Books of*

Moses." Although I believe the Bible to be the inerrant, infallible, inspired and final authority of God, there was a curiosity to know more of what Moses wrote after the Pentateuch (five books).

While growing up in the island of Jamaica, we always heard about the mysterious writings of Moses and the Hebrew Kabbalah, which were hidden from the black man. We would hear songs like, "Bring back Maccabee version that God gave to black man." We heard tales of mysterious happenings on account of the books, such as; *Greater Keys of Solomon* and the Books of Moses. The materials in the *Sixth and Seventh Books of Moses* are extended to the eighth, ninth, and tenth books.

In my early days as a youth growing in Jamaica, I would hear strange stories of people's furniture being removed from their homes and placed on the sidewalk without anyone carrying it. There were also rampant accounts of people's houses being stoned by unseen hands. It was common knowledge that when the poorer people were unable to purchase things, they would arrange loans and credit from organizations very much like the Mafia loan sharks.

One such organization was a family called the "Delawrence's." Tradition tells us that this organization would send spirits to pressure their clients to pay their debts, and quite often when the client was late in paying or neglected to pay the organization would 'conjure-up' (invoke) spirits from the "Books of Moses" and send them to do their bidding. These same books that they were alleged to have used to 'conjure-up' spirits were now in my possession. It was indeed frightening to read, because it opened by warning the reader not to handle the book lightly, or there would be adverse consequences.

Although I was a Christian and a deliverance worker, my curiosity got the better of my judgment. I was aware that the book was occult material and not suitable for believers, so I hid it in a small room in my house next to the kitchen. I thought to myself, "If I could see how the enemy operate, I would be better informed and more knowledgeable about the spirit world," but I was soon to realize how very wrong I was.

Each night I would hear walking in my bedroom, back and forth. I prayed but each night it would return, louder and louder. My wife also would hear it and we would pray the prayer of deliverance but it would still return. We thought the house may have been haunted and began to inquire more about the phenomenon. I decided to ask my father in-law, who was a seasoned Christian what he thought.

He was such a wise man. He asked me one question that was the key, he asked, 'Do you have anything in your home for the enemy?' My God, that was it! I went into the room and tore the sixth part of the book out and burned it. The sixth part of the book contained drawings of pentagrams and Hebrew hieroglyphics, with holy names and secrets.

It even gave the conjurations to duplicate many of the plagues of Egypt, the casting of curses, and more; however, I kept the seventh part in a container hidden in the room, because it contained mostly the power of the Psalms and the undoing of curses and spells.

The next night the walking came back into my room, only this time like a violent decisive march. I rebuked the presence in Jesus' name, and almost immediately it shifted to the small room (pantry) where all the pots, pans, and items that were in the room were violently thrown aside. When I looked into the container the seventh part was gone. I learned a valuable lesson that day: **The enemy is careful to promote and protect what is his, and if you have what is his, he is entitled to have what is yours.**

Far too often I have seen well meaning people, whom in an attempt to better their lives, create a doorway for complications and demonic oppression, by seeking help in the wrong places. How in the world can anyone expect Satan to betray himself or free him or her from himself? It does not serve his own self-interest to be divided in his kingdom.

"... How can Satan cast out Satan? And if a kingdom be divided against itself, that house cannot stand. And if Satan rise up against himself, and be divided he cannot stand, but hath an end. No man can enter into a strong man's house, and spoil his goods, except he will first bind the strong man; and then he will spoil his goods" (Mark 3:23).

It is ironic that you can look all around and not find one bee. Yet as soon as you put down some honey exposed outside, the bees seem to find it. In like manner, the things of darkness attract the source of darkness. The agent of evil will always be attracted to evil.

What's In Your Camp?

Many of the people who go into the enemy's camp seeking help, when they take the charms, amulets, talisman, oils, candles and such-like into their homes, business, or on their person, do so and unwittingly attract demonic spirits. There is an accompanying spirit to every ouija board, tarot card, dungeon and dragons and all that pertain to the occult world. Whenever we bring these things into our lives, we open the door for demonic infestations.

The Bait-and Switch

The entertaining of occult materials, literature, amulets, charms, fetishes, oils, candles, talisman, and gems, are some of the reasons why so many people's lives are *crossed-up* with complications, rebellions, oppressions, suppressions, depressions, deceptions, bondage and demonic infiltrations. Satan gives *temporary* relief in order to secure a *permanent* subject.

Another aspect of the ***demonic bait*** is that while you may be relieved of one problem, a gateway is opened up for a host of other problems. It is only logical then that his workers transform themselves into workers of good deeds to attract the unsuspecting; In Second Corinthians 11:14, the bible declares: *"And no marvel; for Satan himself is transformed into an angel of light."* Satan has recruiters out there, "vessels of dishonor" if you will. The main purpose of these recruiters is to lure the ignorant, unsuspecting, the vulnerable and the curious. Quite often they fascinate with their psychic abilities, that even the skeptic is inclined to show an interest. They promise liberty but they are unable to deliver. They are servants of corruption (2 Peter 2:19).

The enemy specializes in *"bait and switch."* Many satanic recruiters use fortune telling as a means to snare the souls of men. I have seen people expose themselves to the occult for healing from a spirit of infirmity, only to receive a spirit of bondage in exchange. The oppressor exchanges the oppression to check-mate the soul. Deception and lies are the devils prerogative. He will give a six for a nine, and swap a black-dog for a monkey. In other words, he will give you something that looks like what you want, but in reality it is something completely different. That is a bait and switch!

When we use the things that proceed from the dark side we attract the works of darkness. It may just appear in lesser degrees of light, but in the true light of God's Word, it is thick darkness. You cannot put down honey and not attract bees, wherever the carcass is, vultures will gather together.

What my daughter heard when she heard those people in our living room fighting, were the angels that encamp round about us. They were doing battle on my behalf against the demonic spirits which had responded to my challenge to spiritual warfare. I want you to understand that God supernaturally alerted my wife on time to the presence of these invading forces, through the reflection in the mirror. This gave me enough time to launch a counter attack that gave us the victory.

There is Price to Pay

It is unlikely that a fighter would enter into the ring and fight for twelve rounds and emerge untouched; even if he is the victor, there are usually bumps and bruises which are the tell-tale signs that he had been in a fight. The physical fatigue, listlessness, and loss of energy that I experienced after that encounter lasted for several days. There are times when the back-lash of the battle may carry over into other areas as well. We must be vigilant, especially after a great battle; the enemy is a sore loser.

We should not become carless after a victory, but be even more sober and vigilant. Remember; *"be sober, be vigilant; because your enemy goeth about like a roaring lion seeking whom he may devour" (1 Peter 5:8-9)*. Walk in forgiveness and love, *"Lest Satan should get an advantage of us: for we are not ignorant of his devices" (2 Corinthians 2:11)*.

There may be a price to pay in waging effective warfare, but the rewards of victory and deliverance are truly sweet.

Close the Door through Repentance & Denunciation

A Prayer of Faith and Deliverance

If you are one of those who may have gone into the enemy's camp for help, pray this prayer now for your release and forgiveness. Pray,

'Heavenly Father I acknowledge my sin before you, of seeking help from elsewhere (say the source). I ask your forgiveness now; cleanse me thoroughly with your redeeming blood through Jesus Christ my Lord. I denounce every involvement and practice that is displeasing to you, I surrender my will, my life, and my all to you, I return to you now, as the giver of life, my Lord and personal savior. I refute, reject and cancel every satanic retaliation and backlash now, and I stand justified in the presence of my Lord and savior, in Jesus name!'

Now take those things which belong to the enemy and dispose of them. Some of these items should be burnt, while others could be dumped into an incinerator in Jesus name. It is also recommended that certain items be broken, bound, and buried in a remote place in Jesus' name. After you have properly disposed of the items, you must take time now to read your bible regularly. I recommend that you read the New Testament thoroughly. Take time also to pray; prayer is a vital part of our growth, spiritual development, and relationship with the Lord. Fellowship with the people of God is equally as important, it provides the security, the strength, the accountability, and the environment needed to hone your gifts and empower you for your God given calling. Make it your point of duty to assemble yourself in the house of God regularly, growing in grace, and in the knowledge of our Lord and savior Jesus Christ.

READER'S DIGEST

Thoughts to Consider

Let me take this time to provoke your mind into reflecting on the previous chapter.

- When we stand in the gap and make up the hedge where does that put us?

- One should always assess the battle before engaging in it. The spoils of war are usually the determining factor that leads men and nations to war. *Is it worth fighting for?*

- What are some disadvantages in being a lone ranger?

- Does an intercessor only speak on another's behalf?

- Binding the enemy is more than just restricting, hindering, or neutralizing him.

- The enemy recognizes the opportunity for spiritual engagement, when we challenge him, he is ready for a fight, even when we have long forgotten about it, he, still bears it in mind.

- When we have materials and goods from the enemy's camp, he turns up to support or fight for it.

- If sending demons to hell is not biblical, then where should we send them?

- Could our assignment against demonic spirits become a revolving door at any time?

- The doors of entrance should be the doors of exit.

- There are some things that attract evil activities, can you name a few?

- The battle may be unseen, but it is no less real than the things that are sensually perceived.

3

THROUGH OPEN DOORS

Who Opened That Door?

"He that diggeth a pit shall fall into it; and whoso breaketh an hedge, a serpent shall bite him" (Ecclesiastes 10:8).

The sister, whom I had interceded for, unknown to me at the time, had gone into a botanica store (a retail outlet for occult materials, etc.), where tarot-cards were read on her behalf, attempting to foretell her future. She had also received some items which she thought would help her to alleviate some of her problems caused by her enemies. She was told that by carrying some of these items on her body she would get relief from misfortune and attract prosperity.

As a believer, this sister was seeking help in all the wrong places. She was in willful rebellion against God's Word.

"There shall not be found among you any one that maketh his son or his daughter to pass through the fire, or that useth divination, or an observer of times, or an enchanter, or a witch, or a charmer, or a

consulter with familiar spirits, or a wizard, or a necromancer.
For all that do these things are an abomination unto the Lord:
and because of these abominations the Lord thy God doth drive
them out from before thee" (Deuteronomy 18:10-12).

She had broken her own hedge through the sin of disobedience, creating a doorway for satanic activity. She had eroded her own spiritual defenses through her ungodly actions. A breach or gap had been created in her life. It is what we often refer to as "a kink in one's armor."

The Doorway

Because of the disobedience of one man (Adam), a gap was made into this world that allowed evil to enter in upon all of mankind (Romans 5:12).

In recent years there has been such a growing increase of failure in ministries, to the extent that many churches have seen serious decline in their membership, on account of the disillusionment they have experienced within the 'organized churches.' Most of these failures in ministry can be attributed to "open doors." A majority of these failures would not have occurred if persons did not give some place to the devil in their minds. The enemy cannot operate in your life without your conscious or unconscious consent. He has absolutely no power to steal, kill, or destroy without permission or an open door. When an entrance is located, the evil spirits send suggestions and strong impressions that form footholds that can lead to strongholds in your mind, and oppression in your life. Paul cautioned the church of Ephesus:

"Be ye angry, and sin not: let not the sun go down upon your wrath.
Neither give place to the devil" (Ephesians 4:26-27).

The Greek word for *"place"* is the verb *topos* NT: 5117, from (Eng., topic or topography, which is the study of lands and contours, etc.). The word *"place"* is used of 'a region' or 'locality.' Paul warns believers not to give even a piece of ground to the devil. This is to be understood in the light that whenever the devil sizes up your life, his survey includes all that pertains to you.

You cannot give the devil a foothold of ground in your life and he not advance to take all of your property. He is not content to take only the areas that we allow him to have, but he seeks total dominion, therefore we are admonished by Paul not to give him a grain of sand!

Quite often when there is personal failure we hear people say; "The devil is responsible for this!" It has always been the tendency of mankind to shift the blame of personal failure on someone else, or on some external force or situation out of their control.

In Genesis, we read how Adam shifted the blame of his own moral failure to Eve, rather than acknowledge his own willful sin, he said, *"The woman whom thou gavest to be with me, she gave me of the tree, and I did eat" (Genesis 3:12).*

In like manner, Eve shifted the blame to the serpent: *"And the Lord said unto the woman, What is this that thou hast done? And the woman said, The serpent beguilded me, and I did eat" (Genesis 3:13).*

Temptation is Not a Sin!

Temptation is not a sin, but yielding is, therefore if the devil has any influence over us it is only because we have consented to it. He can only operate through what we do, or what we fail to do.

The Old Testament is filled with true life stories of characters that made choices that determined their fate. One such person that comes to mind is Cain, who was admonished by God to be careful to master his thoughts of anger and jealousy toward God and his brother, Abel. If those feelings were not checked, subdued, and brought under control, and if he did not close the door of his mind to these negative thoughts, they would lead to destructive behavior.

"And the LORD said unto Cain, Why art thou wroth? and why is thy countenance fallen? If thou doest well, shalt thou not be accepted? and if thou doest not well, sin lieth at the door. And unto thee shall be his desire, and thou shalt rule over him" (Genesis 4:6-7).

Cain was warned by God to shut the door and keep the devil out! Sin was crouched at his door like a hungry lion waiting for an opening to pounce upon him and overcome him, but he was reminded that he had the power to master it and gain control of his thoughts and mind. These accounts were written for our instruction and admonition. This is why the apostle Paul tells us;

"Now all these things happened unto them for ensamples: and they are written for our admonition, upon whom the ends of the world are come" (1 Corinthians 10:11).

While it is the devil's prerogative to do what he does, it is our responsibility to make choices and decisions that reflect our spiritual position and commitments. Temptation is not a sin, but heeding to the temptation is.

Take Responsibility!

The effects of life that we blame on the devil are usually caused by our own actions or some open door; for example: We blame the devil for drying up our finances, when we fail to balance our check books, we spend-drift, practice bad stewardship, or do not pay our tithe, what do we expect?

The collection agency is not the problem! You can cry broke, from now until Jesus comes about how the devil is messing with your money and your credit, but if you are irresponsible in paying your bills, then you opened the door to that attack. If you are driving down a street at sixty miles per hour on a thirty five mile per hour zone and get a ticket for speeding, it cannot be the devil's fault, now can it? Similarly, you cannot say the enemy is attacking your body with sickness, when your diet is wrong. You have bad eating habits, you overwork yourself, fail to exercise, push your body beyond its capabilities, and deprive it of the adequate rest it needs to function at its full capacity, these are open doors for the enemy!

We must be willing to take responsibility for our actions. Whenever we live carelessly or entertain negative sinful thoughts and behavioral patterns, there are always consequences, and it invites the evil one to *draw alongside* and assist in wrong thinking and wrong living. Jesus recognized this principle of negative identification and declared;

"Hereafter I will not talk much with you: for the prince of this world cometh, and hath nothing in me" (John 14:30).

It is evident from scripture that after Jesus' forty day temptation was ended, *the devil departed from him for a season* (Luke 4:13). But at a later date when the devil would return, he would find Jesus' life impeccably blameless. It is important to note, that the consistency of Jesus extended in and out of seasons. You could say, 'Jesus had been left alone to do His Father's bidding for three years.' Then, at a later date we hear him say, *"Hereafter I will not talk much with you: for the prince of this world cometh, and hath nothing in me" (John 14:30).* Here Jesus refers to Satan as the "prince of this world," coming again, but not to tempt him this time.

This time the wicked prince of darkness was coming to take a spiritual inventory of Jesus' life. Now, what are some of the things you think Satan would be looking for? That's right; he would be looking for the by-product of sin; either in the lust of the flesh, the lust of the eyes, or the pride of life (1 John 2:16). Jesus however, boldly said, *"He hath nothing in me!"*

When the devil came around in that season of inspection or inventory he could find nothing in Jesus that he could identify with. I have found in my own experience that there are seasons in our lives when even the smallest detail must be accounted for.

One's Sanctification is the equivalent to the Power of a well-Seasoned warrior.

Therefore, when Jesus said, *"…he hath nothing in me"* he meant; there is no concord between Satan and I. 'No means by which he can claim equality or equal footing with me; No reason for him to draw alongside my life to help, or aide, in any form or fashion. Nothing that originates from him has influenced or shaped my life to any degree whatsoever. Judicially he has no right to impact my life, or to claim influence over it. There is no room for his operation.'

Jesus walked in complete obedience to the Father. He operated in love, showed mercy and compassion, and did the will of the Father always; therefore he could boldly say of the devil; "he hath nothing in me." This provides a moral, ethical, and spiritual template for aspiring Christians; that we too may boldly say, 'The devil hath nothing in me.'

No Hatching Ground for Oppression

When Jesus said, *"…he hath nothing in me" (John 14:30b),* what he meant was; *there is no hatching ground for Satan in my life,* there is no conducive place to cultivate an evil thought or habit, in neither word, nor deed. There is no potential yield of any kind for him to harvest from my life.

We are commanded by the apostle Paul in his epistle to the church of Ephesus, *"And give no place to the devil" (Ephesians 4:27)*. The word, *"place"* finds its roots in the Greek noun (*topos*).

Topography is a derivative of *topos*, and topography as we well know is the science, drawing, or descriptions of a region, mapping accurate and detailed description of lands and contours etc. To *give no place to the devil* both literally and metaphorically is not to allow him access by any means into our lives. Neither give him a foothold in our lives; lest he maps out a detailed description of the contours of our lives for the invasion of his forces, and the erection of strongholds.

"Giving no place," means not allowing even a grainof sand to be the means by which access is given to erect a strong-hold in our lives.

Hop Scotch

In the early ninety's I conducted a series of warfare seminars in the island of Freeport, Bahamas, for a then-popular pastor and evangelist at the Princess hotel. After one of the morning sessions I was invited by the host pastor to conduct a deliverance session at one of his member's home. I brought the team that I had taken with me from the United States to the sister's home, along with the pastor.

After a brief time of discussion and pre-deliverance counsel, we proceeded to address the entities. Now the sister was sharing a flat with another sister at the time. As the deliverance progressed, we were able to cast out several worker spirits. We however encountered a strange phenomenon. An unclean spirit said, "Wait a minute, let me show you something, I bet I can let the phone ring!" When it said that, both the telephone in the living room and the extension in the master bedroom began ringing.

I had asked the flat mate to excuse herself from the living room earlier, before we began the deliverance session. She removed herself from the living room to the master bedroom. I asked a member of my team to answer the phone in the living room where we were. During this time the young lady that the demon was speaking through became very quiet. At the same time that the team member picked up the phone, the flat mate picked up the extension in the bedroom also. It was then that the demon spirit spoke through the phones and said, "I told you!" and began laughing.

Now when this happened, the other young lady came out of the bedroom terrified. Immediately I sent my wife into the room to counsel with her, and continued to cast out the demon. Then it said, "Alright, alright, I will go but I am going into, [let's call her] Suzie-May for the sake of confidence. The demon proceeded to plead desperately as we pressed the deliverance, then she screamed and said, "I am going out into the room with her, she is a liar, that's right, she lies all the time! I am going to her."

Suddenly, Suzie-May started screaming in the bedroom as the young lady we were praying for collapsed. We ran into the room where Suzie-May was only to find her choking herself, as the demonic spirit laughed hideously. He began speaking through Suzie-May, saying, "See, I can do that, she is a liar." Well, it took us some time, but the demon was cast out, and both young ladies were delivered that afternoon, thank God!

Let me say that in the same way that the Holy Spirit is the "comforter" (John 14:26), (the Greek word is *paraklesis* NT: 3874, means, "a calling to one's side" or, One who draws alongside the believer to help or assist, especially in the work of righteousness), it is in a similar manner that the devil and his demons draw alongside us looking for areas of sin or disobedience in our lives that they can identify with, in order to assist us into further rebellion against God.

That demon was able to play hop scotch between roommates because of an open door. God has empowered us as free moral agents to wage successful spiritual warfare against the enemy. We are admonished to resist him steadfast in the faith (1 Peter 5:9). James also echoes the same admonition when he wrote: *"Submit yourselves therefore to God. Resist the devil, and he will flee from you" (James 4:7).*

Much of the ungodly actions and behavior patterns we see in believers are either fleshly or a result of demonic infiltration, caused by disobedience. If the enemy can find a doorway into the mind, then this high position of advantage enables him to wage a successful campaign against the soul. The Holy Spirit often will sound the alarm by convicting or convincing us of the open door; however, we play a very crucial part in the process of our personal purity or deliverance.

Our willingness to repent and permanently shut the door plays a vitally important part in our continued freedom. Most certainly, there are times when we come under genuine demonic attacks, even when there seem to be no apparent open doors. This is so, especially if you are actively involved in ministry, or advancing Kingdom purposes. When you are on the front line of ministry, you become a direct threat to the enemy, and at such times he wages vicious attacks against you, and against your ministry. The more active and visible you become, is the more vicious the attacks are against you. These attacks of the enemy can come in your finances, health, relationships etc., and the list goes on. It is a fact that he comes only to *steal, kill or destroy (John 10:10).*

The enemy has viciously struck in my own ministry and life, time and time again, to destroy us. So, I am fully aware of what a genuine satanic attack is as opposed to some harvest I am reaping on account of some bad seed I may have sown. These attacks are usually executed at a critical time in my ministry, just as we were about to embark upon some major project for the kingdom of God. The most vicious attacks come mainly to derail and discourage us, and thwart God's plans for our lives, and our ministries.

After a while you will notice that your greatest fight always comes just prior to a great break-through, and quite often it is at that time that you will find yourself alone during the most intense battles of your life. Of course I know the enemy seeks to buffet and hinder you and me as he did the apostle Paul (2 Corinthians 12:7; First Thessalonians 2:18), however he cannot gain ground into your life unless he is given permission, or his goods are accepted and allowed to reside within you. Short of the providential will of God, there must be some grounds of familiarity or identification within us that give the enemy license to afflict us.

Whenever you are on the front lines of battle, advancing God's purposes, or doing something significant for the kingdom of God, the enemy will target you and intensify his assaults against your life. Even Jesus himself came under such attacks when he was on his way to cast out a legion of demons out of the demoniac of Gadara (Luke 8:22-37). We are told how a violent storm arose that put the life of Jesus and his disciples in great jeopardy.

"Whatever happens, conduct yourselves in a manner worthy of the gospel of Christ. Then, whether I come and see you or only hear about you in my absence, I will know that you stand firm in one spirit, contending as one man for the faith of the gospel without being frightened in any way by those who oppose you. This is a sign to them

that they will be destroyed, but that you will be saved-and that by God" (Philippians 1:27-28 NIV).

***Some attacks of the enemy are indications
that he is intimidated by you.
You are a threat and high-risk
to the works of darkness***

It is important to remember also that good things happen to bad people, and bad things happen to good people. Never use your circumstances or trials as a barometer to determine if you are in the will of God. In all your ways acknowledge God, and He will direct your paths (Proverbs 3:5-6). Remember that wherever God guides, He provides, and whatever He orders he pays for.

*"And we know that all things work together for good to them that love God, to them who are the called according to his purpose"
(Romans 8:28).*

Shut the door and keep the devil out!

We must be willing to confess our sins to God, and ask forgiveness daily. We must genuinely turn, (repent), from wrong, evil thoughts and actions and the Lord will: (1) Be Faithful, (2) Be Just, (3) Forgive us, and (4) Cleanse us from all unrighteousness (First John 1:9).

Walking in love and the exercise of forgiveness will also help to keep the door locked against intruders. Our obedience to God is also a definite seal against the enemies of our soul. If we rest in the "redemptive" work of Jesus Christ, as His purchased possession and use the weapons that are provided in scripture (Ephesians 6:13-18), they will move us over into a mode of successful spiritual warfare; giving us victory within and around us.

We must not forget that the real battle against Satan was won at the cross and by the resurrection by our Lord Jesus Christ. That same triumphant Jesus who defeated the devil now lives in us! He has made it possible for us to declare: *"Greater is He that is in me than he that is in the world" (1 John 4:4).*

The enemy may try his best to harm you and me, but he cannot destroy any of us without God's permission, or, unless there is already a crack in our armor, or a defect within us. When such a doorway exist, the hedge becomes lifted inadvertently giving him the permission he needs to enter our lives. Once the evil spirits can locate an entrance, they can begin their evil influence and attacks.

The Holy Spirit will convict, enlighten, and alert us to the vulnerable and accessible areas in our lives. However, it is still left up to us to exercise our wills and close the door and deny access to the evil one. If we do not obey the pleadings and convictions of the Spirit, and permit sin to dominate our lives un-confessed, we create a breach and a doorway in which destruction becomes unavoidable. Therefore, *"shut the door!!"*

4

THE TERRITORIAL WAR

I was invited by a friend to conduct a series of crusades in several churches he presided over in the island of Jamaica. I arrived in Kingston on a Saturday afternoon. As I disembarked from the flight, the crisp clean island air and hot tropical sunshine enveloped and caressed me. Although I was there to conduct a week of meetings, my mind raced forward to the end of the crusade when my team and I would spend a few days at one of the resorts in Ocho Rios, St. Ann.

As I walked from the plane I could almost feel the cool waters of the Dunns River falls cascading across my shoulders and massaging my entire body. The anticipation of my recreational time was almost unbearable because of the extreme ministry activities I was involved in for the past month in New York. It was an intense month of speaking engagements, deliverance services, tent crusades, counseling sessions and pastoral care. I could not wait to repose for a couple of days before returning to New York.

I was rudely brought back to reality by a team member who asked, "Are you ready for tomorrow morning?" to which I replied, "Oh, yea,

yea! That's right I am opening the crusade." That sure jolted me back to reality. As we collected our luggage and took our journey into the country, a somber feeling came over me. I just sensed that this trip was not going to be an uneventful one, and oh, was I right!

We arrived into the parish of Manchester late the Saturday evening. I spent the evening in fellowship with the team and we ended the day with prayer and intercession for the upcoming week of services. The Sunday morning and evening services in which I ministered were dynamic and resulted in many giving their lives to Jesus and the saints making recommitments to the Lord. I have found over the years that whenever I was involved with a week of meetings, it was always important for the first night to be a success. It usually assures me of the success for the rest of the meetings. However, after the fourth night there is usually a tendency to want to "cruise it in," especially after exerting much energy and engaging in spiritual maneuvers.

The ministry team and I ministered in three churches from the Sunday through the Wednesday of that week. When we completed the Wednesday night service, I can remember the sigh of relief that I expressed, thinking that we were over the hump of the half way mark, as the crusade was scheduled to conclude on Saturday with a water baptism. What I failed to recognize however, was that the crusade was just about to begin; this would not be business as usual.

During my devotion on that Thursday morning, the Holy Spirit said to me, "Girt on the full armor for what lies ahead!" As I shared with my ministry team what the Holy Spirit had said to me, the host bishop went on to explain the challenges that lay ahead. He informed us that the church we were going to minister into that Thursday evening was established by his late father four years earlier. It was located in a place called Hibernia, in the hills of Manchester.

The church had been recently completed on two and a half acres, and had a seating capacity of three hundred, although it was not fully furnished at the time. The bishop informed me that although a considerable amount of monies was spent to complete the church building with finished zinc roof, six cedar doors and many windows, yet no services were allowed to be held there. After inquiring further, I was told that in spite of a thriving community, and no other Pentecostal church in the area, the people of the community were afraid to come into the church, and no pastor could remain there for any time on account of the threats and heavy activities of the spiritists in the community.

It was common knowledge in that district that no church would be allowed by these (balm yard) spiritists to be established there. Weeks prior to our team arriving in the island, we had sent fliers and publications announcing the two night crusade in Hibernia, so they knew we were coming!

The Thursday evening was charged with expectation as we prepared ourselves in organizing the teams activity, and delegating duties to the local officers of the accompanying sister churches. We met one hour before the evening service for intercessory warfare prayer for the district and surrounding communities of the area. The time of intercession was electrifying and fervent; the presence of the Lord was indeed there.

When we arrived at the church that evening, the summer breeze blew gently over the greenery of the mountains giving an earthy smell with an accompanying aroma of burning wood. I remember how remarkably clean and quiet the town was, and was quite impressed. The church was located near the heart of a vibrant community. It was well lit, finished and furnished with metal chairs. The technicians had already wired the public address system, and the musicians were already in place. The intercessory team gathered at the altar and the stage was now set. Little did we know what lay ahead!

As the worship team led in choruses and worship songs, the musicians played skillfully, and the ushers stood by the double entrance doors. I wondered prayerfully how well an attendance we would have that night. However, as the night progressed the attendance slowly grew. When the first wave of worship and praise stopped, an opportunity was given for the saints to testify. During the pause between the worship service and the testimony service we were disrupted by loud sounds of rhythmic drumming some distance from the church.

The drumming became louder and louder with every passing moment as it echoed off the hills in the silence of the night. It was at this point that we were informed by some of the handful of local members of that church that the drums were being beaten in opposition to the church service.

With this information, we now moved in aggressive warfare prayers against the regional strongmen over the district and community of Hibernia Manchester. The testimony service came to a screeching halt, as the war was now on; the atmosphere was transformed into spiritual warfare.

Showdown in Hibernia

Our worship service became a power encounter leading to a showdown with the satanic forces operating through the stronghold of witchcraft in that region. While the drums continued their blazing, the prayer team counteracted with warfare prayers of binding and dismantling the satanic arsenals operating through the prince of the power of the air. As the battle ensued, the time grew closer and closer for the breaking of the word. The warfare was so intense that we even considered postponing the preaching. After much deliberating, it was decided that I should still preach the gospel in spite of the hostile interference. I left the rostrum to go to the pastor's study. The host bishop accompanied me, where we prayed together briefly. I removed my jacket and replaced it with my apostle's cape. The Bishop and an accompanying deacon returned with me to the rostrum. Not long after our return, the worship leaders raised a congregational chorus entitled *the blood prevails*.

Immediately after the chorus, the bishop was given the microphone to make an official introduction. As soon as I was given the microphone, I entered into a series of spiritual warfare, denouncing the works of darkness and satanic interference. It was at this point of the evening that the showdown intensified violently. I stepped down from the rostrum to the front of the pulpit where I continued with a series of verbal spiritual assaults of binding and paralyzing the spirits of witchcraft. During this time the drumming from the community intensified, but the intercessory team kept praying quietly. Now the double doors of the sanctuary was at this point of the service closed as the ushers stood by the sides of them.

Suddenly, the two front doors swung open to the outside simultaneously, and a gust of wind entered through the open doors. At the time when this happened I was walking from the landing to mount the rostrum where I was intending to announce my scripture passage. As I looked down the aisle the two ushers were engulfed in a cloud of dust as they rebuked and bound furiously. The entire church was on their feet at this point. What was most unusual about the wind is that it moved in a circular manner like a miniature tornado as it entered into the church, bringing with it the dust from the unpaved streets unto the tiled church floor.

At the time my team members included members of my church, members from the host church in New Jersey, and officers from the sister churches in Jamaica. The host bishop took one of the microphones and joined me in the warfare over the amplified system. We began to discharge the forces that had entered the sanctuary. Now the distance between the front door and the pulpit was approximately sixty to sixty five feet. The gust of twirling wind advanced about twenty five feet down the aisle and remained there like a helicopter hovering in the center aisle. The fearful congregation became frantic and began to run towards the side doors. By this time, the bishop directed the deacons to shut the four side doors, as the congregation now assembled against the two walls and away from the center aisle. Like commandos, the bishop and I advanced down the center of the aisle towards the swirling dusty wind. With one hand holding the microphone and the other hand pointing with my fingers, we advanced towards it rebuking the spirits of witchcraft, and commanding them to return from whence they came in Jesus name.

Back up devil!

What I remember to be a remarkable sight was the strangest phenomenon. As we advanced towards the whirlwind, it went backward towards the open door, with the same spinning intensity it used when it came forward. For every inch of ground we gained in our advance toward it, was every inch of ground it lost in its withdrawal from us. As we moved, it eventually withdrew until it departed through the open doors. We called the congregation to order and realized at this point that the drums had stopped beating. So I said, "It's not over, shut all the doors and let's pray!"

Before the word was out of my mouth, a hail of stones began to be hurled on the zinc roof of the church. If you know anything about zinc roofs, you will know that you can determine the difference between the sound of pebbles and rocks. They were raining upon the church roof. As the deacons manned the side doors and the saints manned the windows, it was obvious from the illumination of the flood lights to the side of the church that the source of the stoning was not human. Needless to say, as we continued bombarding the forces with prayer, and pleading the blood of Jesus Christ, the stoning stopped.

As the people returned to their seats we raised a blood song and praised God with shouts of praise, thanksgiving and adoration for the victory that we had won through the name of Jesus, and the power of His blood. Eventually I was able to preach a short, but power packed gospel message in that church that Thursday night. At the close of the service ten people gave their hearts to the Lord, including some teenagers that came from the community nearby.

We ended the service and went back to the homes we stayed in; however, we did not get much rest that night but remained awake for some time praising God and discussing the events of the evening. The next night we returned for our second night of service. There was no drum beating, no winds blowing, and not one stone thrown. In fact, many of the town's people who heard what had happened came out to the service and gave their lives to the Lord. The crusade was so successful we had to extend it another night, to the Saturday after the water baptism service. After that crusade a pastor was appointed there, and the church was fully established.

While writing this account I had a need to contact the bishop and his wife in New Jersey to confirm the location of the church we were at in Manchester, Jamaica. I shared with them that I was writing a book and was including the incidents that took place there over ten years earlier. Both the bishop and his wife expressed to me how they often spoke of the experience, and how vivid and fresh the memory of it still was in their minds. In fact Mother Brooks, one of our church mothers and long standing members, still reminds me every now and then of that spiritual encounter we had as a team, with the work of witchcraft in the mountains of Hibernia, Manchester.

It is my hope and prayer that my experience in this case will furnish you with holy boldness, a boost of faith, and a better understanding of the power encounters we face with evil supernaturalism in our war for territorial dominance. It is here we learn that the violent take it by force!

I want you to come with me now as we explore the multidimensional warfare of the believer in territorial disputes and power encounters. You are a player in the equation, and you also are involved in spiritual warfare, so fight a good fight of faith, and remember you too are a winner!

The Multifaceted Warfare

I want you to recognize that you are engaged in Spiritual Warfare on a multi-dimensional level. Your warfare is Personal, Social, Natural, Psychological, Physical, Spiritual, Regional, Mental, and also involves Evil Supernaturalism.

As we examine spiritual warfare from a Biblical perspective, we realize that it involves the combatants of the *World, the Flesh, and the Devil*. However, what I have found in my own experience is that spiritual warfare and power encounters are not one and the same.

Here are some facts to consider:

While we cannot have a power encounter without spiritual warfare, in a broader sense, we can have spiritual warfare without a power encounter.

In other words, all spiritual warfare does not imply that you will have a power encounter, but when you engage in spiritual warfare, be prepared for a power encounter.

Understanding Power Encounters

It is very important for us to understand that there is a marked difference between spiritual warfare activities and what we classify as a *power encounter*. We must not confuse a power encounter with evangelism, Christian living, miracles, signs and wonders, and even the casting out of demons. Although evangelism can provide the platform for a power encounter, and in some sense it always involves power encounters because it delivers men from the power of Satan to God (Acts 26:17-18).

Power encounters do not always occur in evangelism. I could have conducted the evangelistic crusade in Hibernia without a power encounter, although Satan's forces generally oppose the gospel coming to the souls of men. However, when I refer to power encounter, I mean an intense resistance on the part of Satan which leads to a spiritual showdown, a face off of the bad guys against the good guys, pretty much like "showdown at O.K. Corral" if you will.

It is observed: "There is a sense in which the whole Christian life is a power encounter, as Satan and his forces will resists every believer at each step of his advancement in his Christian life, but this resistance does not always involve power encounters. It always involves spiritual warfare, but not power encounters." Therefore we can safely say that the whole Christian life involves spiritual warfare and will occasionally involve power encounters.

A Territorial Conflict

My experience in Hibernia, Manchester was spiritual warfare that involved a power encounter. If you recall, you will remember on that crusade in Jamaica how the forces in that region had made it quite clear that they would oppose the planting and establishment of any Pentecostal church in that community. It was announced by them and became public knowledge. Satanic forces may work covertly to gain a stronghold, but once they have secured it, they will brag, boast, intimidate, threaten, and defend that territory vigorously.

The dominant ruler spirits or strong men of that territory will lay their stakes deep in that region, and the only way to overthrow them and dominate the region would be through spiritual warfare and a power encounter with the territorial spirits. There are a number of places in the bible that tells of power encounters with territorial spirits. The level of warfare against these territorial spirits is considered, as *"high-level warfare."* Such a level of warfare took place in the book of Daniel chapter ten.

After 21 days of fasting and prayer, Daniel was informed by the angel Gabriel that from day one his prayer had been answered, but he was withstood, and prevented from bringing the answer by a territorial spirit, the *principality* of Persia.

"But the prince of the kingdom of Persia withstood me one and twenty days: but lo, Michael one of the chief or (arch) princes came to help me; and I remained there with the kings of Persia" (Daniel 10:12-13).

The angel Gabriel proceeded further to announce another principal territorial spirit: the prince of Grecia. *"Then said he, knowest thou therefore wherefore I come unto thee? And now I will return to fight with the prince of Persia; and when I am gone forth, lo, the prince of Grecia shall come" (Daniel 10:20).*

Showdown at Ephesus

In the New Testament book of Acts during the first century of the Christian era, Ephesus was a militarized stronghold for demonic activity; it was a spiritual war zone. It was a center for magical practices for the entire Asia Minor. When I speak of magic, I am not talking about some optical illusion, cheap trick, or sleight of hand. I am talking about spells, charms, incantations, potions, the casting of spells and curses, and the use of power over supernatural forces. This was the prevailing idea of the magic that existed in the Old and New Testament era. Paul's experience in Ephesus as recorded by Luke in Acts chapter nineteen gives three territorial power encounters.

The first territorial power encounter as recorded by Dr. Luke was expressed as an astonishing phenomena, he opens with the first encounter as recorded in Acts 19:11-12.

"God did extraordinary miracles through Paul, so that even handkerchiefs and aprons that had touched him were taken to the sick, and their illnesses were cured and the evil spirits left them."
(NIV Bible)

Although there is much controversy concerning this subject, it is obvious that whether Paul was consciously or unconsciously involved, or even encouraged the distribution of his sweatbands and work aprons among the people of Ephesus, God honored the activity with healing and deliverance. The power of bondage and oppression was broken as these items came in contact with them.

What I have found today is that there are cheap copies of priceless originals. So many people have made merchandise of this phenomenon for filthy lucre, preying upon the simple and superstitious. I am not saying that it does not work authentically as a point of contact. What I am saying is there must be a genuine anointing of God resident upon the life of the minister of the gospel that saturates his or her being, affecting even the things that are personal tools during ministry.

It's like Gahazi, the servant of the prophet Elisha's, being told to place the staff of Elisha upon the Shunammite woman's dead child, and nothing happened (Second Kings 4:29-31), because it does not work in the hands of a hypocrite!

<u>In the second territorial power encounter</u> of Paul in Ephesus, Luke seeks to convey the misunderstanding of the other power workers (exorcists) in the city of Ephesus concerning the *power* the apostle Paul demonstrated. The confrontation with the seven sons of Sceva [some vagabond Jewish exorcists] (Acts 19:13-17), was as a result of the "power deeds" they heard were done by the apostle Paul, in what they perceived to be a power formula, "the name of Jesus."

"Then certain of the vagabond Jews, exorcists, took upon them to call over them which had evil spirits the name of the Lord Jesus, saying, We adjure you by Jesus whom Paul preacheth. And there were seven sons of one Sceva, a Jew, and chief of the priests, which did so. And the evil spirit answered and said, Jesus I know, and Paul I know; but who are ye? "And the man in whom the evil spirit was leaped on them, and overcame them, and prevailed against them, so that they fled out of that house naked and wounded.

And this was known to all the Jews and Greeks also dwelling at Ephesus; and fear fell on them all, and the name of the Lord Jesus was magnified" (Acts 19:13-17).

A Unique Power play

This power encounter here is unique in the entire volume of both Old and New Testaments, because it was not an encounter between God and the no-gods, as is usually the case. It is observed that the encounter here is with the no-gods and the no-gods. Dr. Murphy observes that the demonized person physically attacked the demonized Jewish exorcists. He further argues that all spirit-world practitioners of this type are demonized to one degree or another. That is how they derive their power.

The Jews had access to the Kabbalah (the *art and secret science* of the occult); hence they had set up their own group of exorcists long before the coming of Jesus. In fact, we are told by Jesus in Matthew 12:27, that the Jews of his day practiced the rite of exorcism. Origen and Justin Martyr, two of the early church fathers tell us the Jews were successful in this ministry only when they cast out demons, in the name of the God of Abraham and Isaac and Jacob, and unsuccessful when they adjured in the name of kings, prophets, and patriarchs.

The sons of Sceva in this case were not genuine Jewish exorcists. They were spirit magicians, and occult practitioners who happened to be Jews. They were after a kind of Abracadabra, power names, or such as are found in the six and seven books of Moses and similar occult materials. They couldn't care less where the source of the power came from, as long as it worked, they were just power hungry. You will find that even witches and warlocks will engage in hideous violent crimes against each other in an effort to gain more power than the other practitioner. It's a dog eat dog world amongst these occultists!

The seven sons of Sceva seemed to have had some degree of former success from the demonic powers attached to their lives. In this case the embodied demon residing in the demonized man went to war with the demonized occult sons of Sceva. This should not surprise us as we are fully aware of the positive and negative religious practitioners, a healer removing the spell of a witchdoctor, the Shaman versus the Sorcerer.

Demons will cast out demons to enhance the control of the sorcerer or medium over the person in question. They will do it with force and utter hatred for other demonic spirits (Matthew 7:21-23).

The superhuman ability of the man enabled him to beat all seven of them, strip their clothes off them, and sent them fleeing out of the house *"naked and wounded"* (Acts 19:16). Wow! That demon was serious about keeping that man's body as his house wasn't he?

In-house Territorial Disputes

In my experience with casting out of demons I have seen a common civil war in the kingdom of Satan among his evil demonic spirits. There is no loyalty among them. I have heard the arrogant bragging of strong demonic spirits as they boast in telling me how the weaker spirits had to leave because they were stronger, and they kicked them out with brute force, not being willing to share their house, (the body) with them. They boast insolently, "I am in control!" They are oppressive and dominant even in the ranks of their demonic kingdom.

Division in the Ranks of Satan's Kingdom

The utter contempt and arrogant defiance of the demon which possessed the man in turning against the sons of Sceva who, like him were serving Satan's purpose, shows the independence of their intelligence or lack of it. The dominant spirit that possessed the man turned against his ally (spirits of witchcraft and sorcery) in order to secure his territory. Can you imagine? How much more foolish can they get?

Had the demonic spirit shut his mouth and cooperate with his fellow demons working through the sons of Sceva, their kingdom and territory in Ephesus would not have experienced such a devastating defeat. He shot himself in the leg and with his arrogant dominant behavior managed to single handedly turn the spiritual warfare tables in the favor of the kingdom of God. Together they caused the collapse of an intricate satanic system established in Asia Minor, how much more foolish can they get?

The Scripture declares in the book of Acts 19:17-19 *"And this was known to all the Jews and Greeks also dwelling at Ephesus; and fear fell on them all, and the name of the Lord Jesus was magnified. And many that believed came, and confessed, and shewed their deeds. Many of them also which used curious arts brought their books together, and burned them before all men: and they counted the price of them, and found it fifty thousand pieces of silver."*

It is at such times that the deliverance worker rejoices to see Satan's kingdom divided, knowing that his house will not stand. After all, the bottom line is knowing that as we do battle against the kingdom of Satan, we can count on the internal division within his kingdom becoming an asset to the cause of the gospel in advancing the kingdom of God. Surely, the wisdom and power of God is seen through the preaching of the gospel of Jesus Christ.

Great numbers of people in Ephesus became believers, and publicly confessed and showed their involvement with the occult world of no-gods. Many converted magicians renounced their power publicly rejecting the spirits of bondage that had formerly held them bound. They brought their witchcraft books and occult materials, their parchments and magical papyri and made a bonfire of them.

In this power encounter, Satan's forces suffered a major defeat and a great loss of fifty thousand drachmae's worth of occult materials went up in smoke. From this point onward the power of darkness over Ephesus began a rapid decline, as the gospel of Jesus Christ triumphed, becoming stronger and stronger.

"So mightily grew the word of God and prevailed" (Acts 19:20).

Much of the growth of the early church can be attributed to their aggressive assaults against the gates of hell, namely demonic strongholds, heathen paganism, and Greek demonic mythology.

Paul Breaks up Shop!

At this juncture I pause to remember an old chorus we sang in our Sunday evening revival services, I think it befits the entire nineteenth chapter of Acts, it said, *"Come brother sister mek we mash dung Satan kingdom…!"* Do you know it? Well this entire mission in Ephesus seems to ring out that song as the Apostle Paul's mission statement and theme of modus operandi.

In the third territorial power encounter of Paul recorded by Dr. Luke in Acts 19:21-27, we see the fallout of Paul's two prior power encounters in Ephesus. The previous encounter led to the rapid spreading of the Word of the Lord among the people (v. 20), cutting a gospel trail through the religious-economic life of the city. Psychic shops were closing; candle stores and botanica outlets went out of business. Demetrius the silversmith (v.24f) gathered "the members of the employer's federation, in order to organize a protest demonstration. The reason being that many of the clients and former worshippers of Artemis were turning to Christ, resulting in a decline of the sales of their silver idols and religious crafts which they made for commercial gain. The people denounced the worship of idols made with men's hands, and had turned to the true and living God.

The converts of Ephesus may have come to understand that the idols of the gentiles were demonic. No doubt as Paul continued there in Ephesus teaching and training disciples (Romans 15:22-24), he must have introduced the Old Testament scriptures and their meaning to the newly converted Ephesians; scriptures such as Psalm

106:36-37 which reads, *"And they served their idols: which were a snare unto them. Yea, they sacrificed their sons and their daughters unto devils."*

The [Hebrew, word for devils [idols] is *sheediym* (OT: 7700). The Septuagint renders it *daimoniois* (NT: 1140), "demons." The Vulgate renders it, *"daemoniis."* The word is used only in the plural number, demons or devils, and is applied to idols. It occurs only in this place and in Deuteronomy 32:17, which declares *"They sacrificed unto devils, not to God; to gods whom they knew not…"*

So, in Ephesus these no-gods were badly thrashed by the power of the gospel of Jesus Christ. Demetrius the silversmith knew it, but he decided to appeal on the basis of the unique role the craftsmen played in the cult of Artemis [the goddess Diana] (vv.24-27)

"For a certain man named Demetrius, a silversmith, which made silver shrines for Diana, brought no small gain unto the craftsmen; Whom he called together with the workmen of like occupation, and said, Sirs, ye know that by this craft we have our wealth. Moreover ye see and hear, that not alone at Ephesus, but almost throughout all Asia, this Paul hath persuaded and turned away much people, saying that they be no gods, which are made with hands: So that not only this our craft is in danger to be set at nought; but also that the temple of the great goddess Diana should be despised, and her magnificence should be destroyed, whom all Asia and the world worshippeth" (Acts 19:24-27).

This was a political move and a brilliant diabolic strategy of Demetrius, because had he made his appeal and protest on the basis of his loss of revenue it would not have mattered much, but instead, he showed that the goddess associated with Ephesus which drew worshippers from all over the world was being jeopardized. Diana ran the risk of being dethroned by this new 'God' whom Paul now preached. A brilliant strategy of the enemy, indeed! I have come to realize that the enemy of the cross of Christ does not roll over and play dead, even in the light of his seeming defeat.

From Clinton Arnold's excellent study of Artemis we learn the following facts:

1. The temple of Artemis was one of the Seven Wonders of the World.

2. The Ephesians Artemis, or Diana, was worshipped more widely by individuals than any other deity known in the Asian world.

3. The dissemination of the cult was aided by a strong missionary outlook by its devotees as well as an unusual month-long festival held in her honor.

4. The temple wielded tremendous power through its function as a banking and financial center.

5. The cult also obtained a sizable income from the large amounts of property owned in the environs of Ephesus. Through economic means the religion of Artemis was therefore a crucial factor in the daily lives of the people.

6. Unsurpassed cosmic power is attributed to her (the goddess Dianna). To those who called upon her she was a savior, Lord and Queen of the Cosmos.

7. As a supremely powerful deity she could exercise her power for the benefit of the devotee in the face of other opposing "powers" and spirits.

8. Artemis was also a Goddess of the underworld. Thus she possessed authority and control over the multiplicity of demons of the dead as well as the demons of nature and of everyday life.

Arnold concludes his discussion of the place of Artemis in Ephesians life, by saying that an understanding of the cult may also give some insight into why the author emphasized the "powers" in Ephesians. It may also be helpful in understanding one of the terms for the hostile 'powers.' The power-term that Clinton Arnold alludes to is *kosmokrator*, translated 'world forces' in Ephesians 6:12."

His views provide a good background to the study of spiritual warfare in Ephesians chapter six. The power encounters of the apostle Paul in Ephesus provides a good picture and reference to the reader of how the early church lived in the context of spiritual warfare and power encounters. The early church occupied themselves with the preaching of the gospel and delivering the demonized from evil spirits and spiritual bondage. The brief historical account in Acts chapter 19 provides a conclusive understanding of the role that the church plays in the continuing conflict with the powers of darkness and pulling down of strongholds in territorial warfare. It is a sad commentary, but our modern churches possess a form of godliness, but grossly lack in the power of God. (2 Timothy 3:5) We cannot afford to be complacent anymore!

5

DISMANTLING THE STRONGHOLDS

Several years ago a teenage girl walked into one of our church services. She was not a member of our church, but a friend of one of my daughters. The moment she entered the door she passed out on the floor. She was ushered to a seat in the back of the church where she was attended to by an usher. As the service continued the young lady who I will call Mary to protect her true identity, began to scream very loudly, she cried, "Shut up, shut up I don't want to hear it, shut up!"

In an effort not to embarrass the young lady, I waited for the ushers to control the situation and calm her down or remove her from the service. Their attempt to calm her down was unsuccessful. It only enraged her even more. I had no choice at this point but to suspend my preaching and address the commotion taking place in the rear of the church. She was screaming threats against me, saying, "I hate you, I hate you, and I am going to kill you!" She told the ushers, "I hate him! I hate him, make him shut up!" With an authoritative voice I commanded, "Hold your peace, you unclean spirit and come out of her in Jesus' name!" She began foaming at the mouth as she violently threw herself between the chairs. I stepped down from the rostrum and came to where she laid wrestling on the floor with the deacons and ushers. After some time of rebukes and binding the unclean spirits, her violence and threats subsided. However, when I looked into her eyes I could tell, 'this one had a stronghold! And she was not delivered yet.' At that point I stopped, and made a decision not to expose my congregation to that level of spiritual warfare.

After returning to the pulpit, I finished my message and conducted a brief altar call, where I prayed the prayer of faith, and ministered the laying on of hands. I had instructed the ushers to ask Mary to remain after the service so that I could speak with her. I was raised on the old school teaching which told us, "When casting out devils always do the forty, twenty, and forty. That meant that we should conduct pre deliverance counsel 40% of the time, 20% actual deliverance, and 40% post deliverance counsel.

I have found quite often that the data and information you gather in a pre deliverance counsel gives a greater advantage for the person to keep their deliverance. For example, if you find that the open door is masturbation, then you can better counsel the person how to shut the door to sexual deviance and the spirits of perversion. These principles are most effective in cases when the deliverance worker is available and have the time. Although most cases are done spontaneously, and there is very little time for counseling, a system of post deliverance teachings or workshops should be set in place.

What I find today in the post-modern 21st century church however, is that many Christians who are demonized are being counseled. You cannot counsel a demon, it must be cast out! Counseling is only effective with the person, not the entity. There are times when the entity will try to engage us into a discussion or counseling session, we must discern the different spirits and cast him out.   The old school principle only allotted approximately 20% of the time to the actual deliverance. This is mainly because demonic spirits can only hold out but for so long. When a Spirit filled believer walks in their God given authority devils will have to flee! The deliverance worker marches to the sound of the "great commission," and final command Jesus gave to His disciples and the Church of all ages, found in the book of Mark;

"And he said unto them, Go ye into all the world, and preach the gospel to every creature. He that believeth and is baptized shall be saved; but he that believeth not shall be damned. And these signs shall follow them that believe; In my name shall they cast out devils; they shall speak with new tongues" (Mark 16:15-17).

There are times when I am not able to meet and counsel with a demonized person, and the Holy Spirit will move me to engage in deliverance without any forewarning or preparation. In such cases I just flow with the Holy Ghost obediently and let Him work through me as He wills.

Most of the time however, I use the old school principles because they are tried and proven to work effectively over time. The 40% post deliverance counsel is geared to teach and empower the person to walk in, and keep their deliverance. Quite often as the scripture says, when a demonic spirit is cast out of a person it walks through dry places seeking rest, and when it finds no rest it returns to the person who it was cast out of. If when the returning ex-resident finds the house clean and yet not inhabited he is liable to return with other demonic allies and reclaim the house, compounding the problem. The last state then becomes worst than before the initial deliverance. See Matthew 12:43-45. That is why it is most important to counsel the person after the deliverance. They will need instructions on how to maintain their deliverance and live the overcoming Christian life.

Meeting with Mary

When the service was over I met with Mary. She was a member of another church in the same community. During our first counseling session I learned that Mary would sometimes hear voices telling her that they had the power to kill her. She also shared with me that during services at her church she would also have frequent demonic attacks. I enquired about her personal walk with God and gave her some scripture passages to read after assuring her that I would consult with her pastor, whom I knew.

After consulting with her pastor, he informed me that she had manifested similar outburst and neurotic behavior in his church services also, and that they had prayed for her several times. We shared our thoughts and personal feelings on the matter. I explained to him that I recognized demonic presence in the life of this young lady. He insisted that she was a believer and that demons and the Spirit of God could not exist in the same body. When we recognized that we had some fundamental theological differences, we both agreed that we would continue to pray for Mary.

Over the next few weeks Mary's condition grew worse in that she was unable to attend school. I received a call from her mother asking for a deliverance service in their home. After informing her pastor, he agreed to meet me and my team at her home. During the meeting at Mary's home, the demonic spirits began to manifest themselves. There were many. As we prepared in prayer to engage the spirits in warfare, her pastor called me into an adjoining room. He said, "Let's ask her if she is on drugs or something," to which I informed him that I had already enquired in my previous counseling session, to which she had informed me she was not. We had a lengthy discussion on the subject in which he insisted that faith alone in God makes a believer untouchable, and with such, the presence of a demon could not infiltrate a true believer.

We agreed to disagree on the subject of Christian demonization. After this discussion he informed me of another prior engagement which he had, and was unable to remain for the duration of the deliverance service. He commended Mary to my care and expressed confidence that she was in capable hands.

Can a Christian Have a Demon?

The prevailing thought among many ministers at the time was that "no true Christian can have a demon." Now I am not going to attack their theology or philosophy, but my experience over the years however, has taught me different. In fact I have cast more demons out of professing Christians than I have out of unbelievers, and I would even hesitate to expel a demon from an unbeliever unless he was willing to surrender his life to the Lord.

In my many travels and deliverance seminars over the years, the question about Christians being demonized has been one of major concern. Quite often I allude to what Jesus said to Peter not long after he had brought forth a brilliant revelation concerning who Jesus was. In fact, Jesus told him he must have gotten the revelation from God the Father (Matthew 16:17). Just a few verses later we hear Jesus rebuke the devil speaking through Peter;

"But he turned, and said unto Peter, Get thee behind me, Satan: thou art an offence unto me: for thou savourest not the things that be of God, but those that be of men" (Matthew 16:23).

Maybe we should rephrase the question to be "can a demon have a Christian?"

Can a Demon Possess a Christian?

Whether a Christian can be possessed has been one of the most frequently asked questions. Let me first establish that the word "possessed" should not be used in regard to a true Christian. The word "possessed" as defined by Webster's dictionary means; to have or belonging to one, to have as property, or to own.

With this definition in mind it would not be biblically correct to say that a Christian could be owned as Satan's possession. Jesus paid the ultimate price of self sacrifice to redeem us by his precious blood, and we are now His purchased possession. The scriptures make it very clear that we are **God's own possession**.

"In whom ye also trusted, after that ye heard the word of truth, the gospel of your salvation: in whom also after that ye believed, ye were sealed with that holy Spirit of promise, Which is the earnest of our inheritance until the redemption of the purchased possession, unto the praise of his glory" (Ephesians 1:13-14).

We were redeemed by the Lord from the enslavement of sin. We have been fully paid for. God has secured His possession with a good-will seal of promise that he will pick up what's His at a later time. The apostle Paul tells us in First Corinthians that we cannot even claim personal ownership of ourselves; we are legally God's property.

"What? know ye not that your body is the temple of the Holy Ghost which is in you, which ye have of God, and ye are not your own? For ye are bought with a price: therefore glorify God in your body, and in your spirit, which are God's" (1 Corinthians 6:19-20).

I want to make it abundantly clear to you that the scripture speaks plainly to us in James 4:7, *"Submit yourselves therefore to God. Resist the devil, and he will flee from you."* Let me draw your attention to two aspects of this verse. The first aspect is to submit ourselves to God. This means that we are never to submit to the devil's influence, presence, or his evil ways. If we as Christians are going to have power to resist the devil, we must walk in obedience to God.

Secondly, we are told to "resist the devil." To *resist* is an action that shows will, determination, and strength. It is a military word which indicates offensive action. It means that the one "resisting" should take the initiative. God clearly says in His word, that when we take this action of "resistance" the devil will flee. To flee in this context does not mean to withdraw slowly, or to crawl away, but to run away in terror.

The active, persistent, resistance of a believer is a spiritual act of terror to the devil

When the devil realizes he is being resisted by the Christian who has a strong hold on God and His Word, he will have to flee. It becomes apparent that the believer, who is strong in the Lord, puts up a good resistance against the advances of the devil. We are further admonished by Peter in First Peter 5:9 that, *in no instance should we yield to the enemy, but are in all forms to stand up and oppose him. Even when feeble in ourselves, we are to confide in the arm of God. No matter in what form of terror he approaches, we are to fight the good fight of faith, and resist him steadfastly.*

While a professing Christian cannot become possessed within his spirit because the Holy Spirit resides in that inner chamber, there are two other aspect of the believer's life that we must take into consideration. We must also consider his *body* and his *mind*, or his soul. We are a tri-partite being; consisting of body, soul, and spirit, and it is within our spirits that we experience regeneration and conversion; it is not in the mind (soul). The mind must be renewed daily.

Bearing that in mind, we also see the God-head manifested in three persons, namely Father, Son, and Holy Spirit. The tabernacle of old had three parts to it also, and so did the Jewish temple. There was the outer court, the holy place, and the holy of holies. That is why the apostle Paul reminds us; *"What? know ye not that your body is the temple of the Holy Ghost…" (1 Corinthians 6:19)*. Paul wrote as a Hebrew who understood that the temple had three components.

If you recall on one occasion when Jesus entered the temple, he found merchants within the outer courts doing business, and Matthew refers to it as the *"temple of God." "And Jesus went into the temple of God, and cast out all them that sold and bought in the temple, and over-threw the tables of the moneychangers, and the seats of them that sold doves, and said unto them, It is written, My house shall be called the house of prayer; but ye have made it a den of thieves" (Matthew 21:12-13).*

When Jesus cast out those business people from the outer court of the temple, he made no distinction between it and either the inner court, or the holy of holies. He simply referred to it as *"My house."* The place was called by Matthew, *"the temple of God."* We can safely conclude then that the temple is His house. The name *"temple"* is used here in a collective sense, to include all three components.

Now let us remember that the Holy of holies represents the place where the Ark of the Covenant dwells, where Aaron's rod of power budded, where the manna or bread of life is ever fresh, and where the Word of God resides. This inner sanctuary was certainly not the place where these sellers had gained access to, but where they were was still called *the temple of God.* In fact, a careful study of Ezekiel 8:10 will also support the argument that 'demons existed in *God's temple.*'

In Acts 5:3, Peter said to Ananias, "Why hath Satan filled thine heart to lie to the Holy Ghost?" We can use these truths to see how a Christian can be demonized, but not possessed. He cannot be possessed in his spirit because it is the inner sanctuary or holy of holies where God's Spirit resides. However all we have to do is look around us, and we can see many Spirit filled Christians who are wrestling with sicknesses, diseases and infirmities. These sicknesses are demonic in their origin, and yet they manifest themselves in the bodies of Holy Ghost filled Christians.

Just recently I lost a dear friend and fellow bishop to cancer. He was certainly a Spirit filled man. Yet, I witnessed the awful disease called cancer sap his physical life away. Now I know that the source of cancer is demonic and had no right being in his body, it may have been able to destroy his body, but not his spirit.

A person can be a devoted Christian and love God, and yet be overcome in their body by a sickness that is demonic.

In my early Christian years, I too wrestled with the notion of a Christian being demonized. It became an ideological stronghold that I had to dismantle over time, especially when I examined my own thought process. I knew that I was saved but my mind was not catching up to the spiritual reality. I remember wrestling with the thoughts of Elisha the successor of Elijah, the man with a double portion of anointing. I could not understand how his dead corpse had so much power and anointing still on it, that after his death there was still enough power in his body to resurrect another man from the dead (2 Kings 13:21).

My struggle with the story was that if he had all that anointing on his life, no sickness or disease should find a place in his natural body. I concluded that the power within him should automatically repel the power around him; however I learned later that my theory was wrong. It was an ideological stronghold. My theology had to give room to my Christian experience. The question I am most frequently asked in our Seminary is, "How is it possible for a Christian person to become demonized?"

While casting out a demon once, I asked him, "How did you get into this woman?" The spirit answered back, "When she came to the Mardi Gras, I was there and I have a right to be here." Now I know that this may inflame some people, but let me tell you, this opened up my understanding and changed my thinking. I began to realize that if a Christian is out of bounds, and become open to the dominant evil spirits of that place through disobedience, that believer becomes open to a possible satanic infestation. Their disobedience moves them away from the umbrella protection of grace.

People who claim to know God but live a fleshly carnal life open the door of their soul to the devil. He takes advantages of them and dominates them through evil desires. After a while they find themselves in the clutches of Satan and can only be set free by the power of God. This does not mean that every time you step out of line you will be demonized, but when you step out from a divine shelter the chances are something could very well fall on your head. If it does not, you should thank God, because you have found grace and obtained mercy.

It is then safe to say that a true believer cannot be possessed in their spirit, because God himself inhabits that inner chamber, but on the other hand what can we say about the believer's mind and body? This is the area that often comes under heavy demonic attacks and possession. We are commanded by the scripture to pull down strongholds, and cast down imaginations.

"For the weapons of our warfare are not carnal, but mighty through God to the pulling down of strongholds; Casting down imaginations, and every high thing that exalteth itself against the knowledge of God, and bringing into captivity every thought to the obedience of Christ"
(2 Corinthians 10:4-5).

Remember, the ruling spirits and strongholds within a person ultimately take their orders from Satan and the strongman in the heavenlies.

Mary had Strongholds

At this point I want to continue sharing my encounter at Mary's house. After her pastor left the home, I joined the team I had brought along with me in the family room. Her aunt and mother also joined us there. Mary was quite subdued and somewhat fearful. She had been warned in the past by the demons that if she ever tried to get rid of them they would certainly kill her. I took a few minutes to enquire from Mary how she felt, and if she had heard any voices lately. She expressed such fear as she wrung her hands nervously and bit her nails.

I asked her, "Do you want to be free?" she replied sheepishly, "Yes, but they won't let me." It was important for her to verbalize her desire to be free because this becomes an important arsenal in the hands of the deliverance worker if the battle becomes intense. When I heard her say, "They won't let me," I knew right then and there that this was going to be a long day.

Sometimes during deliverance it is important to know who the strongman of the house is. It can be quite tempting to engage in battle just because you know "they" are there. There have been times in deliverance when I have commanded the strongman to expel his workers. You can ascertain who he is by commanding, "Who is in charge of this house, or who is the strongman here?" Sometimes he may manifest himself arrogantly if he is deeply rooted, but if he is not, he may not answer, but instead withdraw and send up a subordinate spirit.

Engaging a Strongman

I have also found that it is sometimes wiser not to engage with the strongman at first, because if you cast him out immediately the remaining workers may allow him entrance again. This is what I refer to as their "Trojan horse" strategy. Sometimes you may cast him out and the remaining workers allow a different strongman to enter during the same deliverance session. This is not always the case however.

After a while you will come to find that every case is unique and requires its own battle plan. A general rule however, is to "bind the strong man first." Then afterwards when he is neutralized, you can effectively expel his workers. Jesus gave this principle as a standard rule of engagement in Matthew 12:28-29.

"But if I cast out devils by the Spirit of God, then the kingdom of God is come unto you. Or else how can one enter into a strong man's house, and spoil his goods, except he first bind the strong man? and then he will spoil his house."

Let me draw your attention to another very important demonic strategy at this point. Sometimes the *strongman* will hide deep within what I call the thickets and recesses of the soul, and keep the gateway open for his helpers to pass through. They do this to frustrate the deliverance worker and to burn him out. So by the time you reach where he is hidden, you would probably be weakened, grow weary, or become frustrated. An effective deliverance worker should become acquainted with the "art of war."

Before the actual deliverance, I took time to reassure Mary that Jesus was there with us and wanted her to be free. I also reassured her that God was going to use me to free her from these awful demonic powers and that she would be safe from all harm. This was vitally important psychologically and emotionally for Mary, because as the warfare progresses her life and freedom would be viciously threatened. It is also important for the demonic entities to hear you announce your intentions, as this serves them notice of your confidence and faith in God. It also provokes them to manifest themselves. The ego of a strongman will not allow him to let a threat or challenge go unanswered.

I was aware that Mary had a religious spirit, because of her track record of violent outbursts during religious services. The religious spirit is usually in his element in a religious service, however when the anointing is heavy, or the service is "Christ centered" he will become agitated and act up.

When the religious atmosphere changes and becomes charged with the anointing of God, their element also changes. The demonic spirit becomes vulnerable in an atmosphere he cannot control.

Deborah's strategy

That is why Barak was successful in the military campaign against Sisera, the captain of Jabin's army and his mighty host. Debora strategically set up the battle by the River Kishon, knowing very well that Sisera's iron chariots would not function properly on the uneven rocks of the jagged river bed. Debora calculated a strategy to bring the enemies of Israel into an element they could not maneuver in. It resulted in the dysfunction of 900 chariots of iron and the total annihilation of Sisera's army (Judges 4:7-16). Both Sisera (the strongman) and his host dismounted their chariots becoming vulnerable to the onslaught of Israel. They were now at a disadvantage having been lured out of their element.

I want to awaken you to these dynamics. **The very thing that the enemy enjoys and takes glory in is the very vehicle which leads him to his destruction.** Sisera gloried in his iron chariots, but when the chariots were brought into a strange environment, they became the means to an end, and not an end by any means.

In like manner, when a religious spirit enters into a religious atmosphere which is luke-warm and hum-drum, he will go through the motions of religion. He will manifest a pretentious form of praise and worship, almost mockingly, but when genuine praise and worship begins, it disrupts his comfort zone and makes him vulnerable. He will usually do one of a few things: he will either protest orally or demonstratively, or, he may totally shut down or withdraw himself from the immediate area where the true worship is. The art of praise and worship is a master weapon against religious devils.

I began a mini worship service in Mary's family room. I began with this approach for two reasons. My first reason was, I wanted to bring the presence of the Lord into the atmosphere. There are times when I would read selected scripture passages also, but on that day I did not. My second reason for this approach was to lure the religious spirit into manifesting himself in an atmosphere he felt comfortable in.

When we first began the praise and worship Mary began singing and praising along with us. However, as the minutes progressed she became silent and began looking around with a dazed look on her face. Her brow became knitted as she looked around the room with an obviously annoyed look on her face. As we continued with praise and worship, I did so, watching her every move. This is necessary for the deliverance worker because detection, discernment, and timing are of paramount importance in the work of deliverance. She clenched her fists tightly and started screaming, "Shut up, stop it you are hurting me!" to which I replied, "Who are you and what is your name?" She opened her palms and placed both her hands over her ears, while she lapped both her legs tightly twitching her entire body in the chair. I then held both her hands away from her ears and said, "In the name of Jesus Christ of Nazareth, I command you to answer! What is your name?" She then replied and said, "Hanel, I am Hanel" I then said, "What do you want with Mary, Hanel?" She then replied, "I am dominations and I will teach her how to seek God." I replied, "Hanel, I command you in Jesus' name to come out of her now, I cancel your assignment over Mary's life and cast you into uninhabited places in Jesus name!"

Hanel was cast out of Mary, along with demons of lust and perversions, confusion, a seducing spirit, unclean spirits, and spirits of fear. It took several hours to deliver Mary from these demonic spirits, mainly because Mary as a person was very terrified of the personal threats they made against her. There were approximately eleven demonic spirits expelled from Mary that day. Every single one of them was a separate and distinct entity with a different personality, a different name, and sometimes a different voice.

There are two strongmen however that I must draw your attention to. The first one is a spirit of murder named Rabbos.

[I have miss-spelt the names of the demons so there can be no reprisals]

After several hours of grueling and intense warfare which lasted from morning way into the late afternoon, we narrowed down the many demons to a strongman of murder named Rabbos. This evil spirit had entered into Mary through deep hurt and anger. He was so violent and strong, it took five of us to hold her body down. The demon insisted to kill Mary. I bound him in the name of Jesus and commanded him to leave, but this one was no petty officer in Satan's kingdom. During the earlier deliverance, I had allowed my team members to cast out some of the previous demons, and by now everyone was heavily involved in the warfare.

This strongman spoke in a husky male voice through Mary. It was astonishing to hear these harsh masculine tones coming from a teenager. On several occasions during the exorcism, her hands went around her throat violently, choking herself. We had to forcibly peel her fingers from her throat as Rabbos tried to strangle her. His grip was very strong around her throat. On one occasion she began to get blue as her eyes rolled over in her head. We had to pin her two hands down by her side as he reeled and reeled to be freed.

We read scriptures, anointed her with oil, and pled the blood of Jesus over her. At times Rabbos tried to scratch the team members, all the time kicking and biting her lips and her tongue. Whenever he was commanded to leave in Jesus' name, or told that he had no authority to remain in Mary's body, he responded violently, saying, "I will kill her before I leave, I will never leave until I kill her." It was at this point he said, "My master is coming and he is very angry." I then said, "Who is your master?" to which he replied boldly, "Proflas is coming and he is angry because of what you have done, he is in the Gulf but he is coming!" He began bragging like a child brags about their big brother, "He is coming, my master Proflas is coming, he was in the Gulf, but he is coming!"

This deliverance took place during the Persian Gulf War of 1991, on a Saturday in October, right after the Iraqi invasion of Kuwait. I declared that no weapon formed against us would prosper and continued to proclaim Mary's freedom. This continued for some time, as I remained relentless until he became weakened severely. Finally he said, "Alright, alright, but my master is coming and he is going to be mad!"

Mary' Final Deliverance

It was approximately ten minutes later that the demon, with a weakened defeated voice said, "Ok, ok I am going, but my master is here." I said, "Well, in the name of Jesus, your master also will be defeated today. In Jesus name come out!" His hoarse voice then said, "Sit me up, sit me up, he is here!" I directed the team to sit Mary upright. At the time she was laying flat on the carpet. As she sat upright the most hideous scream came out of her mouth as she vomited in a nearby pail.

While one of the team members was wiping her mouth, this powerful masculine voice spoke through Mary and said, "I will destroy you!" I then said, "Hold your peace and come out of her in Jesus' name." Mary flashed off the five of us with such superhuman strength, that it took all we had to subdue her frail, little, body. Her aunt sat on her, and her aunt was not a small woman. The strongman Proflas was at first very confident as we engaged in warfare. However, as the minutes wore on, while we kept binding and rebuking him, he began to weaken. He named all of the worker demons that we had cast out earlier. At the time, we made tapes of the deliverance services, and recorded the names of the demons during the interrogation, and he knew them all.

I watched him wither in strength before my eyes. Then he said; "Let my hands go and I will show you!" So I directed the team to hold her shoulders, arms, waist, and legs. She then clapped her hands together and said, "Prince of the air, come unto me!" It was at that time that I became charged with power. I clapped my hands together in several directions saying, "I break every communication in the spiritual realm and bind all reinforcements through the prince of the air in Jesus name." He called out loudly, "Powers, powers, come unto me." Then I commanded him to look into my eyes, which he did. I then said unto him, "I have broken the powers of darkness, you are defeated, and by the authority of Jesus Christ of Nazareth I command you to come out of her and go into dry places now in Jesus' name!" Then he said in a subdued voice, "Ok I will go, but if I show you where powers are, will you let me stay?" I replied, "I will think about it." He then said, "Ok stand me up." So we stood Mary up. She then proceeded to lead us into a bedroom where she pulled out a package wrapped in several paper bags.

Expelling the Strongman

When Mary brought these bags out of the closet, they subdued her while I opened the bags. The bags contained parchments, occult items and herbs, and what appeared to be bottles of potions. Immediately, I proceeded to neutralize the contents with olive oil and warfare prayers. She just stood there frozen with a terrified look on her face. I turned to her and said, "Now Proflas, you must leave in Jesus' name" She replied in the hoarse masculine voice of Proflas and said, "But you told me you would think about it, and now you have sent powers away!" to which I replied, "I have thought about it, and you have no place in the body or in the life of this child of the Lord Jesus Christ, she has verbally asked for help from the Lord of Hosts. I command you to relinquish every hold and influence you have over her body, mind, and spirit, I expel you from your stronghold, I dismantle the arms that you trust in and scatter your spoil. I command you to return the soul of Mary rightfully to her in the name of her Lord and savior Jesus Christ of Nazareth. Leave now! And return from whence you came in Jesus' name!" Not long after Mary exhaled a very deep mournful breath and fell out.

After some period of praise and thanksgiving, I did what I call a 'sweep.' That is, a series of checks to make sure that Mary was absolutely clean. I began to recall the names of the demons that we had expelled. After several commands of residual manifestations, I did not receive any response. Only Mary was there asking what had happened. I led her in a series of confession and denunciations and asked her to rededicate herself to the Lord, which she did. I removed the items from the home after I counseled with her mother, who was responsible for those items getting into that home. We prayed throughout the entire home and anointed the occupants, leading her mother to the Lord.

Through counsel, Mary's mother came to understand how the items in the bag became a landing strip, a safe haven, and a stronghold for demonic activity in that household; she also realized that these things were the primary reasons for her own oppression.

It is my prayer that you will examine your own life to ensure that there is nothing there that can be used by the enemy as material to build a stronghold in your life.

Pulling Down Strongholds

I want to remind you of the power and delegated authority that Christ gave to His Church. It is not that evil powers are no longer working where the church is located, but that the evil power has erected strongholds and citadels in our very midst, they are not manifesting because they are not molested. Enough is enough; it is now time to dismantle their strongholds!

"For the weapons of our warfare are not carnal, but mighty through God to the pulling down of strongholds; Casting down imaginations, and every high thing that exalteth itself against the knowledge of God, and bringing into captivity every thought to the obedience of Christ" *(2 Corinthians 10:4-5).*

We are called upon to pull down strongholds! What is a stronghold?

I took a considerable length of time previously to tell the story of Mary and the strongmen. Now I want to introduce several definitions of a stronghold to you. Then afterwards I will share with you several types of strongholds.

Let me begin first by informing you that anything that seeks to fortify itself within your life is a stronghold. Any power or entity securing its workers, its goods, or its bi-product in your life, is a stronghold. Anything that seeks to promote its agenda above a growing intimate knowledge of Jesus Christ is a stronghold. We are admonished to arrest every thought and bring it to the obedience of Jesus Christ. Strongholds are just that; anything that Satan can use as a means to fortify his position with a Strong Hold of manipulation or domination in order to secure an ultimate evil end.

You are responsible for what you allow to germinate in your mind. The mind is like a womb, if the seed of thought germinates within it, it will eventually bring forth fruit.

When you sow a seed you get a thought, a thought in time produces an action, action over time becomes a habit, habits formed makes a character, and character alive predicts its destiny.

Strongholds are erected like castles of old. They are built brick by brick. The enemy cannot set up shop, unless he gains access to your mind (soul), thus, establishing a stronghold. There are several types of strongholds. However, I would like to focus on three kinds, primarily because these three categories cover a wide range of subjects respectively. Here are the three in consideration:

1. **Personal Strongholds:** These are attitudes, behavior patterns, ungodly mindsets, personal habitual sins, inordinate affections, deep seated lusts and ungodly

cravings, bondage of any kind, including any unnatural use of the body. The category of personal strongholds relates especially to the imagination, mental slavery, memories that deceive and act as prison wardens and enslave. It includes a fascination with evil, and fanaticizing. A personal stronghold is a mental fortress.

2. **Territorial Strongholds:** These represent the hierarchy of Dominions; Governing-ruler spirits who have been placed geographically in areas to influence and control rulers, nations, communities, families, and those who are authority figures. Their main purpose is to secure and occupy key strategic regions in order to carry out the design of Satan. Certain cities are noted for their strongholds of sexual promiscuity, others for poverty, religious spirits, witchcraft, etc.

3. **Ideological Strongholds:** These are relative to satanic influences. The control and dominance of world view through dogma. These strongholds are ideas and philosophies that shape character, culture and society; Ideologies such as Darwin's theory of evolution; and natural selection. The idea that man is a self-sufficient god; that faith in faith as a principle, does not need to align itself with the sovereign will of God. These and other ungodly teachings that oppose biblical theology are a few of the ideological strongholds.

In fact, Mary's pastor himself had a stronghold in his belief system which prevented him from seeing the work of the enemy. These strongholds are portrayed in 2 Corinthians 10:5; *"Inasmuch as we refute arguments and theories and reasonings and every proud and lofty thing that sets itself up against the (true) knowledge of God; and we lead every thought and purpose away captive into the obedience of Christ, the Messiah, the Anointed One" (Amplified Version).*

In Acts 19:27, we read, *"So that not only this our craft is in danger to be set at nought; but also that the temple of the great goddess Diana should be despised, and her magnificence should be destroyed, whom all Asia and the world worshippeth."*

These evil territorial spirits do not have exclusives to dominate any territory. It is evident from scripture that God's angels have assignments over these territories as well. The Septuagint version of the Old Testament translates Deuteronomy 32:8, as follows: *"When the Most High gave the nations their inheritance, when he separated the children of men, He set the bounds of the peoples according to the number of the angels of God."*

The Septuagint' reading of Deuteronomy 32:8 suggests that the administration of various nations have been distributed among a number of angelic powers. The hierarchy of angelic order is suggested in Ephesians chapter six, and Colossians chapter one. We will expound further on the hierarchy of angels as is revealed in chapter thirteen of this book, but right now, let's take a look at Corinthians;

"For though we walk in the flesh, we do not war after the flesh: For the weapons of our warfare are not carnal, but mighty through God to the pulling down of strong holds; Casting down imaginations, and every high thing that exalteth itself against the knowledge of God, and bringing into captivity every thought to the obedience of Christ"
(2 Corinthians 10:3-5).

It has been noted that the words "war" and "warfare," are taken from the Greek word stratus, which is used in the New Testament. However, we notice that they are never once used in connection with the devil. The war according to 2 Corinthians 10:3-5 denotes the pulling down of mental strongholds and ideologies.

Ideologies and mental strongholds may very well have been set up in your mind prior to your conversion, but salvation did not automatically rid you of them. Neither did salvation rid you of the need to engage in war for your mind. It is quite plain to see that both the use of the word imagination, and thought, are elements of mental engagement. Thus the arena of the mind is the central battlefield for the soul.

6

THE BATTLEFIELD OF THE MIND

There was a young lady who regularly visited our church. I had counseled her on several occasions for depression. She insisted that she was being oppressed by demonic spirits. While speaking to her at times she would contort her face while she wrung her hands together. On our first two sessions I recommended some scripture verses for her alleged depression and prayed for her. After some time had passed, the sister asked for deliverance from what she determined was an evil spirit. She claimed that she occasionally heard voices telling her awful things about herself. We scheduled a deliverance service for her and proceeded to address the attacks of evil spirits upon her mind. However, after about fifteen minutes into the session I looked deeply into her eyes and what I saw was an emotionally disturbed woman, not someone who was demonized.

I came to the conclusion that it was not a demonic problem but a carefully contrived plan to get some personal attention. So, I dismissed my team and proceeded to speak to the young lady one on one. I said, "Sister, I do not believe that your problem is demonic." She folded her hands across her chest and said embarrassingly, "Then what do you think it is, pastor?" I replied, "Tell me sister, how is your family life?" She then broke down crying and said, "Ever since my husband left home, it has been quite difficult for me, and I just feel like a ghost, no one even notices me." I explained to her that manipulation was not the way to get the attention she craved, and that it was not necessary for her to act demonized in order to be noticed. She was quite apologetic, and expressed how deeply embarrassed she was, but that she felt it was the only way to get some attention. I recommended her to the Sister's Keeper's group ministry in our church who gave her the counsel and care she so desperately needed.

Winning the war in the Battlefield of the Mind often requires personal introspection and honesty. Not every mind-attack is a demonic one. There are genuine mental problems found even amongst God's people. There are also psychological maladies and emotional pitfalls that should not be overlooked. Millions of people suffer from anxiety, worry, fear, doubt, self condemnation, anger, confusion, or depression, and the list goes on. They all are involved in a mental war, and the Battle Field is The Mind.

What is The Mind?

In a general sense we can consider the mind to be to the spirit what the brain is to the body. The "mind" is also the term most commonly used to describe the higher functions of the human brain. In computer language we would call it the hard drive, and in mechanical terms it would be the transmission. It is a more subjective consciousness which involves personality, thought and reason, memory, intelligence and emotion. Whenever the mind is disturbed, your peace is disturbed. I am sure that you will agree with me that we can only accomplish very little when our minds are not at peace. The New Testament book of

First Thessalonians 5:23 shows us that we are triune beings, spirit, soul (mind), and body. The scripture declares, *"And the very God of peace sanctify you wholly; and I pray God your whole spirit and soul and body be preserved blameless unto the coming of our Lord Jesus Christ."*

In the original Greek, respectively, they are *pneuma, psuke* and *sarks.* The way to consider it is this, "I am a new creation (spirit) with a mind (soul) wearing a suit called (body)." The Greek word for spirit is; *pneuma* from the Vines Expository dictionary. It primarily denotes the wind, a breath; the immaterial, the invisible; the disembodied, or unclothed, or naked sentient element in man, that by which he perceives, reflects, feels and desires, Matthew 5:3; 26:41; Mark 2:8; Luke 1:47, 80; Acts 17:16; 20:22; 1 Corinthians 2:11; 5:3,4; 14:4, 15; 2 Corinthians 7:1. It is the means by which man becomes "a living soul" or conscious mind.

> *"And the LORD God formed man of the dust of the ground, and breathed into his nostrils the breath of life; and man became a living soul" (Genesis 2:7).*

The Hebrew word used is "naphash." It means to be breathed upon, to refresh one self, to become "a living creature" (a living soul). The Greek word for soul is; psuche, from whence we get the word "psyche" (pronounced "sy-kee"). The soul of man consciously comprises:

- The Mind
- The Intellect
- The Will
- The Logic
- Reason
- The Emotion and
- The Passion

The Webster's Encyclopedic Unabridged Dictionary describes the word "soul" as: "The principle of life, feeling, thought, and action in humans, regarded as a distinct entity separate from the body, and commonly held to be separable in existence from the body; the spiritual part of human regarded in its moral aspect, or as believed to survive death and be subject to happiness or misery in a life to come, the emotional part of human nature; the seat of the feelings or "ness." (happiness, oneness, peacefulness)

Conscious man must express himself as a "Mind" or living soul.

The inward thoughts of man are usually outwardly expressed through what he "says." *"...for out of the abundance of the heart the mouth speaketh" (Matthew 12:34b).* God's main mode of communication is in what He says (breathes). Your breath is coded by your conscious soul (mind) and given sound through your vocal chords. That is why what we believe must be collated with what we say. If we believe in our hearts we must confess with our mouths (Romans 10:9-10). If we believe in our hearts what we breathe from our lips, then we shall experience what we say (Mark 11:23).

Whenever a man is a thinker, he usually expresses his inward thoughts with outward verbal or written expression. God's expressions in His Word are His thoughts toward us. Those who are inspired by God are those who God has breathed upon. It is this "breath" of God that enables inspired men to "speak" on the behalf of God.

It is to be noted that we are inseparable from what we think. We are essentially a house of thoughts. The scripture puts it this way, *"For as he thinks within himself, so is he" (Proverbs 23:7a) NAS.*

The word, heart, Gk. *Kardia*, does not refer to the physical, or to any other aspects of man, but to his immaterial inner nature. Quite often we use heart and spirit interchangeably. Essentially, our words proceed from our hearts. From a biblical standpoint the "heart" is the most frequently used term in describing man's innermost personality and function. It is used inclusively to represent man's whole being.

"O generation of vipers, how can ye, being evil, speak good things? for out of the abundance of the heart the mouth speaketh. A good man out of the good treasure of the heart bringeth forth good things: and an evil man out of the evil treasure bringeth forth evil things. But I say unto you, That every idle word that men shall speak, they shall give account thereof in the day of judgment. For by thy words thou shalt be justified, and by thy words thou shalt be condemned" (Matthew 12:34-37).

Man is also Carnal (Greek: Sarx)

It is here that we must come to recognize the concept of "dualism." That is, we must understand that the body is a distinct and separate substance from the soul. It is the skinless flesh, a temporal body. Vines expository: "flesh" signifies "the substance of the body, whether beast or men" (1 Corinthians 15:39); the human body (2 Corinthians 10:3a); (Galatians 2:20); (Philippians 1:22) i.e. sensual, controlled by animal appetites, the weaker element in human nature (Matthew 26:41); (Romans 6:19; 8:3a) governed by human nature, instead of being dominated by the Spirit of God (Colossians 2:18).

While the body houses the soul, we must remember that the body is temporal and material. The soul on the other hand is an immortal, immaterial substance.

101

> *The Spirit is the engine of man, but it is his soul that directs the body he lives in.*

The Mind is Ground Zero

The enemy will try to attack us in various areas of our lives. It is very difficult for his attacks to be successful when we are in good fellowship and intimacy with God. As I stated earlier in the previous chapter, Satan does not have easy access to our spirit. Our bodies, on the other hand, are often most susceptible to his attacks. However, if and when a physical attack takes place, it is a noted fact that our spirits can permeate our bodies with health again. Proverbs 18:14 suggests that if our spirits are in right standing with God, it can sustain our bodies through physical infirmities. *"The spirit of a man can endure his sickness, but a broken spirit who can bear?" (Proverbs 18:14 NAS).* The same principle applies with the scripture that says, *"A Merry heart doeth good like a medicine." (Proverbs 17:22)* It is against the soul (mind) however, that Satan launches his most vicious attacks. If he can establish defeat in the mind, he can render us ineffective with the least amount of effort from the outside.

Mind This!

The Vines expository gives the Greek verb *phroneo* for (mind), to signify: (a) to think, to be mindful in a certain way, (b) to think of, be mindful of. It implies moral interest of reflection, not mere unreasoning opinion. Under (a) it is rendered by the verb to mind the following: (Romans 8:5) *(They that are after the flesh)* do *mind* (the things of the flesh). This means literally that fleshly people set their minds on the fleshly things; but *they that are after the Spirit,* mind spiritual

102

things. This also means that spiritually minded people are affectionately and passionately inclined to have their mind on spiritual things.

In Romans 12:16, we read, "be of (the same) *mind*," literally "minding the same," and to be 'likeminded,' here and in 2 Corinthians 13:11. Under (b) we read, "Let (this) mind be," literally, **'mind this'** (Philippians 2:5). Again we read, "Let us… be (thus) minded," and "(if) ye are (otherwise) minded, God shall reveal it to you" (Philippians 3:15). "*Set your mind*," literally, 'mind (the things above),' (Colossians 3:2). It is saying "*set your affection*." This actually means to think on, understand, regard, with delight and desire, the things which are not earthly, sensual, and natural, but heavenly, spiritual, and supernatural. *That is; have an appetite, for true "soul food!"*

Why the Mind?

Satan knows that if he could effectively sell us on the idea of failure, defeat, or any negative thing, then his diabolical plans will be almost fool proof. This subtle enemy understands the concept of negative conditioning. I am reminded about the story of an eagle that was wounded in a fight far from her nesting ground. She was unable to return to her nest because of her injuries. She was carrying eggs, during the time of her injury and had to lay them in the nearest convenient nest. It so happened that the nest she found was occupied by the eggs of a Prairie chicken. She laid her eggs in the Prairie chick's nest knowing that the Prairie chicken would incubate the eggs and her eaglets would stand a good chance of survival.

The mother eagle succumbed to her wounds over time and died. However, only one of her eggs hatched along with the baby Prairie chickens.

Over time, the Prairie chicks and the young eaglet grew together. When they were weaned and had molted their feathers, the young prairie chicks were content to do what Prairie chicks do. They scratched and dug into the earth seeking food such as worms and insects. The eaglet also did the same as the Prairie chicks, digging and scratching. One day they looked up and saw an eagle soaring majestically in the sky, the young eaglet said to the young Prairie chicks, "One day I am going to fly high as he is flying," the Prairie chickens all laughed him to scorn saying, "Don't even think about it, you will never reach those heights, you are a Prairie chicken, and that is an eagle!" The story goes on to say, that the young eaglet held his head down and continued digging and scratching. He never attempted to fly to such heights, but instead, he lived and died as a Prairie chicken.

This is how Satan works. He plants seeds of doubt, fear, lies, depression, loneliness, temptation and such things in our minds. They become effective when we allow them to germinate and form strongholds. When we give up the fight within our minds to repel these thought attacks from the enemy, these alien thoughts and suggestions accuse us through our own guilt and past failures. Once we believe the lies and negative whispers of the devil, we are inclined to resign to the mindset, and not aim our faith any higher.

A Flood of Thoughts

Satan attacks us in our thoughts because it is the central control of our minds, our reason, logic, will and emotions. He often uses circumstances, situations, and personal failure to become the reservoir of discouragement and depression. His intention is to overwhelm us with negative thoughts and toxic thinking. He masterminds perplexing situations in order to drown us in a sea of despair, or cause us to plunge into sin.

The sweet psalmist David prays in a state of personal emergency, *"Save me, O God; for the waters are come in unto my soul. I sink in deep mire, where there is no standing: I am come into deep waters, where the floods overflow me" (Psalm 69:1-2).*

When the enemy plants a negative thought or suggestion in our mind, if we allow them to ripple away at our faith and confidence in God, they could overflow the soul. However, when the torrents and down pouring of negative things come to mind, and we pull the plug by casting them down, our minds will be stable and better able to focus on the things of God.

While growing in the island of Jamaica, I witnessed many tropical hurricanes and heavy rain falls. However, there is a flood that I recall as a youth named Flora that was most devastating. I remember seeing the water levels rise to the window of our house. I saw the flood sweep away furniture and debris, but what I recall most amazingly was seeing a big Leyland bus being swept down our street by a large body of water, as if the bus was paper.

In August 2005 we saw the most severe and devastating loss of life and property damage occur in New Orleans, Louisiana, which flooded as the levee system catastrophically failed, in many cases, hours after the storm had moved inland. The federal flood protection system in New Orleans failed at more than fifty places. Nearly every levee in metro New Orleans was breached as Hurricane Katrina passed just east of the city limits. Eventually 80% of the city became flooded and also large tracts of neighboring parishes, as the floodwaters lingered for weeks. At least 1,836 people lost their lives in the actual hurricane, and in the subsequent floods. The storm is estimated to have been responsible for $81.2 billion (2005 U.S. dollars) in damage, making it the costliest tropical cyclone in U.S. history.

Whenever you feel that you are going through a storm, and the winds of adversity and waters of life have overcome your soul, I want you to remember that God always provides a way of escape for His people (1 Corinthians 10:13). He will not allow you to drown amidst the raging tide of recession, depression, or oppression. When all else fails, remember, Jesus never fails! His Word says to you, *"When the enemy shall come in like a flood, the Spirit of the LORD shall lift up a standard against him" (Isaiah 59:19).* The Holy Spirit sets up spiritual boundaries that prevent the floods of negative thoughts from overflowing your soul. The outcome of your battle has already been fixed, and the stage is set for your victory.

When your mind, your heart, and your flesh are kept under the power of the Spirit, you will be able to master yourself and your circumstances. Whenever the enemy attacks your mind with static thoughts, you must be willing to repel them and cast them down immediately. However, there are times when the thought attacks can come in like a flood. If you let them linger and you dwell too long on those thoughts, they can become a stronghold and an irresistible force. That is why we are told to, *"...cast down imaginations and every high thing" (2 Corinthians 10:5a).* The same thoughts and imaginations that you allow to inhabit your mind, can affect you emotionally, physically, and psychologically.

When floods of thoughts comes to your mind that are not of God, you must be willing to seek personal sanctification, and cleansing of the soul from God, through the blood of Jesus. Read the Word, (Ephesians 5:26) and let your soul (mind), be flooded with pure and wholesome thoughts (Philippians 4:8).

You must take decisive steps to shut down every sensually operative arm, and all negativity. If hanging out with negative friends is a means of polluting your soul, then take time out from their company. It means that if you have a sexual fleshly propensity then you should avoid all provocation, such as; sex magazines, pornographic videos etc., dirty talk, and avoid being alone with the opposite sex. Until you are strong enough to master your thoughts and desires, you must be willing to avoid every source of temptation that Satan uses to pull you from the path of right standing, right thinking, and right living.

The Real Personal Warfare begins in the Battlefield of the Mind.

The Mind of Christ

We are told by the apostle Paul to possess the mind of Christ.

"Let this mind be in you, which was also in Christ Jesus: Who, being in the form of God, thought it not robbery to be equal with God: But made himself of no reputation, and took upon him the form of a servant, and was made in the likeness of men: And being found in fashion as a man, he humbled himself, and became obedient unto death, even the death of the cross. Wherefore God also hath highly exalted him, and given him a name which is above every name" (Philippians 2:5-9).

It is in this passage of Scripture that we find the great "kenosis" theory; that is the theory of Christ emptying himself of His divine prerogatives. He never emptied Himself of his divinity, or else He would cease to be God, but he emptied Himself of the glory, splendor and majesty that pertained to his divinity, in order to become a servant. In spite of His servant role, He was never lessened from Royalty and Son-ship. He will always be the *(mono-genes)* the One of a kind, and the *(theos anthropos)*, the God-man.

Whatever the estimate you may have of yourself, you must be willing to plunge it into the blood of Christ at the foot of the cross. We must not allow ourselves to think of ourselves more highly than we ought to think, but to think soberly (Romans 12:3). The apostle Paul understood his sufficiency was predicated on his relationship with Christ (Philippians 4:13). James also expressed pride to be the cause for divine resistance. *"But he giveth more grace. Wherefore he saith, God resisteth the proud, but giveth grace unto the humble" (James 4:6).*

Arrogance, Conceit and Pride are the enemies of the Mind of Christ.

There is much talk today about "who we are in Christ." While this knowledge is very necessary for the believer, he should be careful not to run off "half cocked" about who he thinks he is. The possibilities of becoming who he professes to be are only possible while he remains in Christ. Quite often when someone struggles with low self esteem and low self worth issues, they usually tend to become inordinately preoccupied with the need to boost self. A true estimate of self is vitally important (Romans 12:3), but, there is need to be careful not to overcompensate for the lack of a submissive and humble heart.

Tryon Edwards, the noted philosopher, says: "True humility is not an abject, groveling, self-despising spirit; it is but a right estimate of ourselves as God sees us." Spurgeon also comments by saying, "Humility is to make a right estimate of one's self." Barnes, the theologian, comment's on Philippians 2:8; "Even then, when Jesus appeared as a man, He had not only laid aside the symbols of his glory (Philippians 2:7), and become a man; but when he was a man, He humbled himself. Humiliation was a constant characteristic of him as a man. He did not aspire to high honors; He did not affect pomp and pride; He did not demand the service of a train of menials; but He condescended to the lowest conditions of life." Adam Clarke, another noted theologian says, "He laid himself as low as possible."

Can Satan Read Your Mind?

Many Christians are concerned about the ability of Satan and his demons to read their minds. Satan is not omniscient (all knowing). Only God is omniscient and knows and understands our thoughts afar off. God knows what we think even before we utter it (Psalm 139:2-4). The Word of God is also a discerner of our thoughts and intentions of our hearts (Hebrews 4:12). Neither Satan nor his demons can invade our thoughts. **It is what we say that betrays our hearts.** There are many emissaries of Satan today who would have you believe that they can read your mind. What they do is project a thought to the psyche, and then tells you what you are thinking (what was projected). This craft of the enemy is like sowing a seed of "succubus" (thought projection), and then tell the thought. Such projected thoughts are mind control games. *Only God can search and know your inward thoughts (Proverbs 20:27).*

Arm Yourself Mentally

We must ever be aware that the subject of spiritual warfare requires a tender balance. We cannot imagine for a moment that everything is spiritual or demonic; there are some areas in spiritual warfare where we must take control of our minds, crucify the flesh, and walk in personal holiness. We must not forget that these aspects of our lives are just as vital as subduing devils.

"Forasmuch then as Christ hath suffered for us in the flesh, arm yourselves likewise with the same mind: for he that hath suffered in the flesh hath ceased from sin" (1 Peter 4:1).

There are millions of people around the world today who are imprisoned by the enemy within their own minds. This familiar territory of thought and thought-patterns can sometimes falsely lead us to believe that our thoughts originate from our own creativity, or from the Spirit of God, when in fact they might be warped thinking, or thought attacks from the supernatural realm.

We all have our individual thoughts and ideas which we process personally, however, because the battlefield of the mind is the frontier where wars are won or lost, our minds should be well fortified.

The man who is truly Armed Possesses the Mind of Christ.

We must bear in mind that one can be armed to the tee, and still not be a danger to the enemy. We are told in Psalm 78 about Ephraim, Joseph's seed who was armed with bows and yet turned back in the day of battle. *"The children of Ephraim, being armed, and carrying bows, turned back in the day of battle. They kept not the covenant of God, and refused to walk in his law" (Psalm 78:9-10).*

A true armament of the soul encompasses the Mind of Christ. If a soldier has a loaded weapon, and does not have the disposition to use it, he is not a *force* to be contended with.

There are a number of great bible-teaching churches around today that are ever empowering the saints with the truths of God's Word. Yet, in spite of this empowerment we find that the saints often come so very short of appropriating the truths they are taught. It's because quite often, the Word is never engrafted in them. The Word needs to be internalized until it is crystallized within us and becomes an integral part of our thinking and living.

It's not more teaching, preaching, books, tapes, seminars or workshops we need, but a ready mind to extract from the canvas of our hearts that Word that is written therein. One of our greatest allies in the internalizing and applying of scriptures to our lives is the Holy Spirit. He knows the mind of Christ and is willing to instruct us.

"The Spirit searches all things, even the deep things of God. For who among men knows the thoughts of a man except the man's spirit within him? In the same way no one knows the thoughts of God except the Spirit of God. We have not received the spirit of the world but the Spirit who is from God, that we may understand what God has freely given us" (1 Corinthians 2:10-13 NIV).

If we desire to be like Jesus, then we must aspire for His mind. This aspiration is attainable because of the renewal, regeneration, and the personal work of the Holy Spirit within us. It is the Holy Spirit who makes it possible for our natural to become supernatural.

*"But the natural man receiveth not the things of the Spirit of God: for they are foolishness unto him: neither can he know them, because they are spiritually discerned. But he that is spiritual judgeth all things, yet he himself is judged of no man. **For who hath known the mind of the Lord, that he may instruct him?** But we have the mind of Christ"* *(1 Corinthians 2:14-16).*

Here, the apostle Paul expresses the frustration of the natural man, trying to understand spiritual things without a spiritual awakening, and the active work of the Holy Spirit within him. He makes it clear that sound judgment is possible with a spiritual person. They may be somewhat of an enigma to others, but in actuality, they march to the beat of a heavenly tune. The truly spiritual person is the one who possesses the "mind of Christ."

Prisoners in the Mind

Sometimes we can be our worst enemy, working against ourselves from within and making ourselves hostages of the devil. Paul writing to Timothy says, *"In meekness instructing those that oppose themselves;*

if God peradventure will give them repentance to the acknowledging of the truth; And that they may recover themselves out of the snare of the devil, who are taken captive by him at his will" (2 Timothy 2:25-26).

The apostle Paul told Timothy to meekly *"instruct those that oppose themselves."* That is, those who embrace erroneous ideology, and array themselves against the truth. A true recovery from satanic snares and captivity is based upon our recognition, acknowledgment, and embracing of the *"truth;"* this process takes place in the mind. How often have we seen believers attempt to engage the enemy with tongues and all kinds of strange ideological weapons to no avail? We must be ever mindful that the most formidable weapon the believer has is still the Word of God, rightly divided.

Paul cautioned Timothy not to be angry with those who oppose truth and denounce them as heretics, neither hold them in public scorn, but to patiently *instruct* them. Our business with ourselves and others is to teach the truth, and receive teachings of truth. Only after having received and embraced "truth," can the mental prisoner find true freedom. Jesus said in John 8:32, *"And ye shall know the truth, and the truth shall make you free."*

Night Attacks

There are times when wrong thinking can attract corrupt agents. Have you ever noticed that quite often the people who engage in watching horror movies are most prone to having nightmares?

There are times when the enemy may sow a seed of lust into someone while they are asleep. Maybe they share their dream of sexual fantasy with you. Many times there is no attraction to them until they have shared their dream with you, then, wham! Now all of a sudden, they look attractive. That is a night attack!

When I speak of "Night Attacks" I am referring to the fallout, thoughts, and activities that comes from what takes place during sleep time. I am not limiting the time of attacks to the nighttime only. There is a period throughout the night, from approximately 12:15 a.m. until early dawn, when the works of darkness are most active, however, the attacks of darkness is geared towards the lower threshold of consciousness we experience when asleep; whether at night, or in the daytime. We are usually most prone to these attacks when we are deep in sleep. It is at that time that the incubus and succubus is most active, seeking to lore and infiltrate unsuspecting souls.

Have you ever noticed that if you fall asleep with a particular kind of music playing throughout your sleep period, when you awaken sometimes you may catch yourself singing songs that you may have heard in your sleeping hours. The sub conscious can accommodate these things and regurgitate them during the awakening hours. The same principle applies with the power of suggestion and unconscious conditioning. You may be asleep in a room filled with people talking, and when you awaken you might remember portions of what they were saying.

We must be ever vigilant because whether awake or asleep our minds are an active battle field where victory is either won or lost. So, be sober, be Christ-like, and you will always be victorious over the enemy.

7

A CHANGE OF MIND

Change Is Possible!

It would be madness for anyone to believe that if someone continues to think along a particular line and follows through with the same thoughts and actions every time, they will get a different result the next time. Just because they desire a different experience and outcome does not mean that they will have it. **If you want to change the effects you must address the cause.** We have to be renewed in our minds to experience new things.

"This I say therefore, and testify in the Lord, that ye henceforth walk not as other Gentiles walk, in the vanity of their mind, having the understanding darkened, being alienated from the life of God through the ignorance that is in them, because of the blindness of their heart: Who being past feeling have given themselves over unto lasciviousness, to work all uncleanness with greediness. But ye have not so learned Christ; If so be that ye have heard him, and have been taught by him, as the truth is in Jesus: That ye put off concerning the former conversation

*the old man, which is corrupt according to the deceitful lusts; **And be
renewed in the spirit of your mind**" (Ephesians 4:17-23).*

Reprogram the mind with God's truth, and safeguard against pollutants, viruses, and identity theft.

Our minds are like a computer constantly processing data. There
must be an internal mechanism of the Spirit within us to help prevent the corruption of our files and safeguard against mind viruses.
Only when our hard drive is free of corruption and our minds are
programmed with Godly data is true change possible.

If we truly desire to be like Jesus, then we must guard against our
understanding becoming darkened. Whenever we are unenlightened
by the truths of God's Word, we become vulnerable to all kinds of
thought attacks from the dark side. If this happens, we become alienated from the very life of Christ. On the other hand, when we have
been enlightened by God's Word, it assures us of His wisdom, guid-
ance, and inspiration. The divine enlightenment is a floodlight for the
soul. Whenever we have been dealt with by God, we are never satisfied to live a nominal life, but to aspire for higher heights and deeper depths. **True change becomes possible as we set our affection
(mind) on the things that are above** (Colossians 3:2).

Many believers who aspire for Christ-likeness fail to conform to
basic Christian principles, because their hearts are in the wrong place.
I hear much talk today about "redefining Christianity." This is absurd!
How can we in the western postmodern world seek to redefine a faith
and practice we hardly defined in the first place?

You may agree that one of the most frustrating things for a Christian leader in America is trying to get the professing believer to think and act according to God's Word. I have found in my own experience that this is a difficult task. This is so, mainly because many times the people who we prod to walk the Christian path, are people who never really had an initial conversion experience to begin with. We may manage to get people to conform, but that will not be lasting, because, they were never transformed in the first place. On the other hand, there are those who have had a genuine conversion, but are unable to experience the will of God for their lives for several reasons. Let me put it this way; consider this, someone may get a skin graft, but that does not mean that the graft will successfully become a part of the already existing skin.

The body uses arteries and veins to carry the nutrients to the cells of the new skin, and only when the grafted skin receives and absorbs the blood and nutrients flowing into it can it begin to grow and become an integrated part of the body. In a similar manner, we find so many people who are hearers of the Word, but they fail to apply the principles they have learned. Hence, they will always come short in practicing what they have learned because the Word has not become a working part of their life.

"Wherefore lay apart all filthiness and superfluity of naughtiness, and receive with meekness the engrafted word, which is able to save your souls" (James 1:21).

James here uses the word "filthiness" as one of the things the believer should lay aside. All 'filthiness' is toxic to the mind, and it pollutes the soul. This word 'filthiness' occurs nowhere else in the New Testament. It literally means; filth, foul, vulgar, or vile; and then it is applied to evil conduct considered as disgusting or offensive. He is suggesting that because sin is a violation of God's law, and is evil in nature and tendency, it should be put aside in thought and deed. It may be contemplated as disgusting, offensive, and loathsome. To a pure mind, this is one of its most repulsive characteristics. He encourages his reader to receive the *engrafted word, which is able to save the soul* (mind).

This state of filthiness described by James is as a result of the mind not being renewed. Hence, they become bound to the beggarly elements of life like caterpillars. They fail to be transformed into beautiful butterflies. The apostle Paul wrote these words to the Romans in his epistle; *"I beseech you therefore, brethren, by the mercies of God, that ye present your bodies a living sacrifice, holy, acceptable unto God, which is your reasonable service. And be not conformed to this world: but be ye transformed by the renewing of your mind, that ye may prove what is that good, and acceptable, and perfect, will of God"* *(Romans 12:1-2).*

While there is a need to change our mind and our mind-set, we must be cognizant of the fact that our mentality does not change overnight. We are not going to go to bed with toxic thoughts and wake up with a healthy mind; it does not work that way!

The Renewal and Transformation of the mind is a timely Process!

"The mind is but a barren soil; a soil which is soon exhausted, and will produce no crop, or only one, unless it be continually fertilized and enriched with foreign matter." (Sir J. Reynolds)

The Mind that will experience Change will be willing to incubate the Incorruptible Seed of God's Word.

The Process of Change

Let's look at the process of metamorphosis and equate it in principle *with* our own change. This process called "change," or transformation, is also called, *metamorphosis*. Metamorphosis is a process that takes place over time. No one is going to attain unto maturity and the life of Christ overnight. It is the forging of the soul through a process of breaking, shaping, molding, and making, until Christ is formed in us. In like manner, a caterpillar does not just become a butterfly in all its wonder and beauty overnight, but through a process, and over time.

In order for us to get a clearer understanding of how we change to become more Christ-like by the renewing of our minds, it is necessary that we examine the process of transformation in the life of a caterpillar that emerges into a beautiful butterfly. A butterfly begins life as a tiny egg, which hatches into a caterpillar. The caterpillar spends most of its time *eating and growing*, but its skin does not grow, and so the caterpillar sheds the *old skin* and grows a larger one. It repeats this process several times, and then it spins a cocoon to form a protection for the pupa stage. After the caterpillar reaches its full size, it forms a protective shell called a chrysalis.

Inside the shell, an amazing change occurs. the wormlike caterpillar becomes a beautiful butterfly. The shell then breaks open, and the adult butterfly comes out. The insect expands its wings and soon flies off to find its mate and produce another generation of butterflies.

The apostle Paul alludes to the process of change, (transformation) that the caterpillar goes through, but, before he admonishes the church to be *transformed* by the renewing of their minds, he cautioned them not to be "conformed." *"And be not **conformed** to this world: but be ye transformed by the renewing of your mind" (Romans 12:2)*. The word *conform* is the Greek word *suschematizo* which is defined in the

Strong's Gr. Dictionary #4964 as: To fashion alike, i.e., conform to the same pattern; conform to, fashion self according to. It implies oneness or togetherness, companionship or union, to fit or coincide with to be on the same page with. The Vines expository dictionary renders it: To fashion or shape one thing like another.

While growing in the island of Jamaica we had a lizard called a *croaking* lizard (chameleon). This reptile had the ability to camouflage itself by blending into its environment; if it went on a green leaf it would become green and blend in with the leaf, the same would happen if it went on a white wall; it was always difficult to distinguish the croaking lizard from its environment. This is a true picture of conformity. The Webster's dictionary defines conformity as: to act in accordance or harmony with, to comply, and to act in accord with the prevailing standards, attitudes or practices of the society or a group.

"I beseech you therefore, brethren, by the mercies of God, that ye present your bodies a living sacrifice, holy, acceptable unto God, which is your reasonable service. And be not conformed to this world: but be ye transformed by the renewing of your mind, that ye may prove what is that good, and acceptable, and perfect, will of God" (Romans 12:1-2).

Kenneth S. Wuest has an excellent expanded translation, actually an interpretation of this verse, it reads; *"...And stop assuming an outward expression that does not come from within you and is not representing what you are in your inner being, but is patterned after this age; but change your outward expression to one that comes from within and is representative of your inner being, by the renewing of your mind, resulting in your putting to the test what is the will of God, the good and well pleasing, and complete will, and having found that it meets specifications, placing your approval upon it"* (Romans in the Greek New Testament, p. 290).

The apostle Paul is then saying that the believer should not allow him or herself to be influenced in mind, character, standards or values by the world. We must not allow ourselves to be fashioned, shaped or molded by worldly ideals. There must be a distinction between the believer and the unbelieving world. There must be a clear divide, no ambiguities or subtle differences, but a noticeable difference in what we do with our bodies, our minds, and our spirits. God's people are called to purity and separated holiness; however, we must be moved from our position to our expression.

The theological term is *sanctification* (Greek is Hagiasmos Strong's N.T. #38), which is the word *holy*, finds its roots in the Gr. word *hagios*, Strong's #40 meaning: to be pure, blameless, consecrated or set apart for hallowed use, separated from everything profane, defiled, and unholy. We are called to function on a higher plane, and to set our mind, our life, soul, affection, appetite, and whole being on heavenly things.

While sanctification is a definite work of grace, we have a responsibility to avail ourselves of this grace, by our willingness to walk in obedience to God and His Word, and be renewed in the spirit of our minds.

If we desire to be conformed to the life of Christ, we must be willing to be transformed by Him.

The apostle Paul makes it clear in the book of Romans, that God's foreknowledge and omniscience has moved him to predetermine the image He desires for those who would be brought into sonship through Jesus Christ.

"For whom he did foreknow, he also did predestinate to be conformed to the image of his Son, that he might be the firstborn among many brethren" (Romans 8:29).

The conforming nature of Christ is achieved through the transforming of the *mind*. The word *mind* in the Greek is *nous* Strong's #3563, and it means: the intellect, (divine or human; in thought, feeling, or will); by implication, *meaning*: mind, understanding. It is expressed in "knowing" or to "know."

Vines expository dictionary renders the Greek word *ginosko* NT 1097, which signifies "to take in knowledge, to come to know, recognize, and understand." In the New Testament, *ginosko* frequently indicates a relation between the person 'knowing' and the object 'known,' what is 'known' is of value or importance to the one who 'knows,' and hence the relationship is established.

It becomes apparent then, that as we become renewed in our minds we come to know and understand the will of God for us. The mind of one who knows God is a mind that has been transformed. Such a person recognizes and understands the things of God, because they know God in an intimate and personal way. When an intimate knowledge of Christ takes place in one's renewed mind it gives him a new means of *expression*, which is proven over time in his experience and walk with God. **When you truly know, it is bound to show!**

THOUGHTS TO CONSIDER

We must experience *change* in **our mind**. The word translated 'mind,' properly denotes intellect, as distinguished from the will and affections. The change Paul speaks about pertains not only to the soul, but should have its seat in your spirit also. "No matter what changes we experience externally, if the mind does not experience metamorphosis, then outward change would be useless, or would be hypocrisy. Christianity seeks to reign in the soul; and having its seat there, the external conduct and habits will be regulated in time" (Romans 12:2 Barnes notes).

Let's look at the process of metamorphosis and equate it in principle with our own personal change.

- When the butterfly began life, it began as a tiny egg.
  Your beginnings may be small, but when nestled in the right environment, you will inevitably grow and evolve.

- After evolving from an egg to a caterpillar the butterfly spends most of its time eating and growing.
  In order for God's purpose to be fulfilled in us, we must feed on spiritual things and grow in grace (2 Peter 3:18).

- The skin of the caterpillar does not grow while he himself is growing. It sheds the old skin and grows a larger one.
  While the outer man (fleshly) perishes for non carnal indulgences, the inner man is renewed and grows day-by-day. The body is subjected to accommodate the spiritual.

- The caterpillar spins a cocoon to protect the pupa, and forms a hardened shell called a chrysalis around the pupa. *We must protect the inward man of the heart, by securing its environment. We must Guard the heart with all diligence, for out of it are the issues of life* (Proverbs 4:23).

- The wormlike caterpillar eventually becomes a beautiful butterfly; then the shell opens and the adult butterfly emerges. *You might be in obscurity right now, being groomed and nurtured, but in the fullness of time you will break forth as God's beautiful handy-work, ready for higher dimensions.*

8

RECOGNIZING WHO THE REAL ENEMY IS

Now that you are transformed and have been sanctified by the power of the Holy Spirit, you must know that you have been empowered to have dominion over the dictates of life's circumstances. God has empowered you to subdue and conquer! However, there is a "real" enemy who seeks to neutralize your power of dominion, but he will not go undetected! In this chapter we will come to "Recognize Who the Real Enemy is."

There is a strong tendency among many Christians to be naïve concerning their arch-foe, Satan, and his demon assistants. This is especially so in regard to the effects they may have upon saints. To find ourselves in such a position of ignorance is to court peril, and to be misinformed on this subject is weighed with serious risk. When the Christian soldier realizes that he is the target of demonic strategic attacks, the tables of offensive warfare should be turned in his favor.

In spiritual conflict, ignorance is definitely not bliss. The church of Jesus Christ must become knowledgeable about its foes. During the Gulf war, the Generals and military strategists of the United States forces had to be keenly aware of the need to know the enemy, his strengths and weaknesses, his position, his weapons and arms-build up, etc. Accordingly, they employed an intricate network of intelligence and counterintelligence.

The missions involving espionage are frequently as crucial to the outcome of a war as the actual battles. The results of any military encounter would be highly dubious without the *intelligence* about the enemy's objectives, tactics, weapons, his strengths, weaknesses, and his position.

Don't Play Yourself Into the Enemy's Hand!

Despite the critical need to know, I have found that believers sometimes either display obvious disinterest in what the Bible reveals about Satan and his demons, or even worse, they manifest a morbid fear of such a study. This apathy, fear, and gross indifference are almost as deadly as the opposite extreme of fanatical occupation with evil. Such extremist sees demons in everybody and everything. This unhealthy fanaticism is just what Satan wants to exercise his wiles in outwitting his opponents, thus, gaining advantage over them. The apostle Paul cautioned in his epistle to the Corinthian church, he wrote, *"Lest Satan should get an advantage of us: for we are not ignorant of his devices" (2 Corinthians 2:11).*

Paul realized that the adversary could defraud the believer of what was rightfully his, if the believer was unaware of the schemes and devises of Satan, and fell victim to them. When we walk in our God given authority, we will have our enemy at a disadvantage. God has placed us in a position of power, and He has equipped us with everything we need which pertains to life and godliness, through the knowledge of Him that hath called us to glory and virtue (2 Peter 1:3).

While it is true that God has placed us behind enemy lines, he has not left us alone or ill equipped, but he has armed us, and made us extremely dangerous to the enemy. He declares in His Word;

"Behold! I have given you authority to tread upon serpents and scorpions, and over all the power of the enemy, and nothing shall injure you" (Luke 10:19 Amplified version).

God has fitted you with "power" and "authority." You have been enabled to establish Kingdom dominion here on earth. However, Satan is not going to allow you to walk over him without a fight. You must gain mastery over your enemy, who will do anything within his power to stop you. You will notice that while the scripture makes it clear in other places *who the enemy is,* this verse speaks metaphorically, and just refers to having *power over the enemy.* May we never become so narrow minded that we lose sight of who the combatants are. They can be simplified into three categories: (1) The World, (2) The Flesh, and (3) the Devil.

Played

A certain sister, (who I will call Margie to protect her true identity), frequently visited our church on Sunday evenings for our revival time services. She was a very pleasant person; one who you would say was quite even tempered. I remember in one of our testimony services when she got up and said, "I like this pastor you see, Lord I would love to take him home in my pocket!" I thought it quite amusing that she would want to take me home in her pocket.

Margie had quite an interest in spiritual warfare. She spoke often of chasing Satan and binding demons. Almost every time she testified, she expressed her hatred for the devil, or told of some victory she had won

ARMED AND EXTREMELY DANGEROUS

over the enemy that week. She was perceived as somewhat fanatical; her testimonies were always passionate, with some degree of humor.

Margie worked as a home attendant caring for an elderly woman. She lived on the premises during the week but visited church and her family members on weekends. The elderly lady whom she cared for would often engage Margie into conversation about her deceased husband. She said he spoke to her from time to time, promising that he would someday take her life in order for her to be with him. Margie's mind was set on exorcising the spirit that her client claimed had spoken to her.

As the days progressed she would find herself engaged in long discussions with the woman she cared for. During these conversations with the woman, Margie would often bind and rebuke evil spirits, which she believed had spoken to the elderly woman.

Over a period of time, the woman began to converse with Margie in a male voice, which identified himself as the elderly woman's husband. It was here that things took a turn for the worse. The spirit that spoke through the woman was verbally abusive to Margie, using profane language and calling her a fool and a weakling. Margie became inflamed as she engaged daily with this spirit which spoke through the woman.

On this day in particular, Margie began a series of her rebukes. The woman in return, launched a series of verbal attacks against Margie in a male voice. She slapped Margie and pulled her hair violently.

The woman became more violent as Margie physically restrained her. She continued her verbal abuse against Margie in the same aggressive male voice. Margie became so enraged by the barrage of verbal attacks and physical assaults against her that she lost control of herself and gorged the woman's eyes out. She also fatally strangled her. Margie was arrested and charged for second degree murder. Her defense was that she was only trying to exorcise a demonic spirit from within the woman, and one thing led to another. Margie is presently serving time for the murder of her home-care patient; not for the murder of a demon. You see, Margie failed to separate the actions of the demonized woman from the woman herself. This is an unfortunate but true case.

In this case the demon had found a means by which to deceive Margie, by erecting a stronghold of deception in her mind. She allowed herself to become engaged with him in verbal discourse. This allowed him a greater foothold on the weakened woman, whom he sought to kill. Through subtlety and deception, the evil spirit was able to carry out his plan, and both Margie and the woman became his victims.

Margie may have had a zeal for warfare, but she lost her focus of who the real enemy was, and failed to remember that *"The weapons of our warfare are not carnal" (2 Corinthians 10:4)*. This may be an extreme case, but there are many believers today who are engaged in inter-personal warfare, who believe strongly that the people in their lives are trying to hinder their progress, or interfere with their peace of mind. In many of these cases these people engage in soulish warfare; that is, warfare that is psychological and fleshly.

There are many in Christendom who commit spiritual hate crimes in the name of *"fighting the enemy."* Gossiping, slandering, negative criticism, bad-talking, sowing of discord, fleshly-binding, praying the Psalms against the alleged enemies, touching and agreeing against the other person, etc., are ungodly methods of dealing with what is perceived to be a problem. While not all of these things are evil in themselves, they are not of God. We must operate in love, and be careful how we deal with the precious souls for whom Christ died. Our enemy (a demon), could use a vessel of dishonor (a human), but the vessel of dishonor is not the true enemy.

Know the Enemy

The only balanced approach to effective spiritual warfare is to know the enemy, his methods, and his devices, and then seek God for a plan of action. We must possess a keen sense of discernment. This discernment must provide us with the intelligent distinction between evil spirits, the spirit of man, and the Spirit of God (1 Corinthians 12:10). Along with the discerning of spirits, we must be able to categorize what is of the world, what is of the flesh, and what is of the devil. Only as the satanic-wiles are identified, will the believer be able to anticipate and outmaneuver him. Remember, his main tactic is to camouflage his identity and underplay his assault. The Christian must recognize Satan and anticipate his moves.

We must not be ignorant of Satan's devices (2 Corinthians 2:11). The Webster's unabridged dictionary defines *"device"* as: A thing made for a particular purpose, an invention, plan, or scheme for affecting a purpose; something elaborately or fancifully designed, a fanciful, crafty scheme or trick.

The apostle Paul recognized that Satan is a master strategist. He schemes and contrives weapons, purposes, and plans to destroy the children of God. We must be vigilant and cautious. That is why we are told in Ephesians, *"Put on the whole armour of God, that ye may be able to stand against the wiles of the devil" (Ephesians 6:11).* The Greek translation for *"wiles,"* is *methodos,* which is the etymological root of the word, "method."

His Methods

Paul here cautions the believer to put on the entire panoply of God's armor in order to stand against the devil's wiles. The word, 'wiles' or methods, speaks of a predictable pattern of operation. Some of his methods are almost scientific. When we speak of 'his methods,' we speak of his procedures and techniques; orderly and prepared, systematically planned way of doing things.

He may begin with an attraction to stimulate a desire (lust) that leads into deception. After the lust has been satisfied, with a sinful act, if not dealt with it eventually brings bondage and death. He has narrowed his methods down to an art, let's face it, he has had thousands of years to perfect the art of attraction, deception, and ruin.

One of the devices of the devil that has proven to be most successful over the years is lust. Lust continues to work as a means of man's downfall. If something is working, why change it? Lust is seen in three categories: (1) The lust of the flesh (2) The lust of the eyes, and (3) The pride of life. John informs us in his epistle;

"For all that is in the world, the lust of the flesh, and the lust of the eyes, and the pride of life, is not of the Father, but is of the world. And the world passeth away, and the lust thereof; but he that doeth the will of God abideth for ever" (1 John 2:16-17).

John in his epistle, seemed almost to over-simplify the available tools of the enemy when he said, *"All that is in the world is the lust..."* However, a closer examination of this text suggests a seeming euphemism in the middle voice that carries a much deeper meaning. While John limits man's experiences of temptations to only three categories, he is fully aware that our experiences are all different, and can produce differing results. However, he seeks to apply in principle, the categories in the light of our diverse experiences.

We must understand this verse then, in the light of the *principle*. Principle, as defined by Webster's unabridged dictionary means an adopted rule or method for application in action; a working principle. Satan's methods, (modes) remain the same; to bring about the downfall of humanity.

While the methods, namely; the lust of the flesh, the lust of the eyes, and the pride of life remain the same, the categories themselves may vary. Let's now look at a working *principle* which contains different *categories*. A classical example of Satan's methods is seen in the book of Genesis;

"And when the woman saw that the tree was good for food, and that it was pleasant to the eyes, and a tree to be desired to make one wise, she took of the fruit thereof, and did eat, and gave also unto her husband with her; and he did eat" (Genesis 3:6).

Here we find Eve being tempted by Satan. Notice the common principle he uses as a means of interest, attraction, and, or intrigue.

1. **The lust of the flesh:** "When she saw that the tree was good for food" (sensual desire)

2. **The lust of the eyes:** "It was pleasant to the eye" (eye candy)

3. **The pride of life:** "To be desired to make one wise" (Lofty thinking).

In a message given at Moody Church in Chicago Illinois, Warren Wiersbe, a well known conference teacher, commented on the *progression* of Eve's decision to believe the serpent (Satan).

He presented the progression in four parts:

1. She saw and became curious.

2. She took and became a thief.

3. She ate and became a rebel.

4. She gave and became a temptress.

I have observed that although Adam was standing right there with his wife, he did not object to her picking the fruit from the tree and eating it. When she had eaten of it she shared it with him, and he ate it, also without objection. He was not enticed or deceived in any of the three categories mentioned earlier, but, he was seduced by a satanic *principle,* and he made an independent decision to eat.

The temptation of Jesus in the wilderness was also marked by the same three aspects of temptations encountered by Eve. The devices of the devil had been so effective against mankind from the beginning, that thousands of years later, during Jesus' 40 days of fasting in the wilderness, he employed the same age-old method in his attempt to lure Jesus into disobedience;

> *"Then was Jesus led up of the Spirit into the wilderness to be tempted of the devil. And when he had fasted forty days and forty nights, he was afterward an hungred. And when the tempter came to him, he said, If thou be the Son of God, command that these stones be made bread. But he answered and said, It is written, Man shall not live by bread alone, but by every word that proceedeth out of the mouth of God. Then the devil taketh him up into the holy city, and setteth him on a pinnacle of the temple, And saith unto him, If thou be the Son of God, cast thyself down: for it is written, He shall give his angels charge concerning thee: and in their hands they shall bear thee up, lest at any time thou dash thy foot against a stone. Jesus said unto him, It is written again, Thou shalt not tempt the Lord thy God. Again, the devil taketh him up into an exceeding high mountain, and sheweth him all the kingdoms of the world, and the glory of them; And saith unto him, All these things will I give thee, if thou wilt fall down and worship me. Then saith Jesus unto him, get thee hence, Satan: for it is written, Thou shalt worship the Lord thy God, and him only shalt thou serve. Then the devil leaveth him, and, behold, angels came and ministered unto him" (Matthew 4:1-11).*

As we can clearly see in the preceding scriptures, the devil appealed to Jesus in the "lust of the flesh," by challenging His Sonship and

Power, in suggesting that Jesus turn the stones into bread, to satiate the hunger He experienced because of His fasting.

Satan's first attempt failed, so he introduced "the pride of life" to Jesus, by taking Him up to the holy city, and setting Him on the pinnacle of the temple. He then presumptuously dared Jesus that if His claim of messianic-ship was authentic, then He should cast Himself down from the pinnacle, because God would command His angels to save Him. Finally, he took Jesus up to an exceeding high mountain, and showed Him, (the lust of the eyes), all the kingdoms of the world, and the glory of them. These Satan promised to Jesus if He would fall down and worship him.

It is quite apparent that if and when we recognize who the enemy is, we should resist him steadfast in the faith (1 Peter 5:9). If we take a careful look at the word "resist," we will find militant implications of warfare. Anyone who refuses to be taken captive, or become subjected to the enemy, will dare to withstand and oppose his advances.

Although Satan's enemy does not always know him, he makes it a point of duty to always know his enemy.

He is quite aware of the ignorant and harmless believer, especially those who become ensnared by his traps. The thing he fears most is the believer who knows who they are in the light of their relationship with Christ, and find and fulfill the will of God for their life. These are the ones that Satan fears most, because they constitute the deadliest threat to his diabolical plans and ambitions.

One of the priorities of Satan and his servants is to prevent any teachings about him, his activities, or his operations. As long as people remain ignorant about him and his cohorts he is at liberty to do almost anything he desires to do. The common justification for ignorance of the knowledge of Satan among our churches is that, when we teach about him, we give him glory, and take people's minds off of the Lord, thus leading to Satanic worship.

The bible teaches much about Satan, and warns us not to be ignorant of his devises. Jesus' ministry was truly one of deliverance from evil powers. The Scriptures testify of His mission and work, we are told, *"How God anointed Jesus of Nazareth with the Holy Ghost and with power: who went about doing good, and healing all that were oppressed of the devil; for God was with him" (Acts 10:38).*

Jesus' mission was two-fold; He came to redeem mankind from the awful grips of sin and death, but he also came to destroy the works of the devil. The fact that Jesus said, *"It is finished!" (John 19:30),* implies that His mission was accomplished. John puts it like this;

"He that committeth sin is of the devil; for the devil sinneth from the beginning. For this purpose the Son of God was manifested, that he might destroy the works of the devil" (1 John. 3:8).

The fact that there is an increasingly large number of powerless spirited Christians, and dead churches around today, is an attestation to the reality that Satan's well planned devises are working.

The church of the 21st century needs to know who the enemy is, and how to resist and overthrow him. My prayer is that every Christian, especially leaders, would seek the Lord for a battle plan and strategy of how to fight the enemy and be successful.

The enemy does not like being exposed. He works secretly, because his success depends largely on going undetected. The Holy

Spirit has come to lay bare his stratagems and reveal the enemy; exposing him to the mighty weapons and powerful attacks of God's people. To ignore the weapons of our warfare provided by the Lord against Satan and his kingdom is spiritual suicide.

Wrapped up in the World and the Flesh

There is nothing that pleases the devil more than to see a Christian so wrapped up with what he is and does to *self*, rather than who he is, and what he does in his position in Christ.

The preoccupation with material acquisition and status-quo is another means by which believers are rendered powerless by the enemy. If the believer does not exercise great care in seeking the things which are above, (Col. 3:1a) rather that becoming engrossed with the cares of this life, then they will expose themselves to the *wiles* of their enemy, and run the risk of being taken *captive by him at his will* (2 Timothy 2:26).

We were given the capacity to successfully resist the ability of the enemy. Our faith is the immune system of the body of Christ. We are called upon to resist the opposing wiles of the devil. The greatest form of resistance we can offer is to utilize what God has freely given us. He has given us the whole armor (Ephesians 6:11), and the gifts of His Holy Spirit (1 Corinthians Chapter 12).

The gifts of the Spirit are vital for the end-times, especially as we see more and more satanic manifestations. Any power encounter with the enemy requires supernatural power from God. The prophet Isaiah alludes to two of the power-gifts. The first is wisdom, and the second is knowledge. *"**And wisdom and knowledge** shall be the stability of thy times, and strength of salvation: the fear of the LORD is his treasure" (Isaiah. 33:6).*

Notice that what brings stability to the believer in the end times is wisdom and knowledge. However, it is when we fully know, that we will have discernment, or understanding. The Scripture speaks to us in principle about the men of Issachar; it says, *"And of the children of Issachar, which were **men that had understanding of the times, to know what Israel ought to do"** (1 Chronicles 12:32)*. Like the men of Issachar, when the church has a grip on what's happening in our world at this moment in time, then it will be apt to receive from the Lord a definite course of action. At such a time, the church will definitely *know what to do*.

There are so many believers who are willing to take action, but they are not fully informed. Zeal without knowledge is always a recipe for disaster. God wants his people to be proactive, but their action must be based upon accurate knowledge, not sensual perception.

The Acquiring of Knowledge

The following are some of the modes we use to gather data and intelligence:

1. **Sensual perception:** It is the use of the five senses to gather data.

2. **Perception:** Is an Intellectual ability to consciously and cognitively perceive, or recognize and grasp facts (Acts 10:34).

3. **Detection:** There is also the training of the senses through frequent use, to discern between good and evil (Hebrews 5:14).

4. **Intuition:** Is a sixth sense. Spiritual reality might not always be revealed, but it can be known intuitively. There is an

inherent sixth sense of intuition, where you know and yet you are not sure of the details, you just sense it.

5. **Revelation:** There is the supernatural gift of the "word of knowledge." These two are similar. It is the supernatural ability to know things that you could not have otherwise known without the revelation of the Holy Spirit.

6. **Discerning of spirits:** Is the supernatural gift of the Holy Spirit to distinguish the state, condition, and the work of spirits, namely: Holy Spirit; the human spirit; angelic spirits, both good and evil.

7. **Perception and detection** can at times be inter-changeable. Perceive means to become aware of, knowing and an impression formed.

While we gather data from many sources, we must never rely solely on our own abilities to process the data we gather. It is only when we rely, and depend on the Holy Spirit of God to lead, instruct, and guide us, that we can be assured of accurate data, and the wisdom of God to deal with what we have come to know.

Having knowledge is not an end in itself. It is when we act wisely upon the knowledge we possess, that wisdom is justified of her children. *The Power to Do and Say is predicated on the Power to Know.* There are nine power gifts of the Spirit, divided into three categories. The nine gifts of the Holy Spirit and their categories are:

A. The Power to Know

1. The word of wisdom (1 Corinthians 12:8)

2. The word of knowledge (1 Corinthians 12:8)

3. The discerning of spirits (1 Corinthians 12:10)

B. The Power to Say

1. The gift of tongues   (1 Corinthians 12:10)

2. The gift of interpretation of tongues (1 Corinthians 12:10)

3. The gift of prophecy (1 Corinthians 12:10)

C. The Power to Do

1. The gift of faith (1 Corinthians 12:9)

2. The gift of healing (1 Corinthians 12:9)

3. The working of miracles (1 Corinthians 12:10)

As the final days of the church approach, there will be a power encounter of epic proportion. The believer must have keen insight, and their senses must be exercised to discern both good and evil (Hebrews 5:14). We must come to know the mind and intentions of God in order to do His will.

Only when we truly *know*, can we effectively *do*. One of the reasons the apostle Paul was so effective in conveying the will of God to the church, was because he was intimately acquainted with the *intentions* and purposes of God. He wrote; *"To the intent that now unto principalities and powers in the heavenly places might be known by the church the manifold wisdom of God" (Ephesians 3:10).*

Paul was not short of the knowledge of why God endowed the church with His manifold wisdom. When we have the mind of Christ we will *know* God's *intentions* and purposes. He will also inform us of *'Who the Real Enemy is.'* Now let's take a look at the enemy who comes from *outside* of self.

The Enemy from Without

We have explored 'The Battle Field of the Mind,' and Romans 12:1, which reads, *"Be not conformed to this world: but be ye transformed by the renewing of your mind."* The word translated 'mind' properly denotes *intellect*, as distinguished from the *will* and *affections*. We learned in previous chapters, that toxic thoughts and *worldly thinking* are fought and won in the *renewed* mind. However, I want us to look now at how we should direct our *affections*, in regard to the encroaching world-values all around us. The scripture clearly admonishes us; *"Love not the world, neither the things that are in the world. If any man loves the world, the love of the Father is not in him" (1 John 2:15a).*

The use of the word *world* here refers not to the global world, but to man and his *world* (system) with its values, ideals, philosophy, arrangements, principles and standards; or lack of it. The *worldly system* is that which governs the fallen world in which he lives. There is a way that the world does things, as opposed to how God requires his subjects to conduct their lives. We are told by James;

"Ye adulterers and adulteresses, know ye not that the friendship of the world is enmity with God? Whosoever therefore will be a friend of the world is the enemy of God" (James 4:4a).

A man might deny in general that he loves the world, while keenly following some of the things in it: its riches, honors, or pleasures. Such a person stands convicted by this very passage. James also says, "…Whosoever therefore will be a friend of the world is the enemy of God" (James 4:4b). If making ourselves a *friend* of the world makes us an enemy of God, then, as "New Creatures," (2 Corinthians 5:17), we are naturally at enmity with the world.

The scripture tells us that *"God so loved this world" (John 3:16).* In order for us to see this truth in the light of its context, we must ascertain the kind of love God has for the world. **He loved it with a love of <u>compassion</u>, not of <u>passion</u>,** and we should feel the same kind of love for the fallen world, and not for the things that are in it.

"All that are in the world," can be classed under either one of the three: (1) The lust of the flesh, (2) The lust of the eyes, or, (3) The pride of life.

The Oxford dictionary defines the word world, as: Worldly affairs; the aggregate of things earthly; the whole circle of earthly goods, endowments, riches, advantages, pleasures etc. Although the worldly things are shallow and transient, yet they provoke desires that seduce us away from the love of God, and are stumbling blocks to the cause of Christ. It is of this establishment that Satan is the prince and a god.

"Hereafter I will not talk much with you: for the prince of this world cometh, and hath nothing in me" (John 14:30) & (John 12:31). We are also told by Paul in his epistle; *"But if our gospel be hid, it is hid to them that are lost: In whom the god of this world hath blinded the minds of them which believe not, lest the light of the glorious gospel of Christ, who is the image of God, should shine unto them" (2 Corinthians 4:3-4).*

It is logical from these passages to see how and why Satan was able to offer Christ the *kingdoms of this world,* and the glory of them. He earned the right in the Garden; when Adam committed high treason through his disobedience. Adam inadvertently handed the dominion of planet earth into the hands of Satan; who plunged the world into wickedness, thus, it became his to give. Even now, it remains his greatest asset to ensnare the souls of mankind.

We are admonished by the apostle Paul to make our spiritual interests paramount in our lives. He tells us that *they which buy, should have a mind-set as though they posses not, "and they that use this world, as not abusing it: for the fashion of this world passeth away" (1 Corinthians 7:30b-31).*

*The dangers are not in our possessing
Things but in things possessing us*

If it's necessary, Satan will himself give you all the *"things"* you want, and keep you so busy maintaining them, that you neglect your call and duty as a child of God.

The World is a Social Antagonist

Jesus announced the world's antagonism when he told his disciples what kind of treatment to expect from it. They were not to expect any better treatment from it than He Himself had received; which consequently led to his death.

"If the world hate you, ye know that it hated me before it hated you. If ye were of the world, the world would love his own: but because ye are not of the world, but I have chosen you out of the world, therefore the world hateth you" (John 15:18-19).

*If the world hates you, then why do you
think it would look out for your
best interest?*

The *world*, with all of its glitter and attractions, becomes strangely dim in the light of God's glory and grace. The song writer also declares, "You can have the whole world but give me Jesus, no turning back, no turning back, the cross before me, the world behind me, no turning back, no turning back!" Jesus, in His high-priestly prayer (John 17:14), reminded the Father that He had given His disciples

His Word; and the world hated them, because they are not of it, even as he was not of the world.

I don't think Jesus was a separatist, so to speak, but, he wanted there to be a distinction between the subjects of His Kingdom, and the 'kingdom of the darkness of this world.' It was in the hostile environment of *'this world'* that Jesus left His disciples; that is why he saw it fit to pray a prayer of protection and preservation for them while they were yet in the world.

He prayed, *"I have manifested thy name unto the men which thou gavest me out of the world: thine they were, and thou gavest them me; and they have kept thy word. Now they have known that all things whatsoever thou hast given me are of thee. For I have given unto them the words which thou gavest me; and they have received them, and have known surely that I came out from thee, and they have believed that thou didst send me. I pray for them: I pray not for the world, but for them which thou hast given me; for they are thine. And all mine are thine, and thine are mine; and I am glorified in them. And now I am no more in the world, but these are in the world, and I come to thee. Holy Father, keep through thine own name those whom thou hast given me, that they may be one, as we are. While I was with them in the world, I kept them in thy name: those that thou gavest me I have kept, and none of them is lost, but the son of perdition; that the scripture might be fulfilled. And now come I to thee; and these things I speak in the world, that they might have my joy fulfilled in themselves. I have given them thy word; and the world hath hated them, because they are not of the world, even as I am not of the world. I pray not that thou shouldest take them out of the world, but that thou shouldest keep them from the evil. They are not of the world, even as I am not of the world"* (John 17:6-16).

Get Over It!

We are in the world, but *not of it*. The believer is warned not to *love* the world, not become so *fond* of it with all its trappings, that we begin a courtship of death. But like Jesus our Lord, we too should be able to say; *"I have overcome it" (John 16:33)*.

"I have told these things so that in Me you may have perfect peace and confidence. In the world you have tribulation and trials and distress and frustration; but be of good cheer, take courage, be confident, certain, undaunted, for I have overcome the world.

I have deprived it of the power to harm, I have conquered it [for you]" *(John 16:33 Amplified Version).*

If the Devil is in something, we should have no business loving it, because he told us that the spirit of anti Christ is in it (1 John 4:3-6). In fact, before we were saved we walked after the course of *this world*; 'according to the *spirit* that worketh in the children of disobedience' (Ephesians 2:2) but now, *"let us not be conformed"* to it any more, with its values, lifestyle, and ideals, which are at enmity with God. Another great scripture showing the impact believers have upon the world, when they are not deeply influenced by it, is found in the book of Acts; *"These that have turned the world upside down are come hither also" (Acts 17:6).*

One of the things that made the early disciples so successful was, that "they turned the world upside down!" **They created havoc!** They actually did not esteem the views, ideals, or things of the world worthy of, or equal to, as high an esteem of Christ, or His gospel. I often envision their refusal of the worldly ideals, as a person turning a plate of food upside down, as a sign of refusal to eat what has been served.

The Choking Kind

A close examination of the portion of scripture found in Matthew 13:22, reveals how the germination and fruitfulness of God's Word in our lives can be threatened by the cares of this world, and the deceitfulness of its riches. *"He also that receiveth seed among the thorns is he that heareth the word; and the **care of this world, and the deceitfulness of riches, choke the word** and he become unfruitful" (Matthew 13:22).*

Whatever the nature of your world is, if it chokes you, and keeps you from God it is evil. There must be a definite turning away from the *things of the world*, rather than being *attracted* to them. We must deal differently with the world than how we deal with the flesh, or the devil.

Our non-conformity to it should set us apart from its values, and ideals, making us distinct in our walk and relationship with God. I grew up in a main line Church of God, where you would hear messages that would scare you out of hell, messages like: 'Get right or get left behind! What in hell do you want? Tell hell I changed my mind!' And also, 'Sin, can never enter there!' and many more.

Now, while many of these early Bible preachers were not as theologically adept as our modern-day preachers, it was obvious they cared for our souls enough to preach a gospel that drove the fear of God into us. We believers, from the old school, are a hybrid breed now, but thank God for our foundation! It was a good one. It drove home the moral ideals that provided the spiritual equilibrium needed for a post-modern world.

After we become converted, and have come to acknowledge the Lordship of Christ, when we have fully surrendered to Jesus, we too, can say like the apostle Paul; *"But God forbid that I should glory, save in the cross of our Lord Jesus Christ, by whom the world is crucified unto me, and I unto the world" (Galatians 6:14).* Many of us are caught up in our own world, a world of self indulgence and temporal pleasures.

There are those who might dare to say, "My world only consists of cars and hard work etc." It really does not matter what the essential make-up of your world is; if it preoccupies you away from divine fellowship, it is an idolatrous world of sin. If you are enticed with technological advancement you can become easily entangled with iPods, Mp3s, surround-sounds, high definition televisions, computer games, or even worse; you can become a prisoner of the internet.

It is evident from the Scriptures that no one can know God through the means of the world, *"Where is the wise? Where is the scribe? Where is the disputer of this world? Hath not God made foolish the wisdom of this world?" (1 Cor. 1:20).*

Jesus made it clear that the world could never receive the Holy Spirit (John 14:17), because the world operates entirely by its senses. While we may be prepared to deal with the "world" and all its nuances, let's be reminded that the child of God is in the *world*, but he is not of the *world*.

The things of the world are worldly, sensual, and devilish. We must live in the world, but let me remind you that the world does not have to live in us. The ship "must" sail in the water, but the water does not belong in the ship! While we maintain the tender balance of living in this world physically and holistically, let's stay connected to our Lord Spiritually. Let us never become so subjective in our walk and warfare, that we can only recognize the Enemy Without, let's pray for discernment to also see The Enemy Within.

The Enemy Within

Too often, our focus is placed on the enemies of the world and the devil. Although there is much reason to be concerned about supernatural and social enemies, there is a personal enemy in our fleshly nature, waiting to seize upon the opportunity to betray us; an enemy far more deadly than those from without, *The Enemy Within*. You better believe you can be your worst enemy!

We are faced with battles on every front, but in spite of the many demons, the devil, the world and its allurements that assault us, unless we win the battle from within over self, it becomes almost impossible to win the other battles of life. **The battles within are battles of self-conquest.** The effects of the external things are nothing to be compared to the things that come from within. The things that come from within are essentially what defile a man;

*"And he said, that which cometh out of the Man, that defileth the man. For from within, out of the heart of men, proceed evil thoughts adulteries, fornications, murders, Thefts, covetousness, wickedness, deceit, lasciviousness, an evil eye, blasphemy, pride, foolishness: **All these evil things come from within, and defile the man"** (Mark 7:20-23).*

In the Old Testament book of Jeremiah, we read; *"The heart is deceitful above all things, and desperately wicked: who can know it?" (Jeremiah 17:9)* The heart referred to in the scriptures, does not refer to the cardiac pump, which is responsible for blood circulating through the arterial system, but is only a symbol of the soul of man, which is the center of his being.

It is towards the heart that the enemy directs his weapons of attack, *within the soul of men.* It is here in the soul, the central control system, where his will resides, and the zenith of man's existence that the attacks from fleshly lusts are intended to reach; into the center of man's being. We read, *"Beloved, I implore you as sojourners, strangers and exiles in this world to abstain from the sensual urges, the evil desires, the passions of the flesh [your lower nature], that wage war against the soul" (1 Peter 2:11 Amplified).*

The flesh is to be considered a double agent in some sense, because although we walk in it, it is governed by a different law, Paul calls it *"the law of sin which is in his members" (Romans 7:23)*. When the flesh is activated, its function is to **war against our minds**, seeking to make us "prisoners to sinful habits." This is ideally what Satan wants, because as we operate in the corrupt deeds of the flesh, we place ourselves directly under his influence (Romans 6:16).

Satan's only hope of winning man to his cause, is giving him what his flesh wants, in order for him to sin through his spirit.

Many of the problems that we encounter in life are not caused by the economy, the crime rate, the moral slide, the attacks of demons or any such thing, but by our "self" life. Paul refers to it as the flesh, he tells us to *"reckon ourselves dead indeed unto sin" (Romans 6:11)*. There comes a time that binding is not applicable; all the exorcism in the world could never substitute for "self discipline." However, even the exercise of that last fruit of the Spirit [temperance] (Galatians 5:22-23), can only be done by the help of the Holy Spirit.

Pride also is another area, that, if not annihilated, it could also be a means of one's downfall. To think that we are sufficient in ourselves, to think anything as of ourselves is a set up for self destruction. We are only sufficient through the sufficiency of Jesus Christ (2 Corinthians 3:5).

It is said, *"Pride goeth before destruction, and an haughty spirit before a fall. Better it is to be of an humble spirit with the lowly, than to divide the spoil with the proud" (Proverbs 16:18-19)*. It is truly said, "The arm of flesh will fail you, you dear not trust your own." Being crucified with Christ is a process of mortifying the works of the flesh. If we starve it of its desires, it will be mortified. But, if we gratify its cravings and lusts, we strengthen a formidable enemy. *"For if ye live after the flesh, we shall die: but if ye through the Spirit do mortify the deeds of the body, we shall live" (Rom. 8:13).*

To mortify the deeds of the body literally means to overcome the desire for sin and to strengthen the will; it is the death of one part of the body while the rest is alive, like what gangrene or necrosis does. In its simplest form, it can mean merely denying oneself certain pleasures, such as, abstaining from fornication, alcoholic beverage, pornography, etc. It means to kill flesh!

Internal Foes or External Woes

It is not enough that we fight the good fight of faith against afflictions of our bodies with sicknesses, diseases, and infirmities which we must battle daily, but we must fight the battle also, on the psychological front. The challenges and daily grind of life has driven many precious saints to the breaking point. The vast complexities of emotional and psychological problems have paralyzed many, and have prevented them from addressing other important issues of life.

One can become so preoccupied with internal battles, that there is no energy left for the external conflicts.

It can be noted that the church has been *mutated* with a materialistic, gospel of prosperity, and name it and claim it trend. This mutation is responsible for many of our 21st century Christians losing sight of the virtues of Christian ideals. Yes God wants us to prosper, but not at the expense of our relationship with Him. Our general prosperity is predicated upon our soul's prosperity in Christ.

"Beloved, I wish above all things that thou mayest prosper and be in health, even as thy soul prospereth" (3 John 2).

Many Christian soldiers have suspended their call and duty to pursue worldly dreams of grandeur. The popular messages of health, wealth, and prosperity have mutated the post-modern Christian with wrong sets of values. Let us not be deceived! But instead, **let's reverse the mutation** by returning to the totality of scripture as the guide for conduct and the basis of faith. Let's return to sound theology, balanced practical application of the Word, and Christ-centered living. **We must stay focused!**

The reason for a lack of resistance against New Age theology in the body of Christ is obviously because many believers do not know who the Real Enemy is. What can be even worse is directing our energy of resistance and rebellion toward authority figures, church officials, law enforcements and others that are set to watch over us and protect us. Believers who are wrapped up in themselves are blind, and cannot see afar off, **they often become nothing more than self-willed charismatic witches and warlocks.**

Staying Focused

It is a common problem for those under the attack of Satan to become preoccupied with thoughts about how Satan is tempting, afflicting, or oppressing them, rather than reflecting on the victory Christ has won on the cross for them. To become obsessed with the enemy is unhealthy for us as Christians. It is said, 'the best way to keep the enemy out, is to keep Christ in.' The sheep does not need to be terrified of the wolf; all they need to do is remain close to the shepherd.

> *It is not the praying sheep that*
> *Satan trembles at, but the near presence*
> *of the shepherd.*

The instructed Christian whose senses have been developed and exercised by the Word and the Spirit will not fear the devil. However, there should always be a sense of respect for your enemy, especially one who is so cunning and devious. He has earned his stripes with a high success record.

When necessary, the believer must stand against the powers of darkness. Remember, *we overcome them by the blood of the Lamb and the word of our testimony (Revelation 12:11).* As a believer, we must recognize the perils of the world in which we live, and we must know what to do about it. Frequent worship and engaging the presence of God, will enable us to ever be "God conscious" and never become "devil conscious."

There must be an attitude of confidence in who we are in our union with Jesus Christ. This exudes a radiance of faith and confidence in our risen Lord, and strikes terror in the heart of our enemies. It will cause the very powers of darkness to tremble!

Accounting For Your Own Actions

It is a fact that the Devil's instrument must share in his punishment. Remember, when God called for accountability in the Garden of Eden, He began with the man Adam. Adam displaced the blame of his sin technically on God, and inadvertently on his wife. His argument suggested that had God given him a better wife, he never would have fallen. Genesis 3:12: *"And the man said, the woman whom thou gavest to be with me, she gave me, of the tree, and I did eat."* Eve followed suit by blaming the serpent for her disobedience. When God called her into accountability she said, *"The serpent beguiled me, and I did eat" (Genesis 3:13b).*

Let us not forget that the devil cannot make us do anything that we do not want to do. He is no different than you and I, in this respect; that he too is a created being who has a will of *his* own. His will however, cannot override ours if we resist him (James 4:7).

Satan's subtle attack against Adam and Eve serves as a sobering reminder that those who are in communion and fellowship with God are the very ones who must face the enemy in his most devious schemes. Any believer, who is determined to occupy himself with his call and preaching of the gospel, the winning of the lost, and knowing who he is in Christ, will certainly be a target of Satan.

When God addressed the serpent in Genesis 3:14, he did not ask the serpent to give account for his actions, but instead, He dealt out punishment upon the serpent as a creature that became an instrument in the hands of the wicked one. Although the serpent was used of Satan, even though he was just a mere creature, he also was made to partake of Satan's judgment.

"And the Lord God said unto the serpent, because thou hast done this, thou art cursed above all cattle, and above every beast of the field; upon thy belly shalt thou so; and dust shalt thou eat all the days of thy life"
(Genesis 3:14).

It is quite probable that the serpent was an upright creature before the curse. However, the curse subjected him to be a creeping creature afterwards. From henceforth the serpent was to be looked upon as the epitome of evil; a noxious, venomous and despicable creature; an agent of evil and instrumental in the fall of man.

God has filled us with His Holy Spirit and empowered us with His gifts. The Lord would never expose us to a hostile world, or a diabolic force without giving us the weapons and gifting to overcome them. God wants us to always remember that, *"Wherever sin abound, the grace of God much more abound" (Romans 5:20).* Many of God's people are destroyed for lack of knowledge (Hosea 4:6). The 'knowledge' I speak about is not merely theological knowledge; but "knowledge" of God and the things of God. Some people are extremely proud, and have taken extreme views of faith, not recognizing that God allows trials to make them strong.

You may be from the camp of the 'name it and claim it,' but soon you will find that God's will is going to be done on earth, as it is done in heaven. His will might not be what we will, but it's His will that will ultimately be done!

We may choose to live oblivious to the battles raging around us, but that does not make us exempt from being affected by them. In fact, many believers are P.O.W.'s. (Prisoners of war), and unfortunately many are not even aware of it. They are bound to habits, weaknesses, and ideologies and will not acknowledge it and seek help. Others are C.O.W.'s (Casualties of war), and will not submit themselves to the Lord for inner healing. Have you noticed that there are increasing numbers of 21st century believers who carry around much baggage? Many are not in need of an armor bearer, but a porter!

Now don't get me wrong, I am not speaking as one who have arrived, but as one who has experienced firsthand these same wretched states I have described, and know quite well that we can be functioning in ministry, and still not be delivered.

Lazarus was resurrected from the dead. He was breathing, he was thinking, and I'm sure he could make at least a humming sound; in fact, I will go as far as saying, that although he was wrapped like a mummy, somehow he moved, even if he hopped (John 11:44).

> *"And he that was dead came forth, bound hand and foot with grave clothes: ... Jesus saith unto them, Loose him, and let him go.*

Notice, he that was dead "came forth." Although he came forth, he was still bound and needed to be loosed. This should be a sobering reminder to us that one can experience degrees of freedom and yet not be completely free. Setting the captives free requires the accurate use of the key of knowledge (Luke 11:52). The key of knowledge is the master-key that enables the other keys of Binding and Loosing to work effectively for the believer (Matthew 18:18). However, knowledge without maturity puffeth up (1 Corinthians 8:1). It swells the head and produces a haughty forced-ripe fruit. We need the Holy Spirit to give us accurate discernment and help us to understand and regulate the knowledge we receive with Godly wisdom.

Real knowledge, like everything else of value, is not obtained easily. It must be worked for, studied for, thought for, and more than all, it must be prayed for. It is my earnest prayer that you will be enabled by these teachings, to "recognize" and "know" *Who the Real Enemy Is.* May you be always filled with the Spirit, and may the Lord sharpen your discernment, quicken your understanding, and perfect your perception.

READER'S DIGEST

Total Recall

- We must be careful never to become too subjective in our view of who our real enemy is. They could hail from one or more of three camps: The world, the flesh, or the devil and his demons.

- What is one of the primary means used by the enemy to ensnare humanity?

- Like Lazarus, one can be functional and yet still not be delivered. What should be the next step to being delivered?

- There are several modes that we use to acquire data and intelligence, can you name a few?

- There are nine gifts of the Spirit as recorded in 1 Corinthians chapter twelve. They are divided into three categories; can you list the categories and the gifts that belong to them?

- According to this chapter, what is one of the priorities of Satan and his servants?

- Margie, the health care-giver was tricked by the enemy, can you say how?

- What are some of the hate crimes that professing believers commit?

- There are some methods and devices that the enemy uses to ensnare the souls of men. What categories do they fall under?

- According to this chapter what is the greatest form of resistance we could put-up, or offer?

- According to this chapter, who is the enemy from within? Who is the enemy from without?

- Which key possessed by the believer, is said to be his master key?

9

SHALLOW VICTORIES

I was well prepared for the freshness that accompanied the early spring, with its brisk cool breeze under the shadowed foment of the New York's sun. I wondered if I was the only Jamaican who, after many years of winters in the United States, could not wait to enjoy the cool spring and hot summer months, which followed the algidity of winter. I had recently returned from a weekend retreat in Canada, where I ministered. The drive from Canada back to New York was a lengthy one, but the hours passed with tranquil, scenic views, of meadows and mountainous landscapes, which painted the peripherals of the highway.

On the day of my arrival home, I sensed a renewing and refreshing within me. My joy stemmed from a deepened sense of purpose, which I realized with clarity over the weekend of meetings. Prior to accepting the assignment, there was a heightened sense and a keen awareness of the presence of the Lord in my life. He spoke a word into my spirit. He said, "Mobilize your ministry!" The word from the Lord had provided me with the impetus I needed at the time to drive from New York into Canada. That Word became a new mandate for me in ministry. I ministered in Toronto for three days, and it was truly a success! Upon my return to New York however, I was faced with the usual cares of family responsibilities, and the challenges of a young ministry. I had a secular job at the time as a manager in an auto parts franchise. I occupied myself in ministry as an itinerant evangelist, and pastor of a small group that met weekly in my home in Queens, New York. On the following day after my return from Canada, I was in the study reading when the telephone rang.

I had a friend and fellow-minister, whom I will call Dwayne, who stayed at my home at the time. He took the telephone call. (I have changed the names of the people involved for confidential reasons) As Dwayne handed me the phone he said, "It's Alene." Alene was a recent convert who had a desire to know more about the Lord; she lived in the Bronx, with her teenage daughter, Jenny. She had also made a recent commitment to Christ. I took the phone from Dwayne and answered, "Praise the Lord, Alene!" She answered, "Welcome back Pastor! I hope I am not disturbing you?" Then I chuckled blushingly and said, "Huh! Not at all my sister, is everything alright with yourself and the family?" She then cleared her throat; "Ahem!" and said, "Well, it's not really on my behalf that I am calling, but it's on the behalf of my cousin Manny. He seems to be having some problems spiritually and he may need your help." I said to her, "Well tell me, is he there?" She replied, "Sure, would you like to speak with him?" I answered, "Certainly!"

As I waited on her cousin to get on the phone, I grasped the glass that was next to me and took a sip of the ginger ale which I was drinking earlier. He took the phone and said, "Hello!" to which I replied, "Hello Manny, Alene shared with me that you might be having some spiritual problems, could you explain a little more to me?" Manny began to explain, "Well, pastor, I am a spiritual man who is trying to get closer to God, but there seems to be a blockage." I thought to myself, 'well, is that not like the devil? Every time he sees people drawing close to God he has to start messing?' Manny continued, "You see pastor, I am trying to do the right thing, but I am having some interference. Every time I get close, I get a blockage, and even sometimes I hear voices." I asked, "You hear voices?" In asking that question, Dwayne drew himself closer to where I was sitting; he became sparked with interest, because we knew from former cases that the hearing of voices were the more serious ones. I heard Alene in the background on the other end of the line saying something, and then Manny said, "Pastor, is it possible for you to see me this week some time? I must get past this hurdle so that I can receive the light."

You know, there are times when you hear certain words, phrases or statements that just trigger off an alarm within you, and yet you may rationalize it. Not because someone professes to be spiritual, or even have a desire for "God" means that they seek the same Spirit you do, or desire the same God you long for. I then said to Manny, "So, you would like to meet with me this week, huh?" He said, "Yea pastor, I think you could help me based upon what Alene says about your knowledge of deliverance." I replied, "Is Thursday evening ok with you, Manny?" he replied, "That will be just fine pastor, about what time?" I thought quickly about my schedule for that day and then said, "About seven thirty, by Alene's home, is that all right for you?" He said, "That will be just fine with me," I then said, "So until then, God bless you."

I spoke again with Alene and informed her of the arrangement that I made with Manny and bade her farewell. I arranged the meeting at Alene's home, because at the time, I was living in Queens, New York, and did not yet have an office in the Bronx where she lived.

Minister Dwayne sat on the lounge chair across from me while I spoke on the phone. When I was through speaking on the phone,

Dwayne sat up in his chair and said, "So, he is hearing voices eh?" I replied, "Yea, it seems as if the enemy is oppressing him as he tries to press forward. What are you doing on Thursday evening, at about 7:30? Could you accompany me to assess the situation?" I asked. He replied, "I am not too sure, but if I'm not mistaken I may be engaged at that time, but I'll let you know if I can make it."

The days passed quietly and uneventfully, and soon it was Thursday morning. After morning devotion I asked my wife if she would accompany me in the evening, but she thought it best to ask Dwayne, seeing that she had the responsibility of the home and children to care for. I asked Dwayne if it was possible for him to accompany me in the evening to discuss the situation with Manny, but unfortunately, he said he would be engaged, however he would be praying for me. "Praying for me?" I thought.

I had a hard time reconciling with the idea that after three days notice he could not accompany me. However, I purposed to go anyway. I said to myself, 'Well, all I am doing is just getting a sense of what's really happening with Manny.' At least that's what I thought.

Now, as I recall those days of early ministry, I will agree with the old African adage which says, **"You can't run to the beat of every drum."** God may have called us to the ministry, but we shouldn't try to be a spiritual Florence Nightingale. All things indeed might be lawful but not all are expedient (1 Corinthians 10:23). We must know the mind of God on a particular situation; not because a door opens up to you, means that God wants you to walk through it.

I spent the day at work, pausing occasionally for prayer. When the evening came, I made a short stop at the bookstore to purchase some new convert materials, and then proceeded to go to Alene's home. I arrived there at approximately 7:25pm. On my arrival, I could smell the sweet aroma of curried mutton in the hallway, and hear gospel music playing in the apartment. "Praise the Lord!" I said as I entered the home. Alene and her daughter Jenny, greeted me warmly, and led me to the living room. "This is my cousin, Manny," she said, as she pointed to the small framed, well dressed man that sat on a sofa in the corner of the room. "Thank you for coming pastor," he said softly. "A pleasure to meet you Manny" I said, as I shook his hand and sat in the seat facing him. Alene offered me tea, while she and Jenny occupied themselves in the kitchen, after lowering the music. I made myself comfortable as I sat facing Manny in the living room. He had an anxious look on his face as he watched me intently seeking to ascertain the scope of my knowledge. It is vitally important for a Christian, especially Pastors, to understand the dynamics of the makeup of the human persona. By acquiring this knowledge over time, we are able to minister effectively and meaningfully to the needs of people. Therefore, I was not intimidated by his intense stare.

It is particularly important for those who are engaged in ministry to identify and understand the dynamics that are at work in personality, because people are ministry!

This chapter seeks to aid the Pastor/Minister/Christian worker in understanding the dangers of solo encounters with evil, as well as the power of the spoken word. It also expresses the need to be careful in how we handle threats and issues of recycled evil.

Manny Explains

I sat comfortably in front of Manny and said, "So tell me Manny, what seems to be the nature of your concern?" He replied, "I was

161

deeply involved in ministry many years ago." He sighed deeply, as he continued, "I have even baptized some people, but I fell away from the faith some time ago, now finally, I am making my way back." He went on to say, "I have preached on many occasions and I was instrumental in helping many people. I am a Maroon from the parish of St. Mary, in the island of Jamaica." I said to him, "Tell me; in what way did you help people?" He looked at me with a puzzled look on his face and said, "I used to clear them from voodoo curses and things, and now I am trying to get the light back, but there is interference. I just need your help."

Now when he said that, I thought to myself, 'What in the world did I get myself into this time, Lord?' One particular scripture came to mind; "It is the glory of God to conceal a thing: but the honour of kings is to search out a matter" (Proverbs 25:2). I thought to myself 'where is he going with this?' I took a sip of the mint tea Alene had prepared for me, and with a calm composure I looked him into his eyes and said, "What is this light you speak about Manny?" As I sat there awaiting his response, his face began to contort with an expression of pain. He began to knit his brow as a look of dismay and annoyance came upon his face. I asked, "Are you ok, Manny?" He sat upright, signaling with his hand, as he pointed to his head, "They are talking," he said, "and they are very angry!" I asked him, "What are they saying Manny?"

With heightened interest I sat up in my seat looking at him intently. I could not help but think, 'I wonder if this man is schizophrenic?' As I sat there pondering and praying, awaiting his reply, he looked upward into the ceiling, scanning it from left to right. So, I repeated more assertively, "What are they saying Manny?"

At that moment, he looked at me with a spaced-out look; it was as though he was looking through me. In an amplified, hoarse voice of bass and baritone, he replied, "What do you want with Manny? He is not here, he is mine!" I realized at that point that I had awakened a giant, and by the sound of his forceful tone I was in for a battle!

Alerted by this unexpected but imminent demonic confrontation, I was forced to reckon with my own cautious teachings that believers should never endeavor to undertake a spiritual battle without an armor bearer, an assisting prayer warrior, or an intercessory team. When Jesus sent out his disciples, he sent them out two by two (Mark 6:7). Here I was, facing a demonized man alone with two new converts, who had no prior training or experience in spiritual warfare, and were not yet filled with the Holy Spirit. I purposed not to involve them directly in this battle. I felt I had no other recourse but to fight, and fight alone. My philosophy is, once you have engaged the entity, you cannot retreat by non engagement or silence. You must respond, or else the entity will interpret your silence as fear; and fear is the primary hatching ground for torment and defeat.

Let me pause here to give a balanced warning. You should never let your ego push you into a battle that you are not prepared to fight. It is better for you to retreat with dignity early, than to be forced into a battle you are not ready for. Yes, God is your keeper and your defender, and you have been empowered by the Lord to cast out demons and thread upon serpents and scorpions; but, bear in mind that God's timing is also a vital component in your warfare. You will come to find experientially, that while you may win your battle, the person you are delivering could lose their war and vice versa.

Always consider the well being of yourself and the oppressed person before you engage. I believe the most viable candidate for a life threatening surgery is the one who has a will to live. In fact, I have heard of cases where doctors would not do surgery because their patient was not in a positive frame of mind. The believer will find that like the surgeon, his power is not an end in itself. It is how and when that power is used that makes the difference.

There are times in life where I have found greater success in approaching life's challenges in an unassuming way. At times it would appear that you are non-threatening like a dove; but you are as wise as a serpent (Matthew 10:16). You must be steady in one direction like a serpent's head, while his body shifts from side to side. He appears harmless, but don't be fooled, he is focused! Sometimes this strategy works. This battle however, was not one of those times!

Delivering Manny

Addressing the demonic spirit that spoke through Manny, I said sharply, "You cannot have Manny, Jesus desires to save his soul and you are forbidden to have him!" He proceeded to speak with a deep, hoarse voice, "Manny was a preacher, but he left the faith to practice, Manny is a backslider and he is mine!" I then stood up with my finger pointed at him, while Alene and Jenny stood terrified by the living room entrance watching. I indicated to them that they should pray. At the time, many things flooded my mind, one of which was that, 'Manny must have made a decision somewhere in his life that opened the door to this level of invasion.' I further thought, 'Since God is married to the backslider, then how could this devil be so bold in his claim against a former preacher?'

While these thoughts occurred to me, one particular scripture came to mind, and shifted me into gear to do battle for Manny's soul. *"Shall the prey be taken from the mighty, or the lawful captive delivered? But thus saith the LORD, Even the captives of the mighty shall be taken away, and the prey of the terrible shall be delivered: for I will contend with him that contendeth with thee, and I will save thy children" (Isaiah 49:24-25).*

As this scripture came to mind, it quickened to me the understanding that Manny may have violated some biblical principles, and made himself a legal captive of the devil, but today, God would deliver him from the jaws of the mighty! "Loose this man and let him go!" I commanded. "You will not get him!" He replied defiantly. I stood over him pointing my finger, speaking more authoritatively, "I command *you unclean spirit* to loose him now in Jesus' name!"

It was here that the reality of the power of the spoken word being life or death was crystallized in my mind, as he replied to my rebuke. He said, "I will never leave this body, *you* are unclean!" Now when he said, "You are unclean!" that statement hit me like a ton of bricks in my chest. It was as if his word formed a fist and punched me off balance. In a matter of seconds, all my life's activities scanned through my mind. I reflected upon my life, my experience, and my walk with God. I examined myself, and I could not see anywhere in my life at the time where there were any inconsistencies in my Christian profession.

Now don't get me wrong; since then, I have engaged in spiritual warfare with the enemy, even when things were not 100%, but on this occasion, my heart and conscience were clean before God. It is important to bear in mind, that when the enemy accuses you of something, it should not be taken as mere words or empty rhetoric. *It is spirit and death!* Whether it is true or not, it still holds the potency of a fiery dart, or deadly venom. Therefore, we must be very careful how we engage in verbal exchanges with the enemy. Words are powerful! They can do great damage, or great good; it depends on who is speaking, and what is being said.

When he said, "…*you are unclean!*" he began laughing hysterically. I stood there for what seemed like a very long time. I felt numb and muzzled with unfounded guilt, as my mind raced through many events and experiences. Amidst my racing thoughts and his hideous laughter, I was suddenly jolted back into the awareness of my surroundings; back in the presence of Alene, and her daughter Jenny, who stood by the living room entrance crying frantically; while Manny sat there laughing hysterically.

Although it felt like minutes had passed, all this took place within in a period of approximately twenty seconds. Regaining my composure I said, "I bind you unclean spirit, and command you to hold your peace in Jesus name!" He stopped laughing and sat there pouting with a defiant look. I then said, "You will leave the body of Manny now in Jesus name!" He kept repeating in a low tone, "No I will not leave, this is my house and I am not going anywhere." I felt a sense of help-lessness at this point of the confrontation.

As I looked to my left I envisioned an angel standing with his sword in its scabbard, as if to assure me that help was near, so I drew nearer to Manny. As I came closer to him, he shouted at the top of a crusty voice and said, "When Manny went looking for help I looked for help also." Now what he was referring to was the fact that Manny sought for someone to cast him (the demon) out, so that Manny could be free to pursue his spiritist interests. As we learned in chapter four *The Territorial War;* there are occasions when Satan's kingdom is divided (Matthew 12:26). I have learned that demons will seek to get the advantage over other demonic spirits for personal reasons, etc.

Quite often, when spiritual warfare ensues, we fail to comprehend the magnitude of the battle because it is often on the plateau of the exchange of faith-charged words. We have a tendency of trivializing the reality of the warfare. Many believers take spiritual warfare light-ly, and dare to engage the forces of darkness on a presumptuous premise of super spirituality. In no way am I overemphasizing the need for the believer's readiness and complete armament (Ephesians 6:10-17). This is vitally essential to successfully withstand the attacks of our spiritual opponents.

The demonic spirit in Manny said, "When Manny sent for help, I (the demonic spirit) sent for help." He said this with a look of glee, knowing that his reinforcements were already in place. As I describe to you what happened next, you will understand just how well coordinated they are. Although Manny was not physically violent, the demonic spirit spoke through him in a harsh and violent tone. He said, "Look! Look! When Manny sent for help I sent for help, look!" He said this mockingly as he pointed into the ceiling above the landing of the stairs. Those older homes in the Bronx were made with a skylight approximately nine square feet. They were made that way to allow air and natural sunlight into the stairway. They also had a meshed metal wire on the outside of the glass. The window in the skylight was opened slightly to allow the fresh spring air to enter the house. Two hanging plants dangled from the skylight suspended from the ceiling.

As I stepped backwards away from Manny, I pointed my finger at him as he mockingly said, "Yes, look, when Manny sent for help, I sent for help." As I stepped backward to look into the ceiling, Alene and Jenny started screaming as we all looked into the skylight. There were three pigeons picking aggressively and tearing at the metal wire mesh that lined the outside of the ported roof. The three pigeons were so intent on getting into the house that the bleeding from the cuts they sustained trying to tear through the metal mesh did not deter them at all. I know it may sound a bit absurd to you, but when we saw the inside glass being covered with the blood of the wounded pigeons, we knew how very real the situation was. The demon laughed mockingly, saying, "Ha-haayeh, you see, when Manny sent for help I sent for help!"

With my finger pointed at Manny, I said, "I bind you and command you in Jesus' name to hold your peace." He stopped laughing. I then proceeded to plead the blood of Jesus against the pigeons. I told Jenny to get me a broom or a stick, which she did, while I cursed the prince of the powers of the air and commanded, "In Jesus name, I rebuke you unclean spirits, I forbid your entrance into this home and command you to leave now in Jesus' name!"

Two of the three pigeons flew away but the third one stood on the metal mesh picking aggressively trying to tear the wire with his beak. I gave Alene the broom and told her to keep hitting the skylight and say, "I rebuke you in Jesus name, go!" This she did, as I walked towards Manny. I laid my hand on his head and said, "I command you to come out of him now and go into dry places in Jesus' name!" He began to make deep, groaning sounds, like a wounded animal, as I laid my hand upon his forehead and rebuked the evil spirit within him. I picked up a Bible that was on the side table and turned it to the ninety first Psalm. As I read the psalm, when I reached the third verse, the breakthrough came. I placed Manny's name in the verses and quoted the Psalm on Manny's behalf. I quoted the third verse like this, *"Surely the Lord shall deliver Manny from the snare of the fowler, and from the noisome pestilence..."* As I said, this he screamed, "Ok, ok I will go, but I will kill Manny with a car tomorrow, and I will blind you tomorrow!"

Have you ever been threatened by a demonic spirit? If you have been, you know that such threats are as real as a man holding a loaded gun to your head. What's even more damaging is when a demonized person speaks against your life; you must refute them sharply! When the demon made the threats against Manny and me, I felt a rush of holy indignation rise up within me, so I said, "In the name of Jesus, I refute your words against Manny and I. I bind every evil work and demonic conspiracy now, in Jesus name!" I quoted a powerful scripture that I often use to refute verbal curses, gossips, and demonic counsel. I am sure this scripture will be a blessing to you also; it is taken from the Old Testament. It says, *"Take counsel together, and it shall come to nought; speak the word, and it shall not stand: for God is with us" (Isaiah 8:10).*

After I quoted the scripture from Isaiah, Manny sighed deeply and flopped backward into the chair in which he was sitting. I asked Alene and Jenny to join me as I led Manny to denounce Manichaeism and accept Jesus Christ as his Lord. I anointed all three of them with olive oil and prayed over them. I declared the Lordship and dominion of Jesus over their lives, and proclaimed the covering and protection of God against Satanic backlashes and repercussions. When I was through praying, I asked Manny to tell us how he felt, and if he still heard voices. Ironically, he remembered very little about the deliverance, but thanks be to God he was free and the voices stopped!

What I found out in my discussion with Manny later that night was that he was involved in Manichaeism. He wanted to be free from the familiar spirit, who was preventing him from being flooded with what he called, "the conscious light."

Darkness through Light

The religion of Manichaeism is a religion of "Light." At the time, I was not fully aware of the religion, but some time later I discovered its erroneous teachings. The religion of Manichaeism believes that man can be saved by the knowledge of spiritual matters. They believe that man is a stranger in the world and a god away from home. They believe that man can regain lost paradise, or heaven through knowledge. They believe in a born again experience, but not the same as evangelical Christianity. They teach "born again of lights and of the gods" (which are actually fallen angels or demons). When the light they seek is achieved, they believe their souls to be free from suffering, and that they become equal with the gods (fallen angels); making them little gods also. Once the 'light' is received, they profess freedom of the soul over matter; and power over demons, witches, and warlocks.

169

Had I known what I was getting myself into, I never would have made the appointment with Manny. He knew what he was into; he knew all about Manichaeism, I didn't. Sometimes, zeal without knowledge can be very dangerous; dangerous indeed, especially for the overly zealous. Can you imagine? Manny used me! Although at the time I did not realize it. He used me to cast out the dominant familiar spirit of the occult in order for him to be initiated into the kingdom of 'lights,' *darkness* (Luke 11:34).

The Saga Continued

When I first spoke to Manny on the telephone, I thought he was a backslider. He had expressed to me his need to get over what he called 'this hurdle,' so that he could receive 'the light.' Although something was triggered within me when he first told me that, I rationalized that he must have wanted to return to the Lord, but was unable to, because demonic spirits were preventing him. What I did not know was that he wanted to have equality with the spirits; while they sought to retain their dominance in his life. He was only seeking freedom from them, to be free among them.

After leaving Alene's home that night, I drove from the Bronx, into Queens, N.Y. The forty five minute drive was filled with my audible praise to God, for Manny's deliverance. I felt a personal sense of victory over the enemy. When I arrived at my home in Queens, I awoke Dwayne and Lydia, my wife, to report the victory I had won. I shared with them the events of the evening and my encounters with the demon and the three pigeons. They were both excited about how the evening had gone, and shared in my celebration of seeming victory. We prayed together that night and went to our beds knowing that another victory had been won. Praise the Lord! Little did I know, this was a "shallow victory," and it wasn't over until it was *really* over.

The night passed quietly and uneventfully. On the Friday, morning I awoke quite refreshed and spiritually high from Thursday's victory. It was a beautiful morning, and I was especially happy because the weekend was near. I drove to work the morning, listening to my favorite gospel songs. After arriving at work, the victory from the previous night faded into the background. It was a busy morning, and as the manager of the store, I was occupied with several aspects of the business that did not allow me time to sit.

After the busy morning passed, I was finally able to get a breather. It was approximately 12:30 in the afternoon. I sat around my desk where I had a small copy of the New Testament and the Psalms. As I opened the scripture to read a portion of the Psalms, the Holy Spirit said to me, "Pray!" As I closed the Bible and began to pray, I could tell, something big was on the way!

A Wicked Act

At approximately 12:45pm the telephone rang, it was Alene. She was crying hysterically. She said, "Pastor, oh my God, Manny! Pastor, it's Manny!" I said, "What's the matter with Manny, Sis?" She replied, "He was hit by a car this morning, ooh God no!" I asked, "Is he alive?" She answered, "Yes pastor, but he has a broken leg and some bruises. He is in Montefiore hospital. But isn't that what the demon said? Ooh God, pastor, he is going to try to blind you!" I said, "Alene, let us pray at this time." So we prayed for Manny, for her and her daughter Jenny, and for me. I reassured her that I would be fine and that I would visit Manny some time later. I immediately called my wife, Dwayne, and a fellow minister to request prayer for myself and Manny.

Act Two

As the afternoon progressed, I became extremely vigilant and prayerful. I found myself quoting scriptures and pleading the cover-

171

ing of the blood of Jesus Christ. I repeatedly quoted Isaiah 54:17. I personalized the scripture and quoted it in the first person; *"No weapon that is formed against me shall prosper; and every tongue that shall rise against me in judgment I condemn. This is my heritage, and my righteousness is of the LORD."* (Italics mine.)

The afternoon became busy again at the store. The retail business was booming. This was a fine time for an automobile owner to put some work into repairing and beautifying his car. At approximately 4:00 in the afternoon, a customer entered the auto store with a battery which he claimed had a bad cell. This was his third battery in a year, and I was convinced that his alternator was draining the battery. One of the countermen called me to verify if a cell of the battery was indeed dead before he went outside to check the charge on the alternator. The counterman had already used a hydrometer, to check the acid of the cells, but the finding was inconclusive, so I decided to put a load tester on the battery. As I cranked the load tester, I stood above the battery looking into the cells. I looked for burning bubbles to determine if a cell was defective. As I looked down into the battery, without any warning, it suddenly exploded, and all the acid splashed on my face.

As I felt the acid burning my eyes and my face, I cried out, 'Oh God, no. The devil is a liar!' Some of the employees led me into the bathroom where I washed the acid from my eyes and face. My eyes burned in excruciating pain, as my face began itching intensely. Fortunately, I was wearing my eyeglasses; it deflected the acid and small particles that scattered from the battery during the explosion. As I finished washing my face in the bathroom, I opened my eyes and cried, 'I can see, praise the Lord, I can see!' If you think I was praying before this incident, it was now that I truly began to pray.

I remained in my office for the duration of the afternoon, praying and nursing my eyes with eye wash. The customer was given a new battery, and he left satisfied. I closed the store at 6:00pm without any further incidents. I decided to go straight home after promising Alene that I would visit Manny in the hospital the following day. I did not tell her, what had happened to me earlier that afternoon; how the battery had exploded into my face and the acid almost blinded me.

Act Three

I closed the store for the day and headed prayerfully home. As I entered the car, I invited Jesus to journey with me, to place a hedge of protection around me and take me safely home. I could sense the oppression of the enemy; it was as if a load was sitting on my shoulder. A stiff feeling came over my neck, shooting up into my head. I prayed even harder now as I made my way home. On my journey from the Bronx into Queens, I decided to take a main street called Baychester Avenue to the New England Thruway. As I came to the end of Baychester Avenue leading into the highway, a drunken driver came from 222nd Street; an adjoining road that also led to the highway. He plunged into the passenger side of my Cadillac, shattering the glass into my face and destroying the passenger door and quarter panel. When he came out of his car apologizing for not stopping at the intersection, I quickly accepted his apology and told him, "Never mind, accidents will happen." I was so happy that the broken fragments of glass had deflected from my eyeglasses without injuring my eyes. I shouted, 'Praise the Lord, I can see!' I dismissed the man without exchanging papers; I just wanted to make it home quickly and safely, in Jesus name.

I arrived home in Queens at approximately 7:00pm that Friday evening. 'I made it home safely,' I thought. 'Praise the Lord, safe at last!' I said, thinking to myself. 'If I could just go inside and get beyond this day, the worst would have passed and my victory would be complete.' I parked the damaged car into the driveway of our home and proceeded to go towards the gate. At that moment, my neighbor, Eugene, who lived directly in front of me, called, "Hey Rev., what's up?" I turned around to respond, when he said, "Could you take a look at this lawn mower for me?"

Eugene, like most of my neighbors, knew that I was mechanically inclined, because I often repaired my cars in the double-car garage. I closed the gate of my home and headed across the street to assist Eugene. "This lawnmower started earlier but it will not run," he said. I replied, "Tell me, did you put fresh gas in it, and clean the spark plug?" He said, "Yes I did Rev., but if you lay your hands on it maybe it will start for you." I blushed and said, "Let me see it."

Now, those old lawn mowers were the kind that you pulled with the cord around a pulley to get it started. I pulled the first time and the lawn mower started immediately. So he said, "I told you Rev., you've got the touch!" I said to him, "Praise God Eugene, praise the Lord!" and walked through his gate. The lawn mower ran for a short time and as I reached the sidewalk of my home, it shut off again.

The Final Act

He tried to start it once again, but was unsuccessful, so he yelled, "Hey Rev., I need that touch again!" I recognized at this point that the enemy was messing with me, so, I walked back across the street binding the enemy of interference and saying; "Loose here devil!" I reached down and again placed my right hand on the pull cord and my left foot on the top of the lawn mower and pulled. My God, it started! But only for a brief second, and then it stopped, and "bam!"

The pulley flew off and hit my face. I felt my glasses shatter and warm blood running down the right side of my face. I cried out, "Jesus!" Eugene exclaimed, "Oh no Rev., can you see?" As I held my bleeding brow, he anxiously washed the blood from my eyes with his garden hose, saying, "Can you see Rev., can you see?"

After wiping the blood from my right eye, I covered my left eye with my hand. "I can see!" I shouted. "Praise God, I can see! The devil is a liar, I can see!" By this time my family heard all the commotion outside and came out to assist me into the house and up the stairs. The cut was a deep slash above my right eye that appeared to require stitches. After discussing it, we decided to go to the hospital to have them look at it. After reaching the hospital, the doctor examined it and insisted that I needed stitches. However, I chose not to have it stitched, but chose instead to treat it with peroxide and bandage it. This was the alternative I was unofficially given at the hospital. We went back home that night and had a thanksgiving service at my home, with my family and my friend Dwayne. Everyone was amazed to hear about the savage attacks of that day. I testified of the entire account from Manny being hit with a car earlier that morning, to the battery exploding in my face in the afternoon. We praised God for his protection and his love for me.

The next day I awoke with a black eye. I looked like someone that was punched in the eye. I went to visit Manny in the hospital that Saturday and encouraged and prayed for him. He recovered well and resumed his normal flow of life, attending a full gospel church in Manhattan, where he lived. The wound above my right eye healed well without stitches, and only a small scar remains today, thank God! My victory may have been shallow in Manny's case, but I have ultimately triumphed over the enemy. I may have lost a battle, but thank God I won the war!

As I write this chapter, my heart is warmed with love and appreciation for the Lord, in sparing our lives and displaying His matchless grace towards me. I feel in many ways that I can say like the apostle Paul, *"From henceforth let no man trouble me: for I bear in my body the marks of the Lord Jesus"* (Galatians 6:17). I want to encourage you today in your walk with God, not be terrified at the schemes and attacks of the enemy, but instead, *"Be ye stedfast, unmoveable, always abounding in the work of the Lord, forasmuch as ye know that your labour is not in vain in the Lord"* (1Cor. 15:58). Remember; *"No weapon that is formed against you shall prosper!"* (Isa. 54:17).

It is my sincere prayer that you will win your war, and experience lasting victory in all your undertakings.

POWER POINTS

- It is better to postpone an appointment, than to keep it at the risk of being ill prepared. It could prove to be a costly appointment.

- It's ok to get reinforcements, Jesus sent His disciples out two at a time. Two is always better than one (Ecclesiastes 4:9-12).

- When casting out a demon, it is important for the person who is demonized at some point, to confess Jesus Christ as their Lord and personal Savior.

- Whenever you are called upon to engage in ministering to someone, always build a mental profile on the person.

- If you are taken 'off guard' by a demonic confrontation, and you are not prepared to fight, tell the demon to hold his peace, in Jesus' name! At that point, you should endeavor to engage the person, by calling for *that* person to manifest and respond.

- Never permit a demonic spirit to 'tell you about yourself,' whether it is true or false.

- If you must interrogate a demonic spirit for identification purposes, do not allow him to engage you in any other discussions.

- Never allow an unclean spirit to speak without your permission.

- Be sure to refute and disown every threat and negative thing that is spoken against you, whether by a spirit, or a human agent.

- Take time to memorize defensive, as well as offensive scriptures. They are a vital part of your arsenal.

- Pray for a sharp spirit of discernment, it is most necessary when dealing with the invisible world.

- Walk in a true spirit of humility, and be always vigilant. Remember, God hath not given us the spirit of fear; but of power, and of love, and of a sound mind (2 Timothy 1:7).

10

WINNING THE WAR WITHIN

Quite often we are led to believe that when we first come to Christ and give our lives to Him it is euphoria, and that becoming a Christian is a cure-all. Many believe also that once they become children of God the inward sinful propensity is automatically conquered and subdued, or eradicated by the greater-One living within. Many others also, are led to believe that they need not be concerned with the old nature posing a threat or problem again, ever. But in time, the very opposite will prove true.

Armed and Extremely Dangerous is intended to equip you with the proper tools, furnishings, and weapons you need to live a practical victorious Christian life. My endeavors is not only to deliver the body of Christ 'from,' but to deliver 'to' the believer that which I have received from the Lord. As we advance on our Christian journey we will find that somewhere along our pilgrimage we will face an opponent that we will never forget. I want to be transparent and honest with you right now, and tell you that my greatest opponent thus far, has been 'me.' Sometimes we will find that the greatest of battles we fight as believers are not on the frontiers of the external, but on the front line of the internal. It is an internal conflict with 'self.' In such cases the deliverance we seek is not from demons or outward threats, but deliverance from our very self.

While history has taught us so many lessons through wars and national conflicts, the greatest lessons can be learned from the battle field of the soul. This chapter is dedicated to the person who is in conflict with himself. I pray that at the close of it you will stand victorious as a winner of The War Within.

This Is War!

In First Timothy 1:18-19 Paul admonished his young spiritual son Timothy to *"War a good warfare"* by *"Holding faith, and a good conscience"* which some have rejected and suffered shipwreck in regard to their faith. He encouraged Timothy to remain in the fight of faith and keep true to the call of God upon his life. Paul further reminded Timothy in Second Timothy 2:3-4 *"Thou therefore endure hardness, as a good soldier of Jesus Christ. No man that warreth entangleth himself with the affairs of this life; that he may please him who hath chosen him to be a soldier."*

The war mentioned here in 2 Timothy 2:3-4 relates to warfare, but you will notice that these mental wars do not include the devil as the combatant, but instead Paul encourages Timothy to make a decisive decision to keep his mind clear of the things of the world and remain focused and true to the election of God upon his life.

The soul (mind) is a militarized zone where wars are won or lost.

Paul's emphasis is on maintaining the discipline of a soldier in Timothy's sanctification and Godly call; even when faced with extremely difficult challenges. It is evident that these New Testament passages of Scripture using the words 'war' and 'warfare' are primarily dealing with the believer doing battle against the works of the flesh and worldly lusts, conquering and taking charge of their mind. I am not suggesting that our battles are only in our minds, because we do have the devil and his demons as enemies and they wage war on many fronts, attacking our finances, our minds, our bodies, etc., and provoking and stimulating our flesh. The works of the flesh has become more pronounced in the church of God today.

James, in his epistle makes it clear that *"Where there is bitter envying and strife, there is confusion and every evil work" (James 3:16).* He expressed earlier, (vs.14-15) that bitter envying and strife, were earthly, sensual, and devilish. He pointed out that confusion and every evil work was worldly. It is a bi-product of worldliness in the body of Christ and has been the cause of the rise of many cults, denominations, factions, divisions and cliques in the church today.

Any honest believer that saw Christianity in the 20th century would be quick to admit that the church has become worldlier rather than more Godly in the 21st century. There is a spirit of rivalry and jealousy found in the body of Christ today, which results in confusion and every evil work. It is not the work of devils, but evil works produced by carnal minds. With this observation as a background, we get a good picture of what James is saying in James 4:1 he writes: *"From whence come wars and fightings among you? come they not hence, even of your lusts that war in your members?"*

The war here as described by James is more centered around fighting fleshly lusts that is intended to undermine spiritual growth, development and maturity. It is quite clear that the wars and skirmishes we encounter among ourselves come primarily because of lusts, fleshly ambitions, and the desire for sensual pleasures. There is little need for the devil to wage a campaign against the church if she is self destructive. I have seen too many great ministries destroyed from within. While we may say that the devil is responsible for the ruin of many great ministries, we cannot neglect the inner failures of character or the lack of it. The apostle Peter echoes the same sentiments; he also speaks of war within, he writes; *"Dearly beloved, I beseech you as strangers and pilgrims, abstain from fleshly lusts, which war against the soul" (1 Pet.2:11).*

We are admonished to take our thoughts captive, through a deliberate and purposeful action. We are told plainly *"to stop feeding our fleshly sensual desires"* which wars against the soul (1 Timothy 1:18; 1Peter 2:11; 2 Timothy 2:4; James 4:1). If the inward struggle of a believer is not overcome, it can retard his ministry. It is only as we walk in the light of God's Word that we are assured inward victory.

God has given us His Holy Spirit to lead, direct, and guide our lives. As we follow the leading of the Spirit, we will also escape the pitfalls and snares that are all around us. When we yield ourselves completely to Him he enables and empowers us to do above and beyond our fondest dreams. We have the light of life living within us, and when we walk in that light there will be no occasion of stumbling in us (John 8:12; 1 John 2:10).

We have heard it asked again and again, "Why has my life become riddled with so much conflict since I have accepted Christ?" What we need to understand is this; we have been delivered from the kingdom of darkness and have been made children of God's marvelous light (2 Corinthians 4:6-7; Acts 26:18)). This light of the knowledge of the glory of God does not blind us to the darkness around us, and the evil that lurks within us.

"For God, who commanded the light to shine out of darkness, hath shined in our hearts, to give the light of the knowledge of the glory of God in the face of Jesus Christ. But we have this treasure in earthen vessels, that the excellency of the power may be of God, and not of us"
(2 Corinthians 4:6-7).

The light that God shines upon the renewed mind brings enhanced realization of the two real existences. The two existences are usually diametrically opposed to each other. These can be seen in examples such as; good and evil, light and darkness, strength and weakness, divine nature and human nature, earthly and heavenly, and the natural and supernatural. These diametrically opposing realities become augmented by the light of the personal knowledge of Jesus Christ. There is an inward conflict initiated by God within us. This conflict is intended to break the sinful will with its desires and lusts in us. When God has broken us from within, it causes us to surrender to the power of the Holy Spirit dwelling within us.

"But we have this treasure in earthen vessels."

The treasure that Paul refers to is the gospel with its rich and invaluable truths. The word "treasure" is applied to the precious truths of God's Word, because of their inestimable worth.

We can also consider the "treasure" of the riches as the gifts of the Holy Spirit. Where is it? Paul says it's *"In earthen vessels."* He refers here to the apostles and ministers as weak and feeble; as having bodies decaying and dying, as fragile, and liable to various accidents, and as being altogether unworthy to hold a treasure so invaluable. It is seen as if valuable diamonds and gold were placed in vessels of earth, of coarse composition; easily broken, and liable to decay. The word "vessel" is *skeuos* in Greek and means, any utensil or instrument; and is applied usually to utensils of household furniture, or hollow vessels for containing things, (Luke 8:16; John 19:29).

The term "earthen vessel" is applied to the human body, as made of clay, and can be seen as frail and feeble, with reference to its "containing" anything. The apostle Paul gives us a glimpse of the internal battle that he faced in the flesh (earthen vessels), in the book of Romans.

"For I know that in me (that is, in my flesh,) dwelleth no good thing: for to will is present with me; but how to perform that which is good I find not. For the good that I would I do not: but the evil which I would not, that I do" (Rom. 7:18-19).

The panorama of inward conflict is plainly seen in the epistle to the Romans. Paul takes into consideration the culture, the times and the spirit of the Romans who were rigid, methodical, and regimented. He gives a classical systematic theological exposition on soteriology, (doctrine of salvation), in the light of God's redeeming love. He also shows the depravity of sinful man in the doctrine of harmartiology, (doctrine of sin), in the light of God's redeeming grace.

A Bird's-Eye View of Romans

The epistle to the Romans is considered by many theologians to be the fifth gospel to be added to Matthew, Mark, Luke, and John. In the four gospels we behold the life of Christ, His birth, teachings, works, suffering, death, burial and resurrection. We see what He came to accomplish in the gospels, but, in the book of Romans we see what was accomplished and how it relates to us experientially in the unfolding drama of redemption. It is here that we come to see the true meaning of justification, propitiation, reconciliation, redemption, sanctification, adoption, son-ship, and glorification.

The epistle of Romans gives us a better opportunity to know Christ more personally. It is this knowledge of Christ to the renewed mind that makes the transformation (change) possible. The structure of the book of Romans presents to us how the gospel saves. In chapter one, Paul lays out a sound plausible argument for humanity's condemnation because of his reprobate mind and behavior (Romans 1:24-28). In chapter two, he brings harsh charges against the Jews for boasting in having the law (Romans 2:17-24), and judging others, but not living by it.

In chapter three, Paul declares sin to be universal, *"For all have sinned, and come short of the glory of God" (Romans 3:23).* In chapter four, he shows through Abraham that salvation is not received by the law, but through faith. In the fifth chapter, he shows justification by grace through faith. In chapter six, we see positional sanctification. Throughout the sixth chapter, Paul admonishes the reader not to let sin reign over them.

"Let not sin therefore reign in your mortal body, that ye should obey it in the lusts thereof. Neither yield ye your members as instruments of unrighteousness unto sin: but yield yourselves unto God, as those that are alive from the dead, and your members as instruments of righteousness unto God. For sin shall not have dominion over you: for ye are not under the law, but under grace" (Romans 6:12-14).

Cecil, the great poet writes, "There are three things which the true Christian desires in respect to sin: justification that it may not condemn; sanctification, that it may not rein; and glorification that it may not be."

God wants us to reign in life by Christ Jesus. He wants us to dominate and rule but we must first win the war within.

Let us consider the seventh chapter of Romans. It is in this chapter that we see a real "war within." In this chapter the law shows the futility of someone attempting to live by it. It was weak to enable deliverance from sin, but strong to condemn because of sin.

"For I was alive without the law once: but when the commandment came, sin revived, and I died. And the commandment, which was ordained to life, I found to be unto death" (Romans 7:9-10).

Let me illustrate this. An airplane is a very useful thing, if it is flown by someone who is trained and qualified. However, if it is flown by someone who is not trained or qualified, it could become a dangerous weapon. The problem is not with the airplane, but the problem is with the pilot. In like manner, the problem is not with the law of God, but with the man who attempts to live by it. The Bible is not the problem, man is!

Man's natural propensity is sinful and he is prone to do what is natural to him. The truth is that the law of God without the Spirit is not capable of empowering man; neither can it give him eternal life.

Paul continues his exposition of the inward struggle, and he explains his plight of trying to follow the law of God in the hope that it would enable him to do righteousness. *"For sin, taking occasion by the commandment, deceived me, and by it slew me" (Romans 7:11).* All humanity attempting to follow the law in order to obtain righteousness without God's personal assistance will always experience futility. This is because man keeps falling victim to sin within him, bringing him into condemnation of the law of God.

*"Wherefore the law is holy, and the commandment holy, and just, and good. Was then that which is good made death unto me? God forbid. But sin, working death in me by that which is good; that sin by the commandment might become exceeding sinful. For we know that the law is spiritual: **but I am carnal, sold under sin**" (Romans 7:12-14).*

This dilemma of Romans chapter seven is a natural human dilemma. Man's nature is the "x" in the equation of life. The equation has three components: God, His Word, and man. Man is the shaky one in the equation. Man, being "carnal" refers to much more than his flesh [Gr. *Sarkinos*], but speaks to the old human mind and nature which resides within his flesh and bones. The word "carnal" is defined by the Vines expository dictionary as the Greek word "*sarkikos*," from *sarx*, "flesh," and it signifies sensuality controlled by animal appetites, governed by human nature, instead of by the Spirit of God (1 Corinthians 3:3).

There is a notion that when we are regenerated (born again), we lose our original Adamic nature, otherwise called, *"the old man, the sinful nature, the flesh, the carnal man, or the old Adam."* There can be nothing further from the truth. We may indeed be regenerated in our spirits, but the mind must be renewed daily. The mind has a tendency of regressing to the power of the carnal nature which resides in the dynamics of our sinful "flesh." I am glad that the apostle Paul was inspired to write this epistle of transparency for us. He sure kept it real!

Our bondage to sin was so complete before our conversion, it had us fully bound. Even though we have become born again, our minds still answer the desires of our flesh and carnal propensities. The apostle Paul states it rightly when he said, *"we were sold under sin" (Rom. 7:14).*

The dynamics of the mind influences all the facets of human existence.

We have been redeemed from the curse of the law (Galatians 3:13; 1 Peter 1:18-19) and by the blood of Jesus Christ. Yet, it is unfortunate, but we still possess the mind of the old nature; that nature that has been steeped in the law of sinful desires. The very fact that we still possess the old mind is an incentive to seek the Mind of Christ. Only Christ can give us victory over the flesh, and enable us to overcome the old mindset with its sinful ways.

Living with the Enemy

Any honest believer will agree that even on their best day, and while doing their very best to serve God in the Spirit, their old Adamic nature is right there waiting for an opportunity to be activated. Have you ever found in your own experience that it is the forbidden thing that your mind craves the most? It's like someone on a diet who had a weakness for chocolate, and is determined not to indulge for a while. Yet, as soon as they smell it or see it, it sparks a fire of desire for even a small piece of it. The same principle applies with fasting. You may decide to fast for three days, but if you are not careful, the sensual perception of smell could set you on a hunger fit. Sometimes, you might even be tempted to taste just a spoon full of what's cooking, and then find that you have essentially broken the fast. No one spoon full of anything can fill the sensual desires!

The Old Adamic nature serves only itself, and provides a conduit to bring you into bondage to sin and disobedience. *"For I delight in the law of God after the inward man: But I see another law in my members, warring against the law of my mind, and bringing me into captivity to the law of sin which is in my members" (Romans 7:22-23).*

The old nature will send you evil thoughts at the same time you are doing righteousness. You cannot tame it, mute it, bribe it, bully it, or counsel it. This old nature can only be neutralized and subdued by a renewed mind and the power of sanctification. Although the thought attacks are evil, binding it will not work because it does not come from outside of you it comes from within. Paul informs us in the Scriptures *"I find then a law, that, when I would do good, evil is present with me" (Romans 7:21).*

Many have been made shipwreck in the Christian arena because of their failure to recognize the presence of evil within them in their old nature. That is a typical case of "sleeping with the enemy." It's like having someone with you at all times who is a disloyal double agent. Although you know that this old nature holds no allegiances to your desires you cannot shake it off, it's always there, because it's a part of you. This seventh chapter of Romans has been a cushion and a safety net for so many struggling Christians. It gives great insight into the "inside story". When you are honest enough to acknowledge your own internal fight and reckon with the enemy within, then you are well on your way to deliverance from you. Paul put's it like this; *"O wretched man that I am! Who shall deliver me from the body of this death?" (Romans 7:24).* This is not the cry of an unsaved man, but of the chief Apostle Paul. This is a saved man. He cries, **"O wretched man that I am! Who shall deliver me?"**

Who is going to deliver me?

The feeling implied by this lamentation *"O wretched man that I am!" (Romans 7:24a)* is the result of this painful conflict; and this frequent subjection to sinful propensities. The word wretched carries with it a note of exhaustion, caused from the inward struggle that produces pain and distress. *"Who shall deliver me...?" (Romans 7:24b).* It is often an agonizing struggle between good and evil "Who is going to deliver me?" He is powerless to help himself. His shoulders are pinned to the floor, he has been wrestled down like Jacob, and he is crippled like Mephibosheth. He cries, "Who is going to deliver me?"

Paul makes an appeal outside of himself. He knew that in this case he could not help himself. There are some things that are just too much for 'self' to handle, and when we are honest and true to "self" we will admit to them and cry out like the prophet Isaiah did, *"... Woe is me for I am undone!" (Isaiah 6:5a).*

In order to be successful against the external foes, we must first recon with the internal woes

---

The book of Galatians shows us how the two wills collide. *"For the desires of the flesh are against the Spirit, and the desires of the Spirit are against the flesh; for these are opposed to each other, **to prevent you from doing what you would"** (Galatians 5:17 RSV).* Once we have come face to face with the sinful nature within us and the natural propensity to obey it, we can either, resign ourselves to live with it knowing that it is a double agent, waiting to deliver us over to evil, or, we can cry out to God like the apostle Paul did. It is only then that our praises for Jesus will be from the heart, and our definition of the word "savior" or "deliverer" will take on a whole new meaning.

Deliverance Has Come!

"I thank God through Jesus Christ our Lord. So then with the mind I myself serve the law of God; but with the flesh the law of sin"
(Romans 7:25).

Paul here thanks God who gives deliverance, through Jesus Christ our Lord. This is the answer to Paul's S.O.S. God has provided deliverance! **Our power to deliver is as great as our power to receive deliverance!**

The grace of God that is given through Jesus Christ makes the deliverance from self possible. The freedom from the law of commandments which frustrates us, and the law of sin which captivate us, must answer to the law of the Spirit of life in Christ Jesus, which liberates us through the power of sanctification. *"For the law of the Spirit of life in Christ Jesus hath made me free from the law of sin and death" (Romans 8:2)*. Sanctification is the work of the Holy Spirit in the regenerated life of a believer, delivering the believer from the power of sin, even in the very presence of sin, and empowering the believer to subdue the flesh while performing the will of God in his life.

11

THE FAITH CHARGED WORD

I have been in several services and deliverance sessions over the years, in which everyone present was binding and loosing. I remember once in Europe, while preaching in a revival service, a young woman who was demonized began to flare up at the end of the service. She was yelling at the top of her lungs, "Leave me alone, I am not letting her go! This is my house and I am not leaving it!" The entire church began shouting, "I bind you devil!" "Loose here devil!" One evangelist placed the open Bible on the woman's chest, binding and pleading the blood, while a deacon splashed some olive oil on her blouse. The host pastor led the series of bindings. It so happened that the louder they got, was the more violent and boisterous the young woman became. After some time, the pastor indicated to me to address the situation. I stepped forward towards the woman, indicating to the church to calm down a bit.

Emotional or Spiritual

Many of the saints were stomping violently; shouting and demonstrating vehemently. It took a few minutes to bring order to the assembly. Finally, I said, "Let us be prayerful at this time, as the pastor and elders gather around." You should have seen the look on some of their faces, as they paced back and forth pleading, *"The blood! The blood!"* Because they were not specific about their commands and statements, I was tempted to ask them, 'What about the blood?' I found that they were yelling more in fear than with authority. However, I fixed my eyes upon the demonized woman as she hissed her teeth and rolled her eyes, shouting, "Leave me, just leave me alone, she is mine!"

I then said, "Hold your peace, in Jesus name!" She immediately shut up, and looked upwards into the roof pouting. I proceeded by saying, "Look at me, in Jesus name!" She quickly glanced into my eyes, which reflected fierceness and concentrated boldness. Then she swiftly unfolded her hands and proceeded to choke herself. I discerned the spirit on her to be the spirit of bitterness, so I pointed at her and said, *"By the authority of the Lord Jesus Christ given in Matthew 18:18;* I bind you spirit of bitterness, I command you to break your hold now! Loosen this woman's mind now! I uproot you, spirit of bitterness! You are forbidden to trouble her any more. Leave now! Go into dry places in Jesus' name!"

It took several strong men and women to hold her as she fought violently to strangle herself. I said in an authoritative voice, "Bitterness and anger you are bound now! You are restricted, and hindered from bringing harm to her, I command you to go from her now into dry places; come out in Jesus' name!" After a short protest, she suddenly loosed her grip from her neck looking sideways at me, pouting and puffing as she rolled her eyes. Then with a loud voice she screamed, and gargled as she secreted slimy, foaming saliva from her mouth, and then plopped in the pew in which she had been sitting. Not long afterwards she was peaceful, delivered, and clothed once again in her right mind.

There are times when the name of the spirit is not important. In some cases they can be addressed by what they do. A lying spirit is a lying spirit, a spirit of fear is what it does, etc. The confidence that I displayed was based upon knowledge of what God's Word says. Once I discerned the spirit to be a spirit of bitterness, I remembered Hebrews 12:15b which says, *"...lest any root of bitterness springing up trouble you, and thereby many be defiled."* When I remembered that bitterness troubles the soul, I declared, "You are forbidden to trouble her anymore!" In declaring what God's Word says, the demonic spirit became subject to the Faith-charged Word of God. The same principle applies in regard to what we say and believe. The scripture declares that *"Through faith we understand that the worlds (eon, course) were framed by the Word of God" (Heb.11:3).* Our course of life can be framed by what we say. It is truly correctly stated, *"We shall have what we say" (Mark 11:23b).*

When we understand the power of the spoken Word, we will speak the Word with power, faith, and confidence, knowing it shall not return void but it shall accomplish that which God pleases, and it shall prosper in the things wherewith it is sent (Isaiah 55:11).

The Overcoming Word

I have always been aware of the authority of **"faith-charged words."** The word that we speak is either spirit and life, or spirit and death (John 6:63). The Scriptures declare that Jesus cast out spirits "With His Word," *"When the even was come, they brought unto him many that were possessed with devils: and he cast out the spirits with his word, and healed all that were sick" (Matthew 8:16).* The principle of the authority of the spoken word that applied then, still applies today.

The Roman centurion understood this principle and authority of the spoken word, we read; *"The centurion answered and said, Lord, I am not worthy that thou shouldest come under my roof: but **speak the word only**, and my servant shall be healed" (Matthew 8:8).*

Demons are still driven out by the powerful Word of God and also by the believer's word when that believer's life is in union and right standing with (Christ), the living Word of God. We must remember that it is the spirit that quickeneth (makes alive); the flesh profiteth nothing, the spoken words of a believer can be spirit and life; or spirit and death (John 6:63). Our words can either affirm or infirm, create or destroy.

John believed that the strength of the young men whom he wrote to was attributed to the Word abiding in them, he writes; *"I have written unto you, young men, because ye are strong, and the word of God abideth in you, and you have overcome the wicked one" (First John 2:14).*

The apostle Paul was also aware of the unrestricted mobility of God's Word. He writes, *"The Word of God is not bound!" (2 Timothy 2:9).* This scripture makes it plain concerning the "Word of God." It is not confined (geographically, spiritually, literally, metaphorically, socially or economically). Let it be known that the Word of God is not subject to any other power; neither can be compelled by external forces. It cannot be restrained, or restricted.

"So shall my word be that goeth out of my mouth: it shall not return unto me void, but it shall accomplish that which I please, and it shall prosper in the thing whereto I sent it" (Isaiah 55:11).

Waging War with Words

Once the word has been given a charge or an assignment, it cannot return void. It must accomplish that which God originally designed it to accomplish. When we assign the Word of God by faith, we can expect favorable results. It must be kept in mind that the Word's accomplishments are in the things which it is originally sent (designed).

God spoke a Word, *"Let there be,"* and there was *(Genesis. 1:3).* Also, Psalm 33:6 says, *"By the Word of the LORD were the heavens made; and all the host of them by the breath of his mouth."* Words are powerful; they can be creative and constructive, or negative and destructive. What we say can either build or destroy. We must be careful that *"the words of our mouth and the meditation of our hearts are acceptable in God's sight" (Psalm 19:14).*

The Holy Spirit may give different battle strategies for different wars. We can always rely on a strategic *key* to victory; that is, through the power of the "Word of God." The prophet Jeremiah wrote about this principle of the assigned Word;

"O thou sword of the Lord, (Word) how long will it ere thou be quiet? Put up thyself into thy scabbard, rest, and be still. How can it be quiet, seeing the Lord hath given it a charge against Ashkelon, and against the sea shore? There hath he appointed it" (Jeremiah 47:6-7).

The book of Revelation tells us also that *"we overcome the accuser (Satan) by the blood of the Lamb, and by the word of our testimony" (Revelation 12:11).* If *our word* testifies and attests to the facts of God's Word in its design, then we shall have what *we say* because *we ask* according to the will of God (Mark 11:23; 1 John 5:14-15).

In every aspect of Jesus' temptation, we see the spoken word assenting to the written Word, and thus giving him victory in every area that he was tempted in. He constantly affirmed: *"It is written; and it is written again!" (Matthew 4:4; 7; 10).*

Let me draw your attention to the gospel according to Luke, to the fourth chapter. The temptation of Jesus as recorded by Luke shows us Jesus using the (Logos), written Word, to respond to the temptation of the devil.

"And the devil said unto him, If thou be the Son of God, command this stone that it be made bread" (Luke 4:3).

Jesus responded to the first temptation with a quote from the written Word in Deut. 8:3, *"He answered and said, It is written, Man shall not live by bread alone, but by every word that proceedeth out of the mouth of God"* (Luke 4:4). In the second temptation as is recorded by Luke, we read; *"And the devil, taking him up into an high mountain, shewed unto him all the kingdoms of the world in a moment of time. And the devil said unto him, All this power will I give thee, and the glory of them: for that is delivered unto me; and to whomsoever I will I give it. If thou therefore wilt worship me, all shall be thine"* (Luke 4:5-7). Jesus again used the (Logos), written word to respond to the temptation. He quoted Deuteronomy 6:13 as his basis of faith. *"And Jesus answered and said unto him, Get thee behind me, Satan: for it is written, Thou shalt worship the Lord thy God, and him only shalt thou serve"* (Luke 4:8).

You will notice that the devil has a fairly good handle on what God's Word says. Therefore, we must endeavor to study the Word of God intensely and hide it in our hearts. It is also equally important for us to know how to rightly divide the Word of truth.

The devil realized that Jesus believed in pointing to the totality of Scripture as the guide for conduct and the basis of faith. When he realized that Jesus used the Scripture as his defense, *he* also resorted to use the written (Word), logos, in a perverse way. He quoted Psalm 91:11;

"And he brought him to Jerusalem, and set him on a pinnacle of the temple, and said unto him, If thou be the Son of God, cast thyself down

from hence: For it is written, He shall give his angels charge over thee, to keep thee: And in their hands they shall bear thee up, lest at any time thou dash thy foot against a stone" (Luke 4:9-11).

When Jesus realized that the devil was bold enough to use the written Word, (Logos), as a basis of temptation, Jesus took a different position in the third temptation. The New King James version puts it so well, it says;

"And Jesus answered and said to him, "It has been said, 'You shall not tempt the LORD your God.' Now when the devil had ended every temptation, he departed from Him until an opportune time" (Luke 4:12-13).

Jesus establishes the principle of the "spoken Word" (Rhema). What Jesus declared was the power of rhema. He said, *"I have **heard** it said."* Jesus told the devil that he had received a rhema word from the written word when it was spoken in his presence. Now Jesus chose to respond to the logos that the devil used with a rhema; He declared from Deut. 6:16 and Exodus 17:2, a faith charged Word that was previously preached into his hearing. When we believe what God says and say what we believe, that is what makes the devil flee! Whenever we "**speak**" the Word with confidence in what God says, that "word" comes alive. We have received a Word (Gk. word: *rhema*) that is step ordering, Spirit activated, and life changing. We must also be aware that when **we say** (Gk. word: *epos*) a word and it has its foundation in the *logos*, it will produce life or death. The three Greek words which I refer to are the following:

(1) **Rhema:** Denoting that which is spoken clearly in speech, what is uttered unmistakably, vividly, undeniably, unquestionably, and definite in terms. It is a "quickened" word!

(2) **Logos:** That which is the expression of thought, as embodying a conception or idea, the sum of God's utterance.

(3) **Epos:** That which is the articulated expression of a thought.

The book of Job also expresses the power of a purposeful, faith charged word. *"Thou shalt also decree a thing, and it shall be established unto thee: and the light shall shine upon thy ways" (Job 22:28).*

You will decree a formed purpose or plan, and it shall not be frustrated. It shall not be opposed by the events of divine providence, but whatever you undertake shall prosper. You will prosper in all things, instead of being overtaken by calamity. You can declare with boldness, *"And He has made my mouth like a sharp sword" (Isaiah 49:2).*

The Word that you speak becomes the sword you wield in war. The Word is quick, and powerful, and sharper than any two-edged sword (Hebrews 4:12).

When you release the *rhema* Word from your lips with faith in God's written (logos) Word, things will happen. In the book of Revelation, John gives us some insight into the spirit world, to understand how the "Word," which is Spirit, accomplishes its specific assignments in battle.

*"And I saw heaven opened, and behold a white horse; and he that sat upon him was called Faithful and True, and in righteousness he doth judge and make war. His eyes were as a flame fire, and on his head were many crowns; and he had a name written, that no man knew, but he himself. And he was clothed with a vesture dipped in blood: **And his name is called The Word of God.**" And the armies which were in heaven followed him upon white horses, clothed in fine linen, white and clean. **And out of his mouth goeth a sharp sword**, that with it he should smite the nations: and he shall rule them with a rod of iron: and he treadeth the winepress of the fierceness and wrath of Almighty God.*

And he hath on his vesture and on his thigh a name written, KING OF KINGS, AND LORD OF LORDS" (Revelation19:11-16).

It is evident from the Scriptures that the Word of God is on the *Cutting Edge* of Warfare, *"sharper than any two-edged sword" (Hebrews 4:12).* Jesus is the Living Word (*logos*), and what we speak is the (*rhema*) word. Whenever we speak the Word of God, the armies of heaven follow that Word in fierce advancement to fulfill the counsel of Almighty God.

The Word is a Sure Weapon of Mass Destruction and a Pure source of Creative Construction

---

Jesus made it clear that the believer should abide in Him and His Word in them. *"If ye abide in me, and **my words abide in you**, ye shall ask what ye will, and it shall be done unto you" (John 15:7).* The Word is most effective when it is charged with faith, when spoken (Mark 11:23-24) by a believer who is renewed in the spirit of his mind (Eph. 4:23); One who is in fellowship with the Lord, and whose mind has been truly transformed (Romans 12:2).

12

THE SUPERNATURAL POWER STRUGGLE

Now that you are reminded of the power of the spoken Word, and the different frontiers that we are engaged in doing battle on, let's consider the struggle for power. No nation would enter into an all out war with another country unless the stakes were high. Have you ever wondered, 'What's all this fighting for?' For many of us, we were born fighting; we have lived our lives fighting for everything that we now hold dear. Probably you have fought every step of the way, and for many others of us who are labeled as 'fighters,' we will very well die fighting.

I want to pause here to make a distinction between a person who is a fighter, and one merely struggling. While in a struggle, we do fight, but in a fight, we do not necessarily struggle. There are many professing 'fighters' who, in their fight, do nothing more than merely beat the air. The apostle Paul informed us of how he fought;

"I therefore so run, not as uncertainly; so fight I, not as one that beateth the air" (1 Corinthians 9:26).

When a struggler engages in a battle, it is like shadow boxing, throwing unconnected blows. When the battle is over, his enemy will probably still be there, ready to engage in battle. However, when a fighter engages in battle, he takes on a **warrior's** mentality becoming focused on the enemy and *his* fight. When the smoke clears, the true fighter will be the only one standing.

The Webster's dictionary defines struggle as: To contend with an adversary or opposing force, to strive, to struggle for existence, to advance with violent effort; to cope with inability to perform well or to win; to contend with difficulty. Webster's also defines a fighter as: One who engages in combat, conflict, contest, or war against, one who defends himself against; to subdue, defeat, or destroy an enemy, one who maneuvers all forces and tactics, and fights vigorously until a decision is reached. It is further defined as a person with the will, courage, determination, ability or disposition to fight, struggle, and resist.

A Fighter can be seen as one who seeks out and destroys.

As you can see, the difference between a struggler and a fighter is that a struggler often only stirs-up the atmosphere with static energy, leaving his enemy intact and still on the prowl. On the other hand, when the fighter advances his attacks, his enemy will always be at a loss, and even if his enemy is not completely destroyed, at least he will not be able to continue the fight anytime soon. I would be remiss at this juncture not to introduce a *warrior*, and explain who he is. A warrior is defined as a person engaged or experienced in warfare; a soldier, a person who shows or has shown great vigor, courage or aggressiveness.

Now here is where we need to pause a moment. Let me take the time to point out to you an important reality. While a warrior is a soldier, every soldier is not a warrior. Now there are some believers who are warriors all the time, when it is not necessary, and this can pose a serious problem within an environment that is non threatening, or user-friendly, namely, fellowship.

A truly disciplined soldier will know how to conduct his or herself, follow directives, and observe protocol. A soldier will wait on orders or counsel before undertaking an aggressive action, while a warrior, although he is a soldier, is known to step over several wounded comrades to subjectively engage an enemy. The warrior, if not disciplined, can cause more damage through friendly fire, in his effort to destroy what he perceives to be his enemy. However, when the warrior is truly disciplined, he is like a one-man-wrecking ball, he becomes God's battle axe and weapon of war. Jeremiah 51:20-21 declares;

> *"Thou art my battle axe and weapons of war: for with thee will I break in pieces the nations, and with thee will I destroy kingdoms; And with thee will I break in pieces the horse and his rider; and with thee will I break in pieces the chariot and his rider."*

The Enemy who Fell from Above

Whether you are a seasoned warrior or a disciplined soldier, we all have one thing in common; we have the same enemies to fight! I would like to begin with examining where our enemy Satan and his demons originate from. The Bible says very little about the origin of evil. We are only permitted a brief glimpse every now and then into the mystery of the fall of Satan, who is the main source of evil. The prophet Isaiah tells how the "Day star," or Lucifer, "The Light bearer," as Satan is called, fell from heaven because of his pride and ambition; *"How art thou fallen from heaven, O Lucifer, son of the morning! How art thou cut down to the ground, which didst weaken the nations!*

For thou hast said in thine heart, I will ascend into heaven, I will exalt my throne above the stars of God: I will sit also upon the mount of the congregation, in the sides of the north. I will ascend above the heights of the clouds; I will be like the Most High" (Isaiah 14:12-14).

Another popular scripture that refers to the fall of Satan, and the beginning of evil is found in the book of Ezekiel, which says; *"Son of man, take up a lamentation upon the king of Tyrus, and say unto him, Thus saith the Lord God; Thou sealest up the sum, full of wisdom, and perfect in beauty. Thou hast been in Eden the garden of God; every precious stone was thy covering, the sardius, topas, and the diamond, the beryl, the onyx, and the jasper, the sapphire, the emerald, and the carbuncle, and gold: the workmanship of they tabrets and of thy pipes was prepared in thee in the day that thou wast created. Thou art the anointed cherub that covereth; and I have set thee so: thou wast upon the holy mountain of God; thou hast walked up and down in the midst of the stones of fire. Thou wast perfect in thy ways from the day that thou wast created, till iniquity was found in thee" (Ezekiel 28:12-15).*

In both these passages, we see that the fall of Satan is attributed to his pride and ambitions. However, in Ezekiel 28:15, we read how Satan was perfect in his ways, until iniquity was found in him.

Although God created all things, it is evident that evil was as an inactive force, a passive, consequential effect. It was activated by the sin of Lucifer's pride and rebellion, after his fall; *iniquity* was *founded in him.* Hence, he is the active source of all iniquity and evil.

Some Facts About Satan

Satan is not some ugly monster with horns and a fork as many imagine, but he was created a handsome wise creature (Ezekiel 28:17).

1. His original place of abode was heaven (Isaiah 14:12a).

2. His original name before the fall was Lucifer (Isaiah 14:12a).

3. He is a fallen star (Isaiah 14:12b).

4. God has cut him down (Isaiah 14:12c).

5. The sin of pride began in his heart (Isaiah 14:13a).

6. He is self willed and presumptuous (Isaiah 14:13b).

7. His desire was to ascend above the heights (Isaiah 14:14a).

8. He wanted to be like God (Isaiah 14:14b).

The Old Testament does not give much information about the demons that work along with Satan, but in the book of revelation we are made to understand more about him and his angels.

"And there was war in heaven: Michael and his angels fought against the dragon; and the dragon fought and his angels. And prevailed not; neither was there place found anymore in heaven. And the great dragon was cast out, that old serpent, called the devil, and Satan, which deceiveth the whole world: he was cast out into the earth, and his angels were cast out with him" (Revelation 12:7-9).

It is apparent from Scripture that because of a cosmic rebellion led by Lucifer, there was war in heaven and he and his demons were cast out. We are also told in Revelation 12:4 that his tail drew a third of the celestial stars of heaven and cast them down to the earth. "And his tail drew the third part of the stars of heaven, and did cast them to the earth..." The term here given to the celestial body of angels is stars.

Biblical theology supports the theory of angels as stars, based upon the following scriptures: Isa. 14:12; *"How you have fallen from heaven, O morning star, son of the dawn!" (N.I.V.)* He is known as the "Day star, or, Morning star." Satan was called, Lucifer, "the light bearer" and "shining one." Also, in Job 38:4-6, we read; *"Where were you when I laid the foundations of the earth? Tell me, if you know so much. Do you know how its dimensions were determined, and who did the surveying? What supports its foundations, and who laid its cornerstone as the morning stars sang together and all the angels shouted for joy? (TLB).*

Barnes notes expresses a similar view of Job 38:7, *"When the morning-stars…"* he comments, "There can be little doubt that angelic beings are intended here, though some have thought that the stars literally are referred to, and that they seemed to unite in a chorus of praise when another world was added to their number." The Latin Vulgate renders it, *"astra matutina," ***morning-stars;*** the Septuagint, "hote (NT: 3753) *egeneetheenai* (NT:1096) *astra* (NT:798) - when the stars were made" The Chaldee renders it, "the stars of the zephyr," or "morning." The comparison of a prince, a monarch, or an angel, with a star, is not uncommon. The expression "the morning-stars" **is used on account of the beauty of the principal star.** It is applied naturally to those angelic beings that are of distinguished glory and rank in heaven.

From the connection, it's apparent that the term 'morning stars' refers to the angels. This interpretation is demanded in order to correspond with the phrase, *"sons of God"* in the other parts of the verse of Job 38:7.

Adam Clarke's Commentary says *"When the morning stars sang together.* This must refer to some intelligent beings who existed before the creation of the visible heavens and earth, and it is supposed that this and the following clause refer to the same beings; that by the sons of God, and the morning stars, the angelic host is meant, as they are supposed to be, first, though perhaps not chief, in the order of creation." God has given man dominion, and set him as the head over the works of His hand (Hebrews 2:7-8).

The Power Struggle

There is an old adage which says; **"Two bulls cannot reign in the same pen."** This is also true in regard to the sovereign rule of the universe. Lucifer's ambition was to exalt his throne into the place of ultimate authority, the Scripture says; *"For thou hast said in thine heart, I will ascend into heaven, I will exalt my throne above the stars of God: I will sit also upon the mount of the congregation, in the sides of the north: I will ascend above the heights of the clouds; I will be like the most High" (Isaiah 14:13-14).* He planned a hostile takeover, a coup if you will. This rebellion and power struggle is not confined to the heavens only, but we see it often played out here on earth in many ways.

So many ministries have experienced a split because of some ambitious individual who could not wait on God to promote him with honor, in God's own time. The spirit of pride and rebellion has been a nesting ground for the premature. Quite often, when ego driven people are denied the opportunity to shine, they become critical of the powers that be, and the decisions they make. It is very much like the devil to promote coups, and mutiny, and those who are hungry for power and glory. He is good at dividing and scattering. He is the founder of it. The God who declared; *"I will not give my glory to another" (Isaiah 42:8),* would certainly not allow any created being to exalt himself over Him.

A Legitimate cause for Jealousy

When God created man, he created him *"in His own image"* (Genesis 1:27). He also made man after *"**His likeness**"* (Genesis 1:26). Man was made in the moral likeness of God, with cognitive volition and moral rectitude. He was created a free, moral, "tri-partite" agent, just **like** His creator; who is Father, Son, and Holy Spirit. Man was created spirit, with a soul, and given a body. The fact that God, "Elohim," (compound plurality of the trinity), in divine orchestrated counsel, affectionately said; *"Let **us** make man in **our image**, after **our likeness**: and let them have dominion over the fish of the sea, and over the fowl of the air, and over the cattle, and over all the earth, and over every creeping thing that creepeth upon the earth (Genesis 1:26).*

This was enough reason to provoke jealousy from his arch-enemy Satan, who was violently cast down from heaven because of his ambitious designs **"to be *like* the Most High"** (Isaiah 14:15). *"How art thou fallen from heaven, O Lucifer, son of the morning! How art thou cut down to the ground, which didst weaken the nations! For thou hast said in thine heart, I will ascend into heaven, I will exalt my throne above the stars of God: I will sit also upon the mount of the congregation, in the sides of the north: I will ascend above the heights of the clouds; I **will be like the most High**. Yet thou shalt be brought down to hell, to the sides of the pit."*

The very thing Lucifer was cast down for was the very thing God did for mankind; God made man after His "likeness."

What has upset the devil?

Here is an obvious set-up for jealousy and rivalry. It is apparent that Lucifer's inordinate ambition and desire to be *"like God,"* was partly the reason that he was kicked out of heaven. Now, can you imagine how upset he was because he was kicked out for wanting to be *like God*, and then God makes a creature from the dust of the ground (mortal, earthly), making this creature (man), into *His own likeness*, and then puts this man in charge of the estate, (planet earth)? This was an obvious demotion for Satan, who was the previous supervisor of our earth. Well, that must have made the devil mad!

In creation, God made man in *His own image and likeness*. God dealt a serious blow to Satan, the former viceroy. His ambitious designs were the cause of the cosmic treason which led him into cosmic rebellion. His rebellion resulted in his fall from grace and his expulsion from on high.

The fall of Satan provided a job opening for the new creature, "man." The job description that was given to man was the stewardship of the garden and planet earth, along with the viceroy-ship and oversight of creation. The newly created man was given authority and dominion-power; without solicitation of approval, or a recommendation from the celestial beings. Can you imagine? Here is a terrestrial creation, (man), made a little lower than the celestial creation (angels), and yet crowned with *glory* and *honor*. God the creator honored man with dominion power, this compounded Satan's humiliation and dishonor.

"So God created man in his own image, in the image of God created he him; male and female created he them. And God blessed them, and God said unto them, Be fruitful, and multiply, and replenish the earth, and subdue it: and have dominion over the fish of the sea, and over the fowl of the air, and over every living thing that moveth upon the earth" (Genesis 1:27-28).

I am sure the question "what is man?" comes up quite often from the diabolical lips of Satan and his host. The scripture declares;

"...What is man, that thou art mindful of him? and the son of man, that thou visitest him? For thou hast made him a little lower than the angels, and hast crowned him with glory and honour. Thou madest him to have dominion over the works of thy hands; thou hast put all things under his feet" (Psalm 8:4-6).

The scripture goes on to say in the New Testament book of Hebrews; *"Thou hast put all things in subjection under his feet. For in that he put all in subjection under him, he left nothing that is not put under him. But now we see not yet all things put under him"* (Hebrews 2:8). The psalmist also declares again in Psalm115:16; *"The heaven, even the heavens, are the LORD's: but the earth hath he given to the children of men"* This obviously must have made the devil furious with man.

Can you imagine? Losing your place of authority and viceroyalty to someone who is inferior (in design) to you, and as if that is not enough, to add insult to injury, now he has been given dominion, or power of rule over you? This would most definitely bring the devil out of some of us.

He came to the party Dressed as a Serpent

While Adam and Eve basked in the glory of their purity and innocence, peacefully enjoying the presence of their creator, there lurked a fiendish being, hideous in thought and malignant in his imagination. Day in and day out as they enjoyed the beauty of God's fellowship, shining with the brilliance of glory and honor, a diabolical mind was at work; a fallen star who could himself remember former days of similar honor and glory.

Now moved with jealousy and incensed with envy, Satan must concoct a means by which these lower forms of creation (Adam and Eve), could experience a similar fate such as his. The plot was set; the plan was birthed in the incubator of a jealous heart. The only thing left was the costume, and he would be going to the party. It would appear that the best camouflage for Satan at the time was the serpent, which was said *to be more subtle than any beast of the field.*

Satan was the "crasher" in the paradise of Eden's party

The enemy of mankind presented himself in the Garden of Eden, using the serpent as a social covering. That is why when the prophet, Ezekiel made reference to his fall in Ezekiel chapter 28, he addressed him as the spirit-being who was in Eden, the garden of God, and was covered in precious stones. He is the same anointed angel who was embodied in the king of Tyre (Ezekiel 28:13-14a).

In the Garden of Eden, Satan was successful in his attempt to cause mankind to disobey God and fall from grace as he did, Romans 5:12 says, *"Wherefore, as by one man sin entered into the world, and death by sin; and so death passed upon all men, for that all have sinned."*

The sin of Adam and Eve resulted in their eviction from Eden, just as Satan was evicted from Heaven. This was advantageous for Satan, because this meant that the *dominion power* of planet earth would become his legally. This was only possible because of the disobedience of Adam.

Adam's disobedience plunged him under satanic dominion, and forfeited his right to rule. This Scripture says; *"To whom a man yield himself a servant to obey, he becomes his servant; whether of sin unto death, or of obedience unto righteousness" (Romans 6:16).* Satan earned the right to rule our planet legally and judicially, and only a Champion greater than he could take it back lawfully.

The first promise of the **champion-redeemer** is found in Genesis; *"And I will put enmity between thee and the woman, and between thy seed and her seed; it shall <u>bruise thy head</u>, and thou shalt bruise his heel"* *(Genesis 3:15).*

God Declared War!

Who exactly is addressed here in Genesis 3:15a? *"And **I will put enmity** between thee and the woman, and between her seed and thy seed."* When God refers to *thee* and *thy*; it is quite apparent that God here is addressing Satan. God puts enmity between Satan and the woman; and between *her seed* and his seed. **God started it!** He inadvertently said; **"I declare war!"** It is quite clear from the Scriptures that it was God Himself who first declared war on earth, "I will put enmity…"

This war that God declared was not just limited to the Godly line of humanity against the ungodly offspring of evil; but was to include all mankind. Every man, woman, boy and girl is on one side or another, we are either for God, or against Him; gathering with him or scattering abroad (Matthew 12:30). This means that you are either fighting on His behalf, or another's. It is important for the believer to know that it was God who started this war, as he did in the book of Job. This is especially comforting for the Christian because we know that if God started it, He will finish it in fine style!

The enmity between the devil and "woman" is clearly seen in typology from the perspective of the woman as the life-giver, the seed carrier, and the incubator of mankind. However, the enmity is not just with the woman, but with all of mankind. The devil is especially angry with the (man), because he is the seed giver. You will notice in Revelation 12:4-6 that *the dragon stood before the woman who was ready to be delivered, to devour her child as soon as it was born.* While there is a historical interpretation of this text, it expresses a spiritual principle that the seed (converts) of the church is the primary target of the dragon (the devil). The church recognizes the attacks against her sons. There seems to be a male genocide, as men become targeted by the enemy.

When Satan successfully caused the fall of man, he thought that God would have dealt to humanity the same fate that God dealt to him and his demonic host. However, God's plan of salvation was already in motion through His predetermined will and counsel.

Another one bites the dust!

Man's seduction and fall in the Garden of Eden is well known to every Bible-believing Christian, and some none-Christians as well, however, the consequence of the fall is not as well understood. Something happened in Genesis chapter 3, something more than a prophetic utterance about the coming champion-messiah. Jesus Christ fulfilled (Genesis 3:15) as the pure and Holy seed of God. He came as the promised deliverer, the champion savior, the One who bruised the serpent's head. The serpent's venom is stored in his head; therefore Jesus "bruising his head" symbolizes that the sting of death would be destroyed (1Corinthians 15:55; Hebrews 2:14).

After his fall, man was sentenced to hard labor. From the dust he was taken and unto the dust he would return. The woman was sentenced to the sorrow of travail in child bearing (Genesis 3:16-19). The serpent was cursed and destined to crawl on his belly eating dust. *"And the LORD God said unto the serpent........ Upon thy belly shalt thou go, and dust shalt thou eat all the days of thy life" (Genesis 3:14).*

The curse upon the serpent, *"to eat dust,"* extended from the creature to the very spirit that had possessed it, Satan. The utter humiliation that the devil would experience was equivalent to the serpent being reduced to move upon his belly. Every time a soul gets saved, **another one bites the dust**. Whenever a believer triumphs over the cunning devises of Satan and his demons, *another one bites the dust*. Whenever the Church prevails against the gates of hell, **another one bites the dust!**

David's prayer for Solomon expresses the victory of Jesus Christ and His Church. The glory of Christ' Kingdom and the Church are seen. *"They that dwell in the wilderness shall bow before him; and his enemies shall lick the dust" (Psalm 72:9).* Micah the prophet alludes to the victory of believers over their enemies, he writes; *"They shall lick the dust like a serpent, they shall move out of their holes like worms of the earth: they shall be afraid of the LORD our God, and shall fear because of thee" (Micah 7:17).* Every time we bruise the enemy under our feet, we cause him once again to *lick the dust* of Calvary's victory.

Bite the Dust or get Flushed!

I want to pause here to share an experience I once had many years ago. Maybe this experience can help somebody. My sister in law told me about a woman from the bank where she worked that had a problem, and wanted deliverance. She mentioned that the woman had a pastor whom she had shared her problem with, but he was unable to help her. Being zealous to help this woman in distress, I overlooked the due process of protocol, and neglected to contact her pastor. My sister in law was able to arrange a telephone conversation with the woman one day. After conversing with the woman, I learned that she had a problem sleeping, and had no appetite for food.

The woman complained to me on the phone that a snake was in her body. At first when she said it, I thought she was a crazy woman, but then I rationalized that had she been crazy, my sister-in- law would have known and would not have recommended her to me, neither would she have been working for the bank. When I asked her how she knew there was a snake inside of her, she told me because she felt it and anyone could see it. Well, 'That's interesting,' I thought. I made an appointment to see the woman at my home in Queens, New York.

When the woman arrived at my home, my sister-in-law was not available to come with her, so I had my wife join me as I interviewed the woman. As we communicated, the woman shared how something was dropped into her drink by a relative, and ever since then, she had the problem. Well, to our surprise, the woman pulled up the sleeve of her blouse, and there was the outline of a snake slithering up and down her arm. At one point, I could feel the impression of its movement under her scalp as I laid my hand on her head, while binding and rebuking it. After about fifteen minutes, I sent her to the bathroom with my wife, where she vomited out the reptile, which we flushed down the toilet. In this case, "Another one just got flushed!"

While it is important for people to be free from the oppression of the devil, we should have a place set aside for cases such as these; namely, the church or the oppressed person's home. I caution you, if you can help it, never perform deliverance in your home. It is unhealthy for you and your family.

The Power Encounter

One of the purposes of Jesus coming to this earth was *"to destroy the works of the devil" (1John3:8b)*. The writer of Hebrews declares;

"Forasmuch then as the children are partakers of flesh and blood, he also himself likewise took part of the same; that through death he might destroy him that had the power over death, that is, the devil. And deliver them who through fear of death were their entire lifetime subject to bondage" (Hebrews 2:14-15).

Jesus was led of the Spirit into the wilderness, to undergo a serious power encounter, but it is obvious from the Scriptures that *Jesus was the victor* in His encounter with Satan in the wilderness.

"And Jesus returned in the power of the Spirit into Galilee: and there went out a fame of him through the entire region round about (Luke 4:14). Where the first Adam failed in his disobedience, the second Adam succeeded in obedience to the Father (John 8:29). Jesus pointed to the totality of scripture as the guide for conduct and the basis of faith. This second Adam, (Jesus), took back the dominion and the right to rule, he declared; *"All power is given unto me in heaven and earth!" (Matthew 28:18)* Glory to God! Our champion defeated Satan and reclaimed the power of dominion for man.

The Bucks Stop Here

Jesus is the final authority of power in this universe. He is the ultimate, authentic irrefutable power source, the crowned pinnacle of power in the heavens, on the earth, and under the earth. Jesus gave the believers back the dominion and the right to reign in life by Him (Romans 5:17b). The Scripture teaches that through Jesus, redeemed humanity have victory over Satan also (Romans 16:20). Christ' enemies become our enemies, and His victories become ours also. (Micah 7:17) Only our champion can help us to obtain victory over our enemy. The Psalmist said it so aptly; *"Give us help against the adversary, for vain is the help of man. Through and with God we shall do valiantly, for He it is Who shall tread down our adversaries"* (Psalm 108:12-13 Amplified ver.).

Once we recognize the enemy and his work, we must take the awesome arsenal of God and advance toward him. We are assured of the victory in Jesus name; *the gates of hell shall not prevail against us (Matthew 16:18).* We have been delivered from the tempter's power, Praise God! The Psalmist declares; *"Through God we shall do valiantly: for He it is that tread down our enemies" (Psalm 108:13).* The prophets of old foretold of the coming messiah who would defeat the enemies of man, namely; Satan, sin, death, and the grave. Because of Adam's sin, death reigned until the coming of our champion Jesus Christ; who was made a quickening Spirit (Romans 5:14-17). Jesus defeated death and rose again on the third day from the dead (John 2:19; Matthew 16:21).

"But God raised him from the dead, freeing him from the agony of death, because it was impossible for death to keep its hold on him"
(Acts 2:24 NIV).

Having defeated death and the grave, Jesus became the legal source of authentic 'power' in heaven and earth. **He is the power broker who delegates authority, rights, and privileges to the believer.** He said, *"Behold, I give unto you **power** to tread on serpents and scorpions, and over all the **power** of the enemy: and nothing shall by any means hurt you" (Luke 10:19).*

The first use of the word "power," in Luke 10:19, is the Greek word *exousia*, which means: delegated authority, right, and privilege. God has given us the rights and spiritual privilege to exercise full power of attorney in all God's interest; and complete authority to act in Christ's stead; as if He himself were here doing the work. The second use of the word, power, is the Greek *dunamis*, which means, ability, or might. Therefore, the power that is given to believers, to *"tread upon serpents and scorpions,"* is the power to destroy what Satan is able to do. To *tread upon*, means to have absolute mastery, as is clear in Psalm 91:13, which says; *"Thou shalt tread upon the lion and the adder: the lion and the dragon shalt thou trample under feet."*

The Scripture in Luke 10:19b, says, *"Nothing shall by any means hurt you;"* this assures us that no matter what means that the enemy uses, whether it be discouragement, sickness, disease, oppression, or witchcraft, etc., *"No weapon that is formed against us shall prosper" (Isaiah 54:17).* When we know our authority in Christ, and walk in close fellowship with Him, the enemy trembles, because to touch us is like touching Jesus Himself, it could prove detrimental to the kingdom of darkness.

We are the army of the Lord, fitted with Kingdom dominion power. We are God's battle-axe and weapons of war, according to Jeremiah 51:20. When we walk in faith and obedience, God *always causes us to triumph in Christ (2 Corinthians 2:14).*

The devil's primary goal is to keep us from fulfilling God's purpose and call upon our lives. We need to be aware of his mission and intents to ruin us, and counteract them with God's mighty weapons of war. One of his strategies is to get us to question our God, ourselves, and our worth; he knows that when we are fully aware of whose we are and who we are, there is no stopping us.

God wants you to be Armed and Extremely Dangerous to your enemy and *his* work. Always remember that Jesus won the victory for the believer in the 'supernatural power struggle' between good and evil. You are called to maintain that victory, and dismantle the enemy's weapons of mind control and 'psychological warfare.' We must destroy his works, and render him inoperative in our lives (2 Corinthians 10:4).

13

THE PSYCHOLOGICAL WAR

The motto of an organization named Psywarrior is; "Capture their Minds, and their hearts and souls will follow." This is the strategy Satan also uses against the believers. Psychological Warfare is intended to influence the mind to produce a desired effect. The enemy knows how to push the buttons of humanity through manipulation, intimidation, and fear. When we recognize and understand the moves of our enemy in these present times, it will expel fear, intimidation and dread. The eagle eyed prophet Isaiah declared, *"And wisdom and knowledge shall be the* **stability** *of thy times, and strength of salvation: the fear of the LORD is his treasure" (Isaiah 33:6).* It will also anchor the believer in the saving grace of Jesus Christ; hereby making him a stable, settled Christian.

During World War II, the United States Joint Chiefs of Staff defined psychological warfare by broadly stating that "Psychological warfare **employs** *any* **weapon** to influence the mind of the enemy. The weapons are psychological **only** in the effect they produce, and not because of the weapons themselves." It is a known fact in warfare, that if a weapon is effective, it should not be changed. If your opponent is unable to effectively resist it, there is no need to modify it. Although you may have several other kinds of weapons in your arsenal, don't change the one that works! This also is the philosophy of our arch enemy Satan.

In psychological warfare, Satan also uses any weapons, (means) or methods available at his disposal to negatively influence **our minds**. There are times when it is easy for him to infiltrate our minds through the open doors that we create through our wrong actions. Some of these doorways we create can be as a result of guilt, wrong choices, backlashes, and flash backs, etc.

For centuries Satan has strategically used intimidation, fear, terror, and torment on us through the tactics he deploys. The psychological war that he wages against believers is intended to make the believer second-guess God and His Word, and doubt God's love and care for them. We must be aware of the enemy's mode of operation, which is to persuade, influence and change.

Psychological warfare is used by our enemy to create doubts and fears within us. He masterminds negative events to strategically produce negative thoughts. When these thoughts germinate within our minds, if they are not dealt with, they can produce the reaction intended by Satan, the sower of these thought attacks. The enemy will manipulate the facts in order to discredit "truth" when it suites his diabolical plans. His purposes are always intended to distort the "truth" of God and His Word. He knows that once truth is neutralized, then the "psychological war" takes place behind the enemy lines, giving him the advantage over us. The apostle Paul states in his second epistle to the Corinthians; *"Lest Satan should get an advantage of us: for we are not ignorant of his devices" (2 Corinthians 2:11).*

The apostle Paul said, "lest Satan," the name 'Satan,' denotes an *adversary*, an *accuser*, or an *enemy*. He was quick to join the Corinthian church in forgiving the brother who had offended. He was willing to forgive, knowing the devices of his enemy (Satan). He did not want   Satan to have an advantage over either the church or the repentant offender; he left no room through unforgiveness. He was not ignorant of satanic **devices**. The word "device" means, anything made for a particular purpose; an invention or contrivance; a plan or scheme for affecting a purpose, something used to evoke a desired effect, or arouse a desired reaction. Paul was cognizant of the power of accusation, slander, gossip, guilt, and condemnation, and because he knew the power of these things, he left no room for them.

The brother, who had sinned in the Corinthian church, had committed a gross immoral act by sleeping with his father's wife (1 Corinthians 5:5), and was excommunicated. However, after some time he demonstrated sufficient proof of the sincerity of his repentance and remorse.

Paul expressed his readiness to forgive and endorse the church's reinstatement of the offender, in order to prevent him from being overwhelmed with sorrow and sink into satanic despair and psychological warfare. Not to do so would portray an unkind and unforgiving spirit; and thus injure church and ruin his testimony as the chief apostle. Not to forgive and restore the brother who was disciplined could also be a means used by the devil to destroy his precious soul. Paul said, *"Lest Satan, (the accuser), should get an advantage of us;"* by running a devilish campaign of slander about our unforgiveness or malice; or use our lack of forgiveness to bring ruin or downfall in some other way. Satan is very creative and versatile in the use of his devices.

His demonic devices are similar to the activities of the Midianites against Israel, in Judges Chapter six. It is a terror campaign! Satan and his demons are terrorists who come only to steal, kill, and to destroy (John 10:10).

To understand more about terrorism as strategies of the enemy in 'psychological warfare,' let us look for a moment in the book of Judges with Gideon and the Midianites.

Year after year, the Midianites came up with the Amalekites and the nomadic Arabian Bedouins of the desert from east of the Dead Sea. They came with their camels and livestock like grasshoppers, ravishing and plundering the land of Israel. Whenever Israel planted, the Midianites came and reaped. Can you imagine working hard and someone else collecting your paycheck year after year? Judges 6:6 says that, *"Israel was greatly impoverished because of the Midianites."* The Midianites were so overwhelming in numbers that the Israelites were swallowed up by them. The Israelites resorted to living in caves and dens (Judges 6:2), in terror of their enemies. Many believers today have also retreated from the front lines of life, hiding, because of their enemies.

The enemy has a way of bullying us into retreat and hiding, by playing on our emotions, motives, reasoning, and behavior. He sets up traumatic circumstances, tragedy, and emotionally charged experiences to deliberately drive us into hiding and retreat. These strategies were most effective against Gideon and the Israelites, and they are still proving to be effective against us today. Let's do our best to recognize the wicked one's devices, and guard against becoming victims of satanic terrorism.

The enemy was successful against Israel year after year in their raids and plundering of their crops. That is why Gideon threshed wheat by a winepress; to hide it from his enemy, the Midianites. He lived in fear; expecting the same results year after year. He lived in terror, always afraid of losing what he had to the enemy. **He was a victim of "psychological warfare!"** There are many people who have been victimized by terror and psychological warfare, and have been greatly affected; they are alive, but merely existing, living in fear and dread. To understand more about the strategies of the enemy in "the psychological war," let us look for a moment at the work of terrorists.

The Terrorist

The modern day terrorist has much more than a mere criminal or political agenda. Some of his criminal activities may include; murder, blackmail, sabotage, kidnapping and extortion, etc. These are not his goals, but only means to achieve his much larger goals. Whether his goals are ideological, religious, social, domestic, or retaliatory, he always has an objective in mind, and that is to paralyze with fear and dread. The modern terrorist seeks to make the society unstable and insecure, and undermine the security of the people. The fear of the uncertain is intended to target a country's ability to function; as we have seen in America, from the effects of the fallout of 911.

Terror as a Strategy of Psychological Warfare

Doctor Boaz Ganor, in his report on terrorism dated July 15, 2002, writes; "Modern terrorism, in defiance of the norms and laws of combat, focuses its attacks on civilians, thus turning the home front into a frontline. The civilian population is not only an easy target for the terrorist, but also an effective one; the randomness of the attack contributes to the general anxiety. The message is, anyone, anywhere, at any time, may be the target of the next attack." These threats undermine the ability of the civilian population to live a "normal" life. When every action must involve planning how to survive a potential terror attack at a random time and place, the daily routine becomes full of danger, thus plunging us into anxiety and survival mode. Such are the evils of terror.

The message that is sent to the community targeted by the terror attack is, 'Despite all your defenses, your army, your police force, your military hardware, you are never safe from us.' This is a direct assault against our peace and safety. Once civilians feel unsafe in their own homes and workplaces, daily life is disrupted, causing considerable harm to personal and national morale.

The will of God for our lives is found in His Word. His Word declares, *"I will both lay me down in peace, and sleep: for thou, LORD, only makest me dwell in safety" (Psalm 4:8)*. The Lord does not want us to be anxious or stressed over anything (Philippians 4:6). We are also reminded in the Psalm;

"Thou shalt not be afraid for the terror by night; nor for the arrow that flieth by day; Nor for the pestilence that walketh in darkness; nor for the destruction that wasteth at noonday" (Psalm 91:5-6).

As Christians, we must be aware of the intentions of the enemy in using the media as a propaganda machine, as a strategy to create fear in the world. In like manner, we must also be aware of the strategy of our enemy (Satan), in using the media as a means to create fear and hopelessness in us. Everywhere we turn, there seems to be a crisis of some kind. If it's not one thing, it's another! If we are not aware of the strategy of the enemy in using "psychological warfare," we could easily fall victim to it, and end up barely living from crisis to crisis.

God desires that we live the *"abundant life"* (John 10:10b). He desires that we walk by faith, and not by sight (2 Corinthians 5:7). If we respond to everything that we see in the natural, it could prove detrimental to us in all facets of life.

Fear, the Feared, and the Fearful

"And there shall be signs in the sun, and in the moon, and in the stars; and upon the earth distress of nations, with perplexity; the sea and the

waves roaring; Men's hearts failing them for fear, and for looking after those things which are coming on the earth" (Luke 21:25-26).

Like the terrorists, Satan's primary aim is to create fear within the target population or believer, with the intention that this fear will be translated into pressure. There are different kinds of fears, two of which are; rational fear, and sudden fear. Rational fear can be explained logically; whereas, sudden fear is brought on quickly, and in most cases cannot be explained through logic.

We are told by the wise man, Solomon, not to be afraid of sudden fear; *"Be not afraid of sudden fear, neither of the desolation of the wicked, when it cometh. For the LORD shall be thy confidence, and shall keep thy foot from being taken" (Proverbs 3:25-26).* Here, Solomon reassures the child of God that God will keep our feet from being taken in the snares of Satan, the flesh, the world, and the oppressors. *"Be not afraid"* is at once a precept and a promise to the godly. We shall have no cause to fear evil tidings; therefore it is our privilege that we are not to fear what we see, hear, or feel (Psalm 112:7). *"For God hath not given us the spirit of fear; but of power, and of love, and of a sound mind" (2 Timothy 1:7).*

I can recall at a particular time in my own life and ministry when I was so deeply affected by what I heard people say about me. The enemy made sure that I heard every negative remark that was said because he knew that at that time I did not have a thick skin protecting my heart, and thus, would be adversely affected. The enemy knows enough about us to fabricate lies and wage a campaign against us in the psychological war; especially in areas where he believes he may be most effective.

We become more targeted for psychological war, when we are on the cutting edge of ministry, and creating havoc in the enemy's camp. We are *then* put as high priority on Satan's hit list. He realizes that if we are unaffected by *his* devices, we stand to gain the upper hand against *his* 'age old' strategies, and his defeat is eminent.

Biblical Art of War

We are taught that the 'art of war,' involves strategies that have been deployed since ancient Bible times. These strategies were used to engage the enemy and gain the upper hand of victory. There are times when victories are won, not on the basis of sheer strength, but by particular strategic measures. I am reminded of the battle against Jericho. The historical record of the strategic siege and conquest of Jericho is recorded for us in the book of Joshua. *"Now Jericho was straitly shut up because of the children of Israel: none went out, and none came in" (Joshua 6:1).* The enemies of God's people will lock down what is rightfully yours. This is merely a delay tactic, or a means to hinder you.

There are times when you may encounter hindrances to your progress, but don't give up, your faith in God indicates to your enemy that you know you are unstoppable.

*"And the LORD said unto Joshua, **See, I have given into thine hand Jericho**, and the king thereof, and the mighty men of valour. And ye shall compass the city, all ye men of war, and go round about the city once. Thus shalt thou do six days. And seven priests shall bear before the ark seven trumpets of rams' horns: and the seventh day ye shall compass the city seven times, and the priests shall blow with the trumpets. And it shall come to pass, that when they make a long blast with the ram's horn, and when ye hear the sound of the trumpet, all the people shall shout with a great shout; **and the wall of the city shall fall down flat,** and the people shall ascend up every man straight before him" (Joshua 6:1-5).* When Joshua, the military commander and chief, deployed the divine strategy against the city of Jericho, the city and all its inhabitants with the

exception of Rahab and her family, were destroyed (Joshua 6:21-25). *God always has an ideal battle plan for your war!*

Another great example of "military strategy" is seen with Gideon's army of 300, facing the overwhelming odds of 450 to 1 in battle. He divided his army of 300 into three companies (Judges 7:16). After dividing them into three groups, he gave them three things: pitchers, lamps, and trumpets. The lamps were put inside the pitchers so that the lights could not be seen by their enemies. They held the pitchers with the light in one hand and their trumpets in the other hand. When they went into battle, the cry was to be, "The sword of the Lord and of Gideon." Although neither the Israelites nor Gideon had a sword, God's sword became their sword. They used the element of surprise and 'tactical' psychological warfare to overthrow their enemies. History tells us that Gideon carried out his attack by night, while most of the 135,000 troops were asleep. Gideon posted his 300 men in three groups around the enemy's camp. On his signal, at a certain time, they blew their trumpets and broke the pitchers so that the light shone out. Imagine the Midianites waking out of a sound sleep to all this noise and confusion.

The first thing they did was to grab their swords and started swinging in every direction. It was pandemonium! They turned against each other in the dark. They soon fled over the hills into the forest and out of that area, glory to God! Gideon and the Israelites obtained a tremendous victory by deploying a strategy of 'tactical psychological warfare.'

Finally, I want to look at the art of war as seen in the story of Ahithophel, one of David's counselors. Ahithophel was considered a thinking man and one that had a clear head, and a great compass of thought. His counsels were proverbial in David's time, and when he spoke it was 'as if a man had inquired at the oracle of God' (2 Samuel 16:23). After serving many years with David, he eventually betrayed him by joining with Absalom, David's renegade son. Ahithophel advised the Prince to take his father's harem (2 Samuel 15:12; 16:21). He also advised pursuit of David, the fugitive monarch (2 Samuel 17:1-3), but Hushai, another counselor, thwarted the move (2 Samuel 17:11-13). The counsel of Ahithophel was good military strategy, which providentially was not heeded by Absalom. Had Absalom gone along with Ahithophel's strategy, maybe, he would not have lost his life (18:6-15). We must learn to discern the people who are master strategists in the *art of war* that are in our lives.

Strategies of War

Let me now introduce some historical figures that have waged successful wars using psychological warfare and military strategies. It is my sincere prayer that you will extrapolate from these examples some spiritual principles of the strategies of psychological war.

Alexander the Great, of Macedon

Although he is not always accredited as the first to practice psychological warfare, he undoubtedly swayed the mindsets of the common people he dominated in his campaigns. In order to keep the new Macedonian states from revolting against their leader, he would leave a number of his men behind in each city to introduce Greek culture, control it, and oppress dissident views. He also left his men in these cities to interbreed, because this method of persuasion influenced both loyalist and separatist opinions.

This method became a direct means to alter the mindset of the occupied people to conform to the Greek influence. It is apparent through history that the strategies of Alexander the Great, proved to be successful in his campaigns for world dominance.

Alexander's approach to world dominance, no doubt parallels Satan's deceptive strategies to induce and develop the infiltration of darkness in a world that has fallen prey to his deceptions. Satan relies heavily on his emissaries (demons) to enforce his evil designs upon fallen humanity. Like Alexander's men, Satan's demons are ever at work influencing humanity with evil and rebellion against God. They are responsible for the infiltration of our world with *"seducing spirits and doctrines of devils" (1 Timothy 4:1).* These demonic agents are essentially responsible for deceiving and leading unsuspecting souls into deep satanic captivity and bondage.

The Strategy of Jesus Christ

The strategy which Jesus used for world conquest and dominance was also similar to that of Alexander the great, only better. Jesus used a handful of disciples to propagate the Good News of His Kingdom and Lordship after His departure. He left an 'occupational force' (the Church), in the world to be his change agents. These 'called-out-ones' are the influence of 'salt' and 'light' in this dark and sinful world.

Jesus said to His disciples, *"Occupy till I come" (Luke 19:13).* The use of the word 'occupy' in this text is a military one, as in the use of occupational forces. When He told them to "occupy," he meant that they were to engage in Kingdom mandates and assignments, until He returned with a full invasion at the end of the age. He established a system of government with superior ideals and empowered His disciples to carry out the great commission faithfully (Mark 16:15). His dominion is an everlasting dominion, which shall not pass away, and His kingdom shall not be destroyed (Daniel 7:14).

The Mongols

Genghis Khan, leader of the Mongols in the 13th century AD, united his people to eventually conquer more territory than any other leader in human history. Defeating the will of the enemy was his top priority. Before attacking a settlement, the Mongol generals demanded submission to the Khan, and threatened the initial villages with complete destruction if they refused to surrender. After winning the battle, the Mongol generals fulfilled their threats and massacred the survivors.

Subsequent nations were much more likely to surrender to the Mongols without fighting, because of their brutal devices. Often this strategy, as well as their tactical abilities, secured quick Mongol victories. Genghis Khan also employed tactics that made his numbers seem greater than they actually were. During night operations, he ordered each soldier to light three torches at dusk in order to deceive and intimidate enemy scouts and give the illusion of an overwhelming army. He also sometimes had objects tied to the tails of his horses, so that when riding on an open and dry field, they would raise a cloud of dust that gave the enemy the impression of great numbers.

The strategy of Satan is quite similar to that of Genghis Khan in this respect; he used terror, fear, and intimidation as a means to cause his enemies to surrender without a fight. Like Genghis Khan, Satan uses deceptive means to bluff his opponent into submission. Genghis Khan was not all-powerful, and neither is Satan, but the strategy he uses in appearing more numerous and powerful than he is, gives that appearance.

Jesus, however, is "The All Powerful, All Mighty, All Knowing, and All Sufficient King of Kings." He is the Almighty God! We have nothing to fear from the enemy! (Philippians 1:28a). The acronym F.E.A.R. means, "False evidence appearing real."

Our enemy is a deceiver, and the father of lies. He only "appears" to have overwhelming forces, but it is only an illusion, because, The Greater One lives within you (1John 4:4). The prophet Elisha reassured his servant at a time when the Syrian army seemed overwhelming in their numbers. "And he answered, Fear not: for they that be with us are more than they that be with them" (2Kings 6:16). It is important for you to guard against feeling demoralized and alone when you are under attack, especially when there is no visible support team. This can also be used by the enemy as a psychological strategy against you. Remember, people are not your source, God is!"

The use of Psychological War

During World War II, psychological warfare was used effectively by the military. The enormous success that the invasion of Normandy displayed was a fusion of psychological warfare with military deception. American troops used false signals, decoy installations and phony equipment to deceive German observation aircraft and radio interception operators. This had the desired effect of misleading the German High Command as to the location of the primary invasion, and of keeping reserves away from the actual landings. In June of 1944, the Allied armies successfully landed at Normandy in what is commonly referred to as "D-Day." Through intense fighting, the Allies established a beachhead, and advanced on the German armies. This was the turning point of the war for America and its Allies, and the fate of Hitler and Nazi Germany was sealed.

Most uses of the term psychological warfare refer to military methods and strategies such as:

- Distributing pamphlets, in the Gulf War were used to encourage desertion or (in World War II), supplied instructions on how to surrender. Today, the enemy uses liberal theology and false doctrines as a means of polluting and diluting what is true. This is done to erode our Christian values, our morals, and the principles and convictions on which we stand.

- Propaganda radio stations, such as Lord Haw-Haw, in World War II, on the "Germany calling" station was used to brainwash the listeners into believing that Adolf Hitler and Nazi Germany were superior, and invincible. There is a prominent Christian radio station today that is heard in many nations, whose music is soothing, but its primary message is propaganda. It informs us that the church age is over, and people should come out of the organized fellowship of the church. What propaganda!

- Renaming cities and other places when captured, is a form of divergence, which subliminally paves the way for new values and ideals. Today, we see this happening in the lobbying to remove the words 'in God we trust' from our moneys, and 'one nation under God' from our constitution. While these may be the removal of mere words, we have a responsibility to fight for the values we believe in.

- Projecting repetitive and annoying sounds and music for long periods at high volume towards groups under siege, has proven to be most effective in psychological warfare. This is one of the strategies that Jim Jones used in his brainwashing technique, in the Jonestown, Guyana tragedy in 1978. He played subjective messages over the public address system loudly, and constantly. This strategy violates the inner peace and sends the message that the defender is not even in control of his own thoughts. Similarly, Satan projects repetitive negative thoughts, lies, and opinions to us and about us. This is done to violate our inner peace, and break our wills to effectively resist him, and to fight the good fight of faith. This is the art of 'psychological warfare.'

Free, but Still Bound

I am reminded of a story that I once heard, about *the Hindenburg bear*. He was held in captivity for many years in a 12x12 cage in the Hindenburg Zoo. He was known to pace each day back and forth in the confines of his cage as the visitors watched. Eventually, he was released into his natural habitat of several hundred acres. After being released, he was observed to pace back and forth; he limited himself to walk twelve feet forward, and twelve feet backward. He was free, but did not know it. In his mind he was still programmed for captivity. Having been conditioned mentally during his captivity, he became accustomed to the narrow confines of his cage, and resigned to live out the rest of his life going merely twelve feet forward, and twelve feet backward. That is the power of conditioning!

In a similar way, many people who were subject to Satanic bondage all their life and were finally set free at some point by the power of Jesus Christ, find little difficulty in returning to their former way of life, and to the bondage of sin. This is mostly due to the conditioning that they received in their former sinful state. That is why it is important to be transformed, by the renewing of our minds (Romans 12:2). The psychological games that the enemy plays are deadly mind games, and if we fall victim to them, we run the risk of becoming prisoners in our minds. **If Christ does not have our mind, He does not have us; hence, whoever has our mind is ultimately in control of us.** That is 'mind control!' When you are a child of God you have the mind of Christ, remember, you should not be limited by the lies and opinions of the enemy, God has given you power, love, and a *sound mind* (2 Timothy 1:7).

14

Fully Dressed for Battle

Now that you can fully recognize who the real enemy is, and know how to recognize and overcome psychological war, it's time to get *'fully dressed for battle.'* One thing that becomes apparent for most of us is that life is full of conflict, struggle or war. The believer is engaged in battle, and that battle is being fought along *spiritual* lines. Throughout the ages, wars have been a part of civilization. Conflict of neighbors has escalated to world wars. Nations have been at war; from the early dynasty of the Egyptians to the most recent war in Iraq. Many people are engaged in war and are not even aware of it. Don't be fooled, if you are not fighting, you will be fought! Ignorance to the war around you is no excuse, and it comes at a high price. Many of God's people are destroyed because of ignorance; *"My people are destroyed for lack of knowledge" (Hosea 4:6).* Many believers have also been taken captive because of their lack of knowledge in the subject of warfare. *"Therefore my people are gone into captivity, because they have no knowledge" (Isaiah 5:13).*

In this chapter, I want to present to you an unwrapped version of the arsenal, and whole armor (panoply) of God, their functions, and their use in warfare. The Scripture speaks to us concerning the weapons of our warfare; its nature, purpose, ability, and aim.

"The weapons of our warfare are not human but mighty in God's sight, resulting in the demolition of fortresses, demolishing reasonings and every haughty mental elevation which lifts itself up against the experiential knowledge [which we believers have] of God, and leading captive every thought into the obedience to Christ"
(2 Corinthians 10:4-5 K. S. Wuest N.T).

The King James Bible renders vs. 4; *"For the weapons of our warfare are not carnal, but mighty through God to the pulling down of strong holds."*

The enemy who the Christian is called to fight, is not flesh and blood, neither are our weapons fleshly in nature. The enemy is spiritual, the warfare is spiritual, and so are our weapons; that is why we need spiritual power. It is only the armor of God that can withstand the strategy and onslaught of Satan, who has all kinds of weapons and spiritual missiles in his arsenal. God has given us an array of powerful weapons, including an antimissile system by which to overcome every fiery dart of the enemy. *"Stand therefore, having your loins girt about with truth, and having on the breastplate of righteousness; And your feet shod with the preparation of the gospel of peace; Above all, taking the shield of faith, wherewith ye shall be able to quench all the fiery darts of the wicked. And take the helmet of salvation, and the sword of the Spirit, which is the word of God: Praying always with all prayer and supplication in the Spirit, and watching thereunto with all perseverance and supplication for all saints"* (Ephesians 6:14-18).

Be Strong in the Lord

As the apostle Paul drew near to the conclusion of his epistle to the Ephesians church, he commanded them to be strong in the Lord.

"Finally, my brethren, be strong in the Lord, and in the power of His might. Put on the whole armor of God, that ye may be able to stand against the wiles of the devil" (Ephesians 6:10-11). Being 'strong in the Lord' is the basis of one's willingness to put on the whole armor of God and stand and fight the 'good fight of faith.' The Amplified version renders it; *"In conclusion, be strong in the Lord-be empowered through your union with Him; draw your strength from Him-that strength which His [boundless] might provides. Put on God's whole armor-the armor of a heavy-armed soldier, which God supplies-that you may be able successfully to stand up against [all] the strategies and the deceits of the devil."*

It is only when we draw our strength from the Lord that we are able to successfully withstand the devil. Paul is literally commanding believers to avail themselves as vessels or containers to house God's explosive power. He said, ***"Be strong in the Lord!"***

The word "strong" is taken from the Greek word *endunamoo*, which is a compound of two Greek words; en, pronounced "in" and the word *dunamis*, which means; explosive strength, ability, or power. The word *dunamis* is etymologically where we get the word "dynamite" from. Therefore, Paul is literally saying; ***"Be infused with an excessive dose of dynamic inner strength and ability."*** He knew that we needed this special supernatural endowment of power from God, in order to successfully combat the attacks of the enemy against us.

It is absolutely necessary for the Holy Spirit to deposit God's explosive supernatural ability within us. Paul was fully aware of the need for this infusion of power. He knew that we were recreated in Christ to house this power of God's might. We are reminded of that in his epistle to the Corinthians. *"But we have this treasure in earthen vessels, that the excellency of the power may be of God, and not of us" (2 Corinthians 4:7).*

Paul's argument was very strong on the need for being empowered with this special inner strength, because he knew that believers needed to receive *this power* before they commenced in their fight with unseen forces. Without this power of God, none of us could be any match for the schemes, or devices of Satan. He is crafty, slick, intelligent, brilliant, and shrewd; he is strong, tenacious, capable, engaging, and determined. Satan is a master strategist, a wise and organized leader, orderly in his planning, and systematic in executing his attacks on mankind. He is an opportunist, who knows and understands timing, he knows just when to assault viciously and destructively, and when to approach mildly and stealthily.

We are no match for him naturally, and our strength cannot be compared with his. We must remember that our sufficiency is found in Christ (2 Corinthians 3:5), and it is only by His grace and power alone that the enemy is defeated. Satan's power is no match for the All-sufficient power of the Holy Spirit, and he knows it. We must not fear the devil, but we should have a healthy respect for him as a worthy opponent. He may be a fallen angel, but he still possesses much of the intelligence and power he had before his fall, therefore, on our own we are no match for him.

Let us learn from the example of Michael, the archangel as he contended for the body of Moses. Jude, in his epistle, describes a protocol in the dispute between the archangel Michael, and the devil; *"Yet Michael the archangel, when contending with the devil he disputed about the body of Moses, [durst] not bring against him a railing accusation, but said, The Lord rebuke thee" (Jude 9).*

Although Michael was an archangel who stood by the throne of God, yet, even in doing battle for God against the devil, he dared *not* presumptuously accuse him, but left it up to the Lord to deal with him. He only said, "The Lord rebuke thee." Like Michael, we also should know our limitations, and know when to allow God to deal with the devil.

Paul believed that the only hope of the believer reinforcing Jesus' victory, and sustaining Satan's defeat, could only be attained with the help and power of God's special supernatural endowment. This was evident when he began the sixth chapter of Ephesians on spiritual warfare and armor, with a command to "be strong" (*endunamoo*). He made it clear that this special power, strength, or ability that we need, can only be found in one place, in the Lord. This supernatural power cannot be obtained through any other source or means, other than from a personal relationship with Jesus Christ. He alone has the exclusive right to this kind of power, and only He alone can dispense or impart the 'power of *His* might.'

The Power of His Might

The power of His might denotes the same unseen power working to inculcate the believer with energy to combat the forces of darkness. This demonstrative power of God's ability is seen quite clearly in Paul's intercession for the church at Ephesus. He prayed that they would come to understand the riches of their glorious inheritance in Christ; the kind of supernatural enabling that God has made available to us. Paul uses the word power twice in the text, when he said, *"...The exceeding greatness of **His power (dunamis)** to us-ward who believe, according to the working of **His mighty power (kratos)** which He worked in Christ when He raised him from the dead, and set him at His own right hand in the heavenly places" (Ephesians 1:19-20).*

The second use of the word power in the text, is taken from the Greek word *kratos*, and it means; vigor, active strength or effective force, dominion, might or power. It describes a visible effective force; not merely a power which can be identified intellectually and believed in, but, an outward show of "might" (Gr. *ichuos*), strength of force, and an outward manifestation of active strength, one that has corresponding action as proof.

It is asked, 'What is the significance of these Greek uses of the word power?' It is very important, because, the Greek words used to define the *mighty power* that God used to raise Christ from the dead, is the very same words used to describe the 'supernatural power' we operate in. It is described as *"the power of His might"* (Resurrection and Ascension power).

God's able power, (*dunamis*), made it possible for Christ to be resurrected from the dead. However, it took his *'mighty* (ischuos) *power'* (**kratos**) of *vigor, effective force*, and *active strength* to cause him to ascend, from the earth's atmosphere, past the stratosphere, past the ionosphere beyond gravity, through the hemispheres, and beyond; *"...far above principality, and power, and might, and dominion, and every name that is named, not only in this world, but also in that which is to come" (Ephesians 1:21).*

This particular kind of *endunamoo* power that Paul describes in Ephesians 1:19-21 and Ephesians 6:10, is so strong that it can withstand any attack, and it can successfully oppose and override any kind of force in this universe and beyond. Can you imagine how the demons of death, hell and the grave fought viciously to keep Jesus in the grave? However, Luke says, *"Whom God hath raised up, having loosed the pains of death: because it was not possible that he should be holden of it." (Acts 2:24)* It was impossible for the powers that be, to withstand the power of resurrection. Ephesians 1:19b from the King James Version says, *"...according to the working of His mighty power."*

While Ephesians 6:10 reads somewhat different, it says; "...*in the power of His might.*" However, it is noted by Greek scholars that the original Greek of Ephesians 1:19b reads, *"according to the working of the power of His might."*

These similar uses are important, because the same power that was used to raise Jesus from the dead, *far above* all existing powers, is the very *same* power that God infuses within us to combat the unseen forces of darkness. Through the power of the Holy Spirit, **we operate in the kratos of resurrection and ascension power!**

This is the strongest flow of power that is known in the universe. This power is so supreme, that reference to its use in Scriptures is only used in connection with God's power. No other created being possesses this kind of power; neither can it be accessed by anyone. This power can only be given by God. The *kratos* power that raised Jesus from the dead, when directed towards evil is more overwhelming and conspicuously disruptive than all the earth's volcanoes activated at once. It is more devastating than ten thousand tsunamis, and more irresistible than the blast of a thousand atomic bombs. *Kratos* power is the greatest power known to God and man.

When Paul addressed the subject of spiritual warfare and the armor of God in Ephesians chapter six, he knew that before he could discuss the warfare of believers with unseen enemy forces, he had to introduce and discuss the issue of power. If the power of God is not operating in our lives, there is no base for war. He knew that we could not carry the armor of God in *our human strength*, even if we tried. Paul sets the priorities in order and introduces the *kratos* power of God first, knowing that without this power there would be no war. He knew that Satan's host was committed to obstruct the Christian soldier by any means, and hinder the work of Christ.

He also knew that the objectives of the enemy were to knock the believer out of commission and combat. The more effective a believer is for the Lord, the more he will experience the savage attacks of the enemy; the devil does not waste his ammunition on nominal Christians, but targets those who are most progressive. In our own strength we are no match for the devil, so Paul's first preparatory command is that we should be continually strengthened in the Lord and in the unlimited power of His might. We are but mere mortals without the supernatural power of God, but when God's 'super' is infused into our 'natural,' we become a "supernatural" force of God to be contended with.

God's most excellent soldiers are those who are conscious of their limitations and ineptness without him, and who rely solely on Him. God has chosen the weak things of the world to confuse and bewilder the things which are mighty (1Corinthians 1:27b). Paul wanted the believer to know that our only chance for victory in the spiritual battle is when we are strong in the Lord, and in the power of *His might*. He was fully aware, that only with God's supernatural strength could we execute our duties as a Christian soldier, and that in order to be effective against such great and formidable foes, we needed to be clothed in the whole armor of God. When we are strong in the Lord we can function in His armor.

Prepared for Battle

Having such awesome *kratos* power at our disposal, we are now ready to successfully engage in the battle against the unseen forces in the spirit realm, which wage war against us on every front. With these facts in mind, Paul continues to command us, *"Put on the whole armour of God that ye may be able to stand against the wiles of the devil" (Ephesians 6:11).*

The phrase "whole armour" is derived from the Greek word *panoplia.* It describes a Roman soldier dressed to the tee, from head to toe. Paul says, *"Put on the whole armour of God that ye may be able to stand against the wiles of the devil." (Ephesians 6:11).* The instruction given here by Paul is, "Put on..." This phrase, "put on" is taken from the Greek word *enduo,* and it refers to the act of putting on the 'whole armor,' as one puts on a new set of clothes. In Ephesians 4:24 and Colossians 3:10, Paul urges us to, *"put on the new man."* He tells us to, 'put on' (enduo), the new man, as a new garment. This was not a mere recommendation or suggestion, but in the imperative tense, it was the strongest kind of command that could be given. Paul is commanding us with great urgency to put on the 'whole armor' (panoply), which originates from God.

The whole armor entails seven pieces of defensive and offensive weapons *[I have included the prayer of Ephesians 6:18 as a weapon].* The apostle Paul was fully acquainted with the full uniform of a Roman soldier. He was a Roman citizen himself, and no doubt was familiar with the full regalia of the Roman soldier.

It could be that he became familiar with the Roman soldier's armor from his observation in Tarsus or from his many imprisonments. Paul noted the six pieces of armor that the Roman soldier of his times wore; *[I have included prayer to make a total of seven pieces of weaponry]* everything that the soldier needed to successfully combat his enemy was at his disposal. In a similar manner, God has made available to us everything that we need to combat our enemy successfully. Paul describes the whole armor in Ephesians 6:14-18, as follows: The girdle or **loinbelt** of truth, the **breastplate** of righteousness, **shoes** of peace, the **shield** of faith, our **helmet** of salvation, the **sword** of the Spirit, and **prayer**. We have been given the whole armor of God, and it is this armor that the apostle Paul commands us to pick up and use in our daily lives.

The armor of a believer is functional only while there is ongoing fellowship with God. I have seen so many people who fell out of fellowship with God and still claim to wear the whole armor of God, but this is not possible. The Christian armor originates with God, and proceeds from God as our source. If our fellowship with the source of our armor is suspended, or broken, then the armor itself is automatically suspended by the source. The armor is not something we put on once, and then it remains on us forever, it must be fitted daily. The belt of truth can become corroded with heresy, just as the breastplate of righteousness could be an irritant to a heart gone cold, etc. We should not expect to reap the benefits from a company we are no longer employed by, so why should we expect the available use of the armor of God, without a right relationship with Him?

The armor of God then, is ours by virtue of our union and relationship with God. The spiritual armor is always accessible to the child of God for his use, but as long as he suspends his relationship with God, he has suspended his rights and privileges to walk in the armor of the Lord. The armor is God's property, and by default, it returns to Him when we choose not to be "in Him."

Enabled to Stand

The apostle Paul, in his command to the church proceeds by telling us why we should put on the whole armor (panoply) of God. *"Put on the whole armour of God, that ye may be able to stand against the wiles of the devil" (Ephesians 6:11)*. He states that we should put on the whole armor in order to successfully '**stand**.' It is noted that the phrase, '**to stand**,' taken from the Greek word *stemai* literally means; to take an erect posture. It gives the picture of a soldier fully armed and prepared for battle; one standing erect with his shoulders squared, and his head lifted high, confident and reassured. In using the Greek word, *stemai* (stand), Paul alludes to a Roman soldier *standing in a specific, strategic position* on the battle field, ready and enabled to engage objectively in battle, or to subjectively stand guard over a person (self), place, or thing.

Paul tells the believers to 'stand' against **the wiles** of the devil. The word 'wiles,' as I have stated in an earlier chapter, is the Greek word *methodos*, and is the etymological root of the word '**method**.'

Methods

Methods speak of Satan's predictable pattern of operations. When I say pattern, I refer to a distinctive style, or method; a procedure or technique, an orderly and prepared systematically planned way of doing things. This is the reason we need the 'whole armor of God.' Without the armor of God, we will not be able to *stand* against the devil, or his methods (planned way of doing things). On the other hand, when we *stand* fully dressed in the 'whole armor of God,' we stand in the winning position of a soldier of the Lord.

The methods that Satan and his demons use are geared at breaking down your resistance. He is proficient in the art of slander, allegations, and accusations. When he launches an attack against you, he targets your mind. He will bombard you with a series of vicious attacks, with the intentions of breaking you down, hoping to neutralize you and take you into captivity when you are most vulnerable.

This is the reason why Paul commands us to *"Put on the whole armor of God"* [the loinbelt of truth, breastplate of righteousness the gospel shoes, the shield of faith, the helmet of salvation, and the sword of the Spirit, and prayer as a weapon]. This panoply comes from God, and is given to you in order that you may be victorious, being fully equipped with God's 'mighty' arsenal. Paul knew that none of us could stand against the organized forces, devices, or strategies of our unseen enemy. Now he could inform us of our invisible foes, and introduce to us the classifications of the satanic hordes. Paul knew that the source of our attacks, whether they are against our minds, bodies, or our souls do not originate with other human agents. He wanted you and me to know that our opponents do not fight fairly, nor do they observe any rules.

He was careful to point out that, "We do not *wrestle* against flesh and blood." The word 'wrestle' is the Greek word pale, and it refers to struggling, wrestling, or hand to hand fighting. It is from this word that the Greeks derived the name Palastra, which means 'a house of combat sports.' It is similar to what we call (blood-sport) or 'cage fighting' today. It is an extremely dangerous sport, where two opponents wrestle, punch, kick, elbow and beat each other mercilessly. The *pale* (wrestling) or fighting in Paul's day was a violent, aggressive, vicious fight, sometimes to the death. It was a 'fight' without rules, where anything goes, and only the best man would remain *standing*. Such is the believer's fight that Paul describes.

Paul wanted us to know that although we have been given weapons and a spiritual arsenal that could be used from a distance, there are times when the fight is personal, close, and so intense that we can hear the enemy breathing, or gasping for breath. He writes; *"For we wrestle not against flesh and blood, but against principalities, against powers, against the rulers of the darkness of this world, against spiritual wickedness in high places. Wherefore take unto you the whole armour of God, that ye may be able to withstand in the evil day, and having done all, to stand" (Ephesians 6:12-13).* Paul here, and in Colossians chapter one, gives us a list of the angelic beings that are ever at work behind the scenes to deceive, ensnare, manipulate, and control the human race.

"For by him were all things created, that are in heaven, and that are in earth, visible and invisible, whether they be thrones, or dominions, or principalities, or powers: all things were created by him, and for him" (Colossians 1:16).

These forces are working even harder against the child of God because we were delivered from Satan's evil power, equipped with dominion power, and called to *rule* and *reign* with Jesus Christ (Revelation 20:6).

Choirs of Angelic Hierarchy

A serious study of Biblical Angelology reveals a choir of angelic beings. The order, rank, or function of this angelic hierarchy that I will provide does not by any means present a comprehensive knowledge of the subject.

The Hebrew word for angel is *mal'ak*, which means to dispatch as a deputy, messenger, and ambassador. A messenger sent whether by God, (benevolent), or by Satan, fallen (as demons, malignant). The Greek word for angel is *angelos*, which means, to bring tidings; a messenger. They are an order of created beings superior to man, (Hebrews 2:7; Psalm 8:5; they are spirits Hebrews 1:14).

1. **Seraphims:** One of the heavenly beings surrounding the throne of God in His service. Considered of the highest order of angelic beings (Isaiah 6:2). The Hebrew: *Seraph* is to burn, implying the burning, dazzling brilliance. It also suggests rapidity; like lightening (Ezekiel 1:13-14). These angels serve in expressing worship to God, they celebrate the praise of Jehovah's holiness and power (Isaiah 6:3), and they act as a medium of communication between heaven and earth (vs.6).

2. **Cherubims:** One of the winged heavenly beings that support the throne of God, or act as a guardian spirit (Genesis 3:24, Exodus 25:18-20; 26:1; 36:8); One of the second order of angels (Ezekiel 1:10-22). In the Hebrew Scriptures they are described as the throne bearers of God.

In Christianity they are celestial attendants of God and praise him continually. This is the order from which Satan belongs (Ezekiel 28:14a).

3. **Archangels**: Greek, *Archos*, a chief angel; first ruler, where rule begins. A Prefix, main, chief, principal of high rank; one who rules kingdoms. Such as Michael, the chief prince, (Daniel 10:13; 10:21), who rules over the nation of Israel, (Daniel 12:1). A Disputer, (Jude 9); A Warrior, (Revelation 12:7-9); An Announcer (1 Thessalonians 4:16).

4. **Thrones**: Hebrew, *'kisse'* Greek, *'Thrao'* (*bema*). To sit in a stately seat, an elevated seat of authority. The Chief potentate. This is Satan's big shot, if you will. He is a prime ruler in the chain of satanic command. This class of celestial being seeks to secure governments and rule through the use of dominions (Daniel 7:9; Colossians 1:16).

5. **Dominions:** The Greek word is *Kuriotes*, which comes from Gr. *'kurios'*, meaning; Supreme in authority, controller, Lord or Master. He is the enforcer, the one who seeks to secure the sovereign governing right or authority over a territory or country for the ownership or legal control on the behalf of Thrones (Colossians 1:16).

6. **Principalities:** Greek, *'Archas,'* *chief ruler*, the beginning of earthly government. This marks the highest level of *earthly rule*. The power that enforces legislation. The Prince ruler of a jurisdiction or territory, (Daniel 10:13-21; Romans 8:38; Ephesians 1:21; 3:10; 6:12; Colossians 1:16).

7. **Powers:** Greek, *'Exousias,'* denotes the freedom or right to act on another's behalf. They are the *delegated authority* of Satan who are empowered to execute the will of the chief ruler, as they will. They are sent to promote superstition,

fear, supernatural manifestations, and magic, paranormal and occult activities. They provoke an interest in the spiritual world, and in the supernatural. They are like recruiters (Romans 8:38; Ephesians 6:12; Colossians 1:16).

8. **Rulers of the Darkness of this world:** The Greek '*Kosmo-krateros,*' taken from two combined words: ***kosmos***, meaning order and arrangements and ***kratos***, signifying *raw power*. This is *raw power* harnessed in an orderly arrangement. They promote the agenda, of the age; such as crimes, violence, drug epidemics, sexual perversions, spiritual blindness, errors, seductions, deceptions, and rejection of the truth, etc.

They are wicked world rulers of the darkness of this age [world], (Ephesians 6:12). These forces of Satan understand rank and file. They work with disciplined, organization, committed to loyally enforce the agenda of their master (Satan).

9. **Spiritual Wickedness in High Places:** The Greek is '*Pneumatika ponerias*', taken from two Greek words, *Pneuma* (spirit), and *poneros*, which is used to depict something very bad, vile, abominable, atrocious; awful, vicious, impious, detrimental, unhealthy, malevolent and malignant. These spirits are sent on assignments from on high, to afflict humanity in a vile, abominable, vicious, detrimental and malignant way (Ephesians 6:12c).

It is evident from the list of angelic choirs in Ephesians chapter six and Colossians chapter one, that the apostle Paul was fully knowledgeable of the alignment of Satan's kingdom. We can tell by the military language Paul used that he understood the direct confrontations that Christians would have in a face to face combat with theses organized, unseen, evil forces. These forces are the ones assigned to assault and afflict humanity. Paul wanted us to know that Satan was so serious about doing damage to humanity, that he organized his demons like troops. He wanted us to be fully aware of our enemy and his organization. He instructed the Ephesians earlier in the chapters, knowing well that they could only be successful in battle if they were prepared beforehand.

Imperatives before Spiritual Warfare

Paul emphasized the need for believers to put on the whole armor. However, before he commanded them to dress for war, he admonished them to:

1. *Put away lying* (Ephesians 4:25a).

2. Every man must *Speak truth with their neighbor* (Ephesians 4:25b).

3. *Be angry, and sin not* (Ephesians 4:26a).

4. *Let not the sun go down upon your wrath* (Ephesians 4:26b).

5. *Neither give place to the devil* (Ephesians 4:27).

6. *Let him that stole, steal no more* (Ephesians 4:28a).

7. *Let no corrupt communication proceed out of your mouth* (Ephesians 4:29a).

8. *Grieve not the Holy Spirit* (Ephesians 4:30).

9. *Let all Bitterness...be put away from you with all malice* (Ephesians 4:31a).

10. *Let all Wrath... be put away from you with all malice* (Ephesians 4:31b).

11. *Let all Anger... be put away from you with all malice* (Ephesians 4:31b).

12. *Let all Clamour...be put away from you with all malice* (Ephesians 4:31b).

13. *Let all Evil Speaking, be put away from you with all malice* (Ephesians 4:31c).

14. *Be Kind one to another* (Ephesians 4:32a).

15. *Be Tenderhearted, Forgiving one another* (Ephesians 4:32b).

Understanding the function of each piece of Roman armor Paul described in his epistle, will better enable us to be *"Fully Dressed for War."* If we are not aware of how each piece of armor is related to the other, we may find ourselves naked amidst the greatest battle of our age. Let us examine the armor piece by piece.

"Stand therefore, having your loins girt about with truth, and having on the breastplate of righteousness; And your feet shod with the preparation of the gospel of peace; Above all, taking the shield of faith, wherewith ye shall be able to quench all the fiery darts of the wicked. And take the helmet of salvation, and the sword of the Spirit, which is the word of God: Praying always with all prayer and supplication in the Spirit, and watching thereunto with all perseverance and supplication for all saints" (Ephesians 6:14-18).

Paul begins in the text of Ephesians 6:14 by saying, *"Stand therefore..."* The Greek word for 'stand' is the word *'stemi,'* which means to "stand upright." It pictures a soldier with his head held upward, his back straightened, and his shoulders squared with confidence. This is the picture of a Christian soldier who is dressed in the whole armor of God, standing confidently in the Lord. Paul states; *"Stand therefore, having your loins girt about with truth..."*

The Whole Armor

The Roman soldier of Paul's day was completely covered by his armor. He wore a large, highly structured, decorative, intricately designed, attractive helmet on his head; a breastplate which encased his upper torso and midsection, which started at his neck and went down past his hips to his knees. It was made of rings, fastened together so that they would be flexible, and yet guard the body from swords, spears, or arrows. It is referred to in the Scriptures as a *"coat of mail"* (1 Samuel 17:5), made to resemble the scales of a fish, or metal plates. It was the heaviest piece of armor he wore.

The soldier also wore a metal greave skirt, which was covered with large metal scales overlapping each other, also called, "a coat of mail." He also wore greaves on his legs, which wrapped around his calf and extended down to his ankles and continued down to the spiked shoes which he wore. The soldier was also equipped with a very large shield, or *scutum*, which was a hallmark of the Roman legions. Its large size and rectangular curved shape let the soldier deploy the "tortoise" formation, which made him practically invulnerable to the attacks of missiles and archer fire.

Another vital part of the armor was the loinbelt, girdle, or sash, as it was also called. It was made of a cincture of iron or steel, and it connected the breastplate to the metal greave skirt. The loinbelt kept all the armor securely together, thus insuring the safety of the soldier. In addition, he also carried on his back, a javelin or spear, which was held by the loinbelt. His scabbard which housed his dagger or sword was also connected to the loinbelt. The *gladius*, or the short sword, was primarily used for stabbing or thrusting, and it was generally eighteen to twenty four inches long.

Eventually, the *gladius* was replaced by a *spatha* or long sword. This sword went up to thirty nine inches in length, and was as sharp as a razor on both sides. Look at how the Roman soldier was well protected; he was covered in metal from head to toe! His helmet was metal, his breastplate was metal, and so was his greave skirt. The spiked shoes which he wore were also metal; he had a metal two edged sword, and a spear which had a metal head. In addition to his armor, he also had a large shield made of leather, wood and brass.

As we get the picture of the Roman soldier fully dressed for battle, we should know that God has given us *His whole armor*, and be assured that God has not left us vulnerable to any satanic assault, but has provided all the armor we need to obtain total victory.

Gird with Truth

"…Having your loins gird about with truth" (Ephesians 6:14a).

Let's examine the pieces of armor that God has given us, beginning with the loinbelt of truth. Just as the Roman soldier's belt was the main support that held his breastplate securely to his greave skirt and centrally connected all his armor together, it is as important to know that it is the "truth" of God's Word that upholdeth all things (our armor), by the Word of His *power* (Hebrews 1:3).

Certainly we must be faithful in holding the "truth" of God's Word, but it is also necessary for the "truth" to *hold* us. The truth is secured through thorough study, and rightly dividing the Word (2 Timothy 2:15). The Gospel of Jesus Christ is the ultimate truth of God, and unless this is known, and conscientiously believed, no man can enter the spiritual warfare with any advantage or prospect of success. By this alone we find out who our enemies really are, and how they come to attack us. We also ascertain where our strength lies, and as the truth is great, and must prevail, we realize we are to gird ourselves with this against all false religion, and the diverse winds of doctrines by which cunning men and insidious devils lie in wait to deceive (Ephesians 4:14). Our armor will not be held together if we operate in error (2 Corinthians 6:7).

The Breastplate of Righteousness

"...And having on the breastplate of Righteousness" (Ephesians 6:14b).

The second piece of armor that Paul mentions is the breastplate of Righteousness. Notice, it's called the "breastplate." This is important, because it covers a very vital organ; *the heart.* Barnes, the well-known expositor, in his comments on Ephesians 6:14, notes; "Integrity, holiness, purity of life, and sincerity of piety are some of the components that make up the breastplate which defends the vital parts of the body. The idea here may be that the integrity of life, and righteousness of character, is as necessary to defend us from the assaults of Satan, as the coat of mail was to preserve the heart from the arrows of the enemy. It was the incorruptible integrity of Job, and, in a higher sense, of the integrity of the Redeemer Himself, that saved them both from the temptations of the devil. And it is also true now that no one can *successfully* overcome the power of temptation unless he stands in God's righteous (integrity), and that a soldier could not defend himself against a foe without *such* a coat of mail.

The lack of integrity will leave a man exposed to the assaults of the enemy, just as a man would be whose coat of mail was defective, or had missing pieces. The king of Israel was smitten by a stray arrow, "between the joints of his harness" or the "breast-plate" (1 Kings 22:34). He was not completely covered, and thus not completely protected. Many a man who thinks he has on the "Christian" armor is smitten in the same manner. Where there is some defect in character, some want of incorruptible integrity, some point that is unguarded, that will be sure to be the point of attack by the enemy. It may be added here, that we need a righteousness which God alone can give;

the righteousness of God, our Saviour, to make us perfectly invulnerable to all the arrows of our foes."

Righteousness is a weapon, according to Paul's list in Ephesians six. We have been made the "righteousness" of God according to the Scriptures. *"For He hath made Him to be sin for us, who knew no sin; that we might be made the righteousness of God in Him" (2 Corinthians 5:21).* Righteousness is a defensive weapon, as well as an offensive one. The enemy of the cross hates righteousness.

When we are conscious of our righteousness, we will walk in a new level of integrity, confidence and boldness. In Proverbs 28:1, we are told, *"The wicked flee when no man pursueth: but the righteous are bold as a lion."* In a messianic passage written by the prophet Isaiah, reference is made of the Messiah canopied in the armor; He put on righteousness as a breastplate. *"For he put on righteousness as a breastplate, and an helmet of salvation upon his head; and he put on the garments of vengeance for clothing..." (Isaiah 59:17).* It is apparent from this Old Testament prophecy, that when Jesus entered into this militarized zone (earth), He was clothed with righteousness as *His* breastplate; let us learn from his example, and stand ready for war clothed with the breastplate of righteousness.

Feet Adorned with the Gospel of Peace

"And your feet shod with the preparation of the gospel of peace"
(Ephesians 6:15).

Your feet represents your stance, your foundation, and your mobilizing power. The sense is that the Christian soldier is to put on the Gospel shoes, and advance the good news to a captive dying world. The word rendered "preparation" Gr. *hetoimasia* means, properly fit and ready for; and the idea according to Robinson (Lexicon), is, that they were to be ever ready to go forth to preach the gospel, as an advancing invasion into enemy territory. An old hymn says, *"Take my feet and let them be Swift and beautiful for Thee" [F.R.Havergal].*

"And how shall they preach, except they be sent? as it is written, How beautiful are the feet of them that preach the gospel of peace, and bring glad tidings of good things!" (Romans 10:15).

Christians are to have the principles of the beautiful gospel of peace; the peaceful and pure gospel, to facilitate them; to aid them in their marches, to make them firm in the day of conflict with their foes. They were not to be furnished with carnal weapons, but with the peaceful gospel of the Redeemer, and, sustained by this; they were to go on in their march through the world. The principles of the gospel were to do for them what the greaves and iron-spiked sandals did for the soldier, to make them ready for the march, to make them firm wherever their feet thread, even upon serpents and scorpions, and upon all the power of their enemy, and nothing shall by any means hurt them (Luke 10:19).

The Shield of Faith

"Above all, taking the shield of faith, wherewith ye shall be able to to quench all the fiery darts of the wicked" (Ephesians 6:16).

Paul uses a phrase to describe the importance of this piece of armor; "above all." The phrase, "above all," is taken from the Greek phrase *epi pasin*. The word *'epi'* means "over," and *'pasin'* means "all," or can be translated, 'everything.' The phrase expresses a note of importance; Paul says, "...above all." *Above all* does not necessarily refer only to the importance of faith, but also to its scope. Paul is saying literally that our shield of faith is intended to *stand out*, cover us completely, and protect us entirely from *all* harm and danger, especially in our advance to establish the Kingdom and dominion of God.

The shield was an ingenious device by which blows and arrows might be parried off, and the whole body defended. It could be made to protect the head, or the heart, or thrown behind to meet all attacks there. **As long as the soldier had his shield, he felt secure; and as long as a Christian has faith, he is safe.** It comes to his aid in every attack that is made on him, no matter from what quarter; it is the defense and guardian of every other Christian grace; and it secures the protection which the Christian needs in the spiritual war.

Paul says, *"Taking the shield of faith" (Ephesians 6:16)*. What is interesting is the use of the word *"taking,"* from the Greek word *analambano*. It is a compound of Greek words, '*ana*,' which means 'up back, or again,' and '*lambano*,' which means 'to take up,' or 'to take in hand.' When combined together, *analambano* means to take something up in hand, or to pick something up again. This tells us that our shield of faith can be taken up or laid down; it is not activated or utilized without our engagement and effort.

The shield was usually made of light wood or a rim of brass, and covered with several folds or thicknesses of stout hide, which was preserved by frequent anointing. The outer surface of the shield was made, more or less, round. From the center to the edge of the shield, was polished smooth or anointed with oil, so that arrows or darts would not stick, but glance off, or rebound.

"Prepare the table, watch in the watchtower, eat, drink: arise, ye princes, and anoint the shield" (Isaiah 21:5). What we need today is an anointed shield of faith!

Fiery Darts

Paul continues by emphasizing the effectiveness and extent of the active shield of faith against the bombardments of fiery attacks. *"Wherewith ye shall be able to quench all the fiery darts of the wicked"*

(Ephesians 6:16b). The allusion here is that no matter what the *Wicked* one throws at us, faith can "quench" it. It can be "put out" by being thrown "against" the shield of faith. "The fiery darts" that were used in war were small, slender pieces of cane, which were filled with combustible materials, and set on fire, then shot "slowly" against a foe.

The object of firing this dart was to make the arrow fasten in the body and increase the danger by burning as it exploded. When Paul used the term, 'fiery dart,' he probably referred metaphorically to the temptations of the great adversary, which are like fiery darts; or those furious suggestions of evil, and excitements to sin, which he may throw into the mind, like fiery darts. They are blasphemous thoughts, such as, gross doubt and unbelief, an overwhelming enticement to do wrong, thoughts of deep hurt and inner wounds, and regret that torments the soul.

Such thoughts are like fiery darts that come suddenly, like arrows speeding from a bow. They come from unexpected quarters, like arrows shot suddenly from an enemy in ambush. If they are not intercepted and quenched, they pierce, and penetrate, and torment the soul as arrows would that are on fire. They set the soul on fire, and enkindle the worst passions, as fiery darts do a ship or a camp against which they are sent. The only way to meet them is by putting up the "shield of faith," by having confidence in God, and by relying on his gracious promises and aid. It is not by our own strength that we are victorious, and, if we have no faith in God, we are wholly defenseless. We should have a shield that we can turn in any direction, on which the enemy's arrows can be deflected and by which it may be quenched. [Excerpts from Barnes' Notes]

The Helmet of Salvation

"And take the helmet of salvation..." (Ephesians 6:17a).

The helmet of salvation is one of our defensive weapons. **There are three defensive weapons:** The breastplate, the shield, and the helmet. These are weapons that protect us and secure us with confidence and assurance, enabling us to grow in grace, and advance in the things of God. **There are three offensive weapons:** The shoes, the sword, and prayer. Although Paul did not list prayer as a part of the armor, it is an offensive weapon which he names in Ephesians 6:18. **There is one neutral piece of armor** and that is the loinbelt. The loinbelt represents the Word of God, in that it is the central piece of weaponry that holds all the other pieces of armor together. If the Word of God is not paramount in our lives, then none of the other pieces of armor will do us any good. Everything revolves around the Word of Truth.

The helmet of a Roman soldier in Paul's day was made of bronze, and was constructed with solid pieces of armor especially designed to protect the head, cheeks, and the jaw of the soldier. The material that made the helmet of the soldier was so strong that no conventional weapon of its time; such as a sword, a war club, or the short handled, battle-axe could pierce or penetrate it. No soldier would go to war without his helmet, it would be suicide. Hence, Paul being quick to see a spiritual lesson in the natural realm makes the application of the helmet to represent the believer's salvation. Thus, no believer dare go to war without his helmet; he would be sure to lose his head.

The helmet God provides is salvation. *"For he put on righteousness as a breastplate, and an helmet of salvation upon his head" (Isaiah 59:17).* If you are going to be an asset in the Kingdom of God, you must cover your head [mind] with the helmet of salvation. If the enemy will invade a believer's life, he will usually aim at neutralizing the mind, because it is your central control unit. If he could seize your mind, then he could control and manipulate you. Whoever has your mind has control of you. To protect you from falling captive to the enemy, God has given you the helmet of salvation.

No doubt Paul was fully acquainted with all the facets of redemption and salvation; he was a scholar and understood the full compass of salvation. When we are fully cognizant of the multifaceted aspects of our salvation, such as: deliverance, healing, justification, acceptance, son-ship, reconciliation, redemption, sanctification and glorification, we will have good reason to make sure that the helmet of salvation remains securely on our head. It is only as our head is covered with God's helmet of salvation that we are able to keep our minds stayed on God, and free to clearly discern psychological warfare, as well as the wiles of the enemy.

"But let us, who are of the day, be sober, putting on the breastplate of faith and love; and for an helmet, the Hope of salvation"
(1 Thessalonians 5:8).

The idea here is that a well-founded hope of salvation will preserve us in the day of spiritual conflict, and will guard us from the blows which an enemy would strike. A soldier will fight well when he has hope of victory.

The Sword of the Spirit

"And take...the Sword of the Spirit, which is the Word of God"
(Ephesians 6:17b).

Paul proceeds to tell the believer to *"take the sword."* This makes clear to us how available the Word of God is. It's accessible to all those who desire it. The classic illustration of this is our Lord's use of this **sword** in His encounter with Satan in Luke 4:1-13; He quoted the Word three times while refuting the devil.

Luke's version of the account of Jesus' temptation is most fitting to show the use of a *rhema* word, (sword), against the enemy. In Jesus' temptation by the devil in the wilderness, Jesus quoted the Word of God, not just random verses, but the appropriate verses which the Holy Spirit gave Him for the occasion. The Word of God here, does not mean the whole Bible, but the particular portion of the Bible which best suites the occasion.

On two occasions during His encounter with Satan, Jesus responded to Satan by saying, "It is written," and on another occasion he said, "It is written again." Jesus establishes the principle of using the written Word as a sword.

In Luke 4:12, He uses the "spoken Word" *rhema*, as His weapon. He declared the power of *rhema*. He said, *"I have **heard** it said."* Jesus told the devil that he had received a quickened *rhema* word from the written word when it was spoken in his presence. He declared from Deut. 6:16 and Exodus 17:2 a faith charged Word that was previously preached into his hearing. What makes the devil flee is when we believe what God Word says, and say what we believe! Whenever we "**speak**" the Word with confidence in what God says, that "word" comes alive. The Scripture declares the power of the Word (sword).

"For the Word of God is quick, and powerful, and sharper than any two-edged sword, piercing even to the dividing asunder of soul and spirit, and of the joints and marrow, and is a discerner of the thoughts and intents of the heart" (Hebrews 4:12).

The Greek word, 'rhema,' denotes that which is spoken clearly, what is uttered in speech unmistakably, vividly, undeniably, unquestionably, and definite in terms. It is a "quickened" word! *"He has made my mouth like a sharp sword" (Isaiah 49:2).* *This principle is seen in Chapter Eleven of this book, "The Faith Charged Word."

Praying Always

*"Praying always with all prayer and supplication in the Spirit,
and watching thereunto with all perseverance and supplication
for all saints" (Ephesians 6:18).*

This final weapon of prayer is the mobilizing power of the soldier's lance (spear or javelin). I have included the lance of prayer, because Paul said, *"Put on the whole armor" (Ephesians 6:11).* The Roman soldier would not be considered fully armed without his lance; neither would the Christian soldier be wholly armed without his lance of prayer. Paul said, ***"Praying Always."*** It is evident from the original language that Paul meant, 'Pray, every opportunity you get.' The Amplified Bible renders it, *"Pray at all time, on every occasion, in every season."* The New International Version says,

*"And pray in the Spirit on all occasions with all kinds of prayer
and requests."*

Paul was fully aware that along with his sword and his dagger, the Roman soldier possessed different kinds of lances for war. That is why he says, *"With [all kinds] of prayer" (Ephesians 6:18a).* The soldier had access to diverse arsenal of lances, of all shapes and sizes; however, there were two main lances which were frequently used in combat, the short lance, and the long. The short lance can be likened to prayer against an unseen foe that has come too close with hostile intentions. This kind of prayer disrupts, dismantles, and destroys. Similarly, the Roman soldier had a long lance to hurl at his opponent from a distance, it was very heavy at the tip; which when used against the enemy from a distance, inflicted deadly wounds because of its thrust. This lance of prayer is similar to an intercontinental missile. When this kind of prayer goes forth, it confounds satanic conspiracies and decimates demonic arsenals. Arsenals such as: Evil plots and schemes, gossip and slander, witchcraft and hexes, evil disruption in families, businesses and ministries; incidents, accidents and occurrences, etc.

No Christian soldier, in spite of how successful he or she may be, is of any consequence in the army of the Lord without prayer. Prayer is our lifeline to God, it is our communication system, uniting us with headquarters, and it is the satellite link to intelligence in the spirit world.

Prayer is the key to locking or unlocking doors in the spirit realm. It is a formidable weapon against the enemies of the Kingdom of God.

Paul continued in his admonition to pray, he said, *"Praying always with all prayer and supplication" (Ephesians 6:18a)*. He literally means to pray *'with [all kinds] of prayer.'* There are different kinds of prayers, just like there are different kinds of lances. Here is a short list of different kind of prayers that I have compiled for you.

Different Kinds of Prayers

1. **Prayer of Communion:** The word 'prayer' is *proseuche* in the Greek. Objectively, it means, 'prayer to God.' The Greek word koinonia, is communication with God by which we express our dependence on Him. God knows what we need, and He is more ready to meet our needs than we are to ask, but until we express our dependence on Him in prayer, God may not act. God loves to have us approach Him as His children, expecting Him to hear and to answer, and He loves to have us call Him, "our Father." He gives us the privilege of calling the infinite God, our Father.

2. **Prayer of Supplication**: This prayer involves petitioning or entreating God for something. Prayed with a passionate zeal and hunger for something specific (Luke 11: 9 - 13, James 5: 17-18, 1 Kings 8: 37-40, 54 - 55). The prayer of

supplication will quite often be accompanied with fasting (Nehemiah 1: 1-6).

3. **Prayer of Intercession:** It is the pleading or mediating on the behalf of someone else. Jesus is interceding for us (Hebrews 7:25). When we occupy ourselves with concern for others and earnestly pray for them, we enter into the realm of intercession. In order to enter into intercession, we must have a heart that loves God and people, and possess a deep love for the things of God. (Genesis 18: 22-33 Abraham); (1Kings 18: 41-46 Elijah); (2 Kings 4: 32-36, Elisha); (Acts 12: 1 - 18, the early church).

4. **Prayer of Faith:** The prayer of faith is rooted in our confidence in God's word. It stems from an assurance that what you are praying for is biblically the will of God. It is to know the will of God and to pray it; expecting only to receive the answer (Mark 11:25; James 1:5-8).

5. **Prayer of Adoration:** Also called, "*the Prayer of Praise and Worship.*" Praise and worship brings us into the presence of God (Psalm 100:4), or brings the presence of God where we are (Acts 16:25-26). This is similar to the prayer of Hanna, when God gave her a son, Samuel (1Samuel 2:1-10). Her prayer of adoration was similar to Mary's prayer of being chosen to give birth to Messiah (Luke 1:46-55). It tells of our fervent and devoted love for God. This kind of prayer is powerful to dispel negative situations and fears. When we express praises and adoration to God, He comes to occupy it (Psalm 68:1-2).

6. **Prayer of Agreement:** This is when two or more people come together and agree with one another and with the Word of God that something specific will be done. God has

given power and authority to His Church, and when we stand together in unity we see more of God's awesome power released (Matthew 28:16-20). Unity is standing together with one purpose, sharing a joint vision and trusting God's Word to be fulfilled (Genesis 1:1-9; Matthew 18:19-20; Exodus 17:8-13; Psalm 133:1-3; Acts 4:23; Hebrews 10:24-25).

7. **Prayer of Confession:** *Homologeo* in the Greek, is to speak the same thing (*homos*, same *lego*, to speak). This prayer is the acknowledgment of what God says about us and agreeing with Him when He convicts us of sin (Psalm 32:5-7). He wants us to know that He readily forgives us. He wants us to be specific in our prayer for the confession of sin, not generic (Daniel 9:4-19).

8. **Prayer of Affirmation:** This is the positive assertion of the truths of God, as they relate to His people (Titus 3:8). It expresses an agreement with the blessings and promises of God, and upholds and supports them by declaration or agreement.

9. **Prayer of Petition:** This prayer is the type we are most familiar with; it is where we ask God for things we need i.e., The Lord's Prayer (Luke 11:3). It is the primary request for spiritual needs, but physical ones as well. Our prayers of petition should always include a statement of our willingness to accept God's will, whether He directly answers our prayers or not (Daniel 9:3; Ephesians 6:18).

10. **Prayer of Travail:** This prayer is a form of intense supplication given by the Holy Spirit, whereby an individual or group is gripped by something that grips God's heart. The individual or group labors with Him for an opening to

be created so that the new life can come forth. The Webster's dictionary defines "travail" as, very hard work, the pains of childbirth, intense pain, agony or toil. Travail takes place after you have borne something in your heart for a period of time, then it comes on you suddenly. It is often accompanied with deep groaning which cannot be explained. It is the deepest wrestling or agonizing of the soul (Genesis 32:24-26; like Jesus did in Luke 22:44; and Paul in his prayers in Colossians 4:12-13 NASB).

11. **Praying in the Spirit:** It is mentioned three times in Scripture. 1 Corinthians 14:15, Ephesians 6:18, and Jude 20). The Greek word translated, "pray in" the Spirit, can have several different meanings. It can mean 'by means of, with the help of, in the sphere of, and in connection to.

Praying in the Spirit does not refer to the words we are saying. Rather, it refers to how we are praying. Praying in the Spirit is God's way of helping us pray when we don't know how. "The Spirit also helps our weakness" (Rom. 8:26). For we do not know how to pray as we should, but the Spirit Himself intercedes for us. "Helps," depicts the Holy Spirit's role in coming alongside us in our condition of human frailty and spiritual vulnerability. It is also the communication of *our* spirits infused by the Power of the *Holy Spirit*, (1 Corinthians 14:15). Paul mentions *"I will pray with my spirit."* It is also interpreted as praying in the Spirit or Heavenly language (1 Corinthians 14:15). This is interpreted by evangelicals as 'praying in tongues.' This kind of prayer is a direct line to God, where the spirit is edified.

12. **Warfare Prayers:** This kind of prayer is not directed to the Lord, but it is directed as a lance (missile, spear or javelin), towards the unseen evil forces of Satan, by the believer who

stands in his union and authority in Christ. God has given us authority over the forces of evil (Luke 10:19), and has empowered us to bind the enemy, and loose His mighty power (Matthew 18:18).

Some causes of unanswered Prayers:

1. Having secret or unconfessed sins (Psalm 66:18).

2. Lack of forgiveness (Matthew 6:14-15).

3. Having a spirit of indifference (Proverbs 1:28).

4. Neglecting to show mercy (Proverbs 21:13).

5. Despising the Law of God [His Word] (Proverbs 28:9).

6. Our iniquities separate us from God (Isaiah 59:2).

7. Being stubborn and hard-hearted (Zechariah 7:13).

8. Being double minded and unstable (James 1:5-8).

9. Pride (2Chronicles 7:14).

10. Lack of compassion (Proverbs 21:13).

11. Hypocrisy (Luke 18:9-14).

12. Broken relationships [unreconciled] (1Peter 3:7).

13. Praying amiss (James 4:3).

14. Having wrong motives (James 4:3).

15. Neglecting to ask (John 16:24).

Having outlined some of the different "*kinds*" of prayers, we are admonished by the apostle Paul to pray, (Ephesians 6:18a); we can boldly advance towards the enemy prayerfully knowing that the arsenal which God has given to us cannot be depleted. God has given us a vast array of weaponry in our armory, both offensive and defensive, and when deployed, makes us *Armed and Extremely Dangerous.*

After getting fully clothed with the '*whole armor* [panoply] *of God*' and being cognizant of our unseen foes; we advance with confidence and courage toward the gates of hell, and surely; they cannot prevail against us. "*...And upon this rock I will build my church; and the gates of hell shall not prevail against it*" (Matthew 16:18). We fight alongside our great Commander and Chief, along with a host of angelic beings; we have a mandate to fight the good fight of faith, under the banner of the Almighty God.

We must put on the whole armor so that no part of us will be left uncovered or exposed to the enemy. As we advance towards Satan's strongholds and high places, we must march undaunted, fearless, confident, secure, valiant, bold, and unflinching. Let us now prayerfully discern the battle, and Identify, Select, and deploy the most effective weapon for our warfare, from the arsenal God has given to us.

15

IDENTIFYING AND SELECTING YOUR WEAPONS OF WAR

Now that you are fully dressed in the whole armor of God, it is time to identify *and Select Your Weapons of War*. In our last chapter, I expounded on the "whole armor" of God, which the apostle Paul commanded us to "put on." Having examined the pieces of armor which the Roman soldier of the New Testament times wore, and applying these pieces in the spiritual realm, we have been made to see how completely Armed and Extremely Dangerous the Christian soldier is. Although most of Christendom is unaware of how much God has given to us to use against the enemy, the enemy is not ignorant of the weapons that are at our disposal. Satan trembles whenever the least of us take unto us the whole 'armor of God' (Ephesians 6:13), and begin our advance towards his gates. Gates here refer to the protected strongholds, prisons, and fortresses where Satan holds many precious souls in captivity. Notice; gates never move, they are fixed to walls and fences which surround something that is valued or precious.

When we say, *"The gates of hell shall not prevail against the Church,"* we mean; that when the army of the Lord advances its assaults against the gates of the enemy with the battering ram of faith, it shall not prevail against us (the Church). For too long now the gates of hell have stood secure amidst the "Church of God;" it's time to take the battle to the enemy and assault his gates, because God Himself has declared war against Satan and his hordes, and the child of God is summoned to arise and fight the good fight of faith!

The enemies of faith has stepped up to the front lines of our homes and families, our schools, our churches and learning institutions, our cities, our nation and our world; it's time to select our weapon and fight. Quite often, it is in a crisis situation that most people find the incentive to become active in the fight of life. Some people strangely shut down in the face of adversity, while others use adversity and opposition to get ahead. There was a time when men counted the spoils, (or bounty) of war before they would join the fight; such men were mercenaries, they did not fight for a cause but for personal gain. Others fought for what they believed in, while some men would fight just for the sake of fighting; it didn't matter what side they were fighting on, they just lived to fight. I would be remiss not to mention those who fought out of obligation, to save face, while others fought because they were forced to. Then, there are those, who, like some rogue nation with nuclear capabilities, live as bullies and antagonists with their neighbors, and just because of their weapons of mass destruction they go looking to pick a fight.

The Christian soldier is enlisted into God's army to fight, because that's what soldiers do, but let's not fight for any other reason, except for the cause of righteousness, and the establishment of the Kingdom of God, through the Lordship of Jesus Christ. When our motives are right, our fight will be a *good fight of faith* (1Timothy 6:12).

Have you ever found yourself in a position like Sampson, the deliverer? Although he possessed supernatural power, God did not activate it until a young lion *roared* against him! (Judges 14:5-6). The Scripture says that Sampson tore the young lion apart with his bare hands, like a little goat. That's what an anointing will do! It will teach your hands to war, and your fingers to fight (Psalm 144:1). You need not be concerned about your ability to use the weapons of your warfare, just prayerfully take them up! God will teach you how to use the weapons of your warfare which you select.

Do you remember what happened when Sampson broke free from the bondage, how he went searching? The bible says;

"And when he came unto Lehi, the Philistines shouted against him: and the Spirit of the LORD came mightily upon him, and the cords that were upon his arms became as flax that was burnt with fire, and his bands loosed from off his hands. And he found a new jawbone of an ass, and put forth his hand, and took it, and slew a thousand men therewith" (Judges 15:14-15).

Observe, it was when the Philistines shouted against Sampson, that the Spirit of the Lord came mightily upon him. In the midst of eminent danger, the Spirit of God will turn on your 'turn on!' It seems to be a common thing with Sampson that whenever hostile intentions were directed towards him, that's when the anointing would come upon him. What lion has roared against you lately, or, what Philistine enemy shouted against you in your situation? These are occasions to fight!

The Scriptures says that, *"Sampson found a new jawbone of an ass."* He found a weapon, because he was looking for one. The weapon which he found was deliberately searched for; he purposefully discriminated in his choice of a *new* jawbone. There was often a place where the bones of dead animals were heaped, usually outside the town, like the garbage dumps of Gehenna, and that is probably where he found the bones. He found a *new jawbone of an ass* [donkey], (Judges 15:15).

You must understand Sampson went looking for a weapon which he could *select* and use to inflict mortal wounds upon his enemies; he became *Armed and Extremely Dangerous.* The fact that he slew a thousand men with this one jawbone, tells us that had he stopped fighting he could have easily been overcome by the mere numbers of his enemies. He selected a new jawbone because an old one would have been too brittle to withstand the strong blows, and constant use, but the new one was durable and strong.

Like Sampson, we need to come to a place where we are motivated to engage the enemy with the weapon we have prayerfully selected for that battle. What does it have to take to get us riled up? Whether it is a roar, a shout, pending danger, bondage, oppression, attack on our families, loss of a job, or mere jeopardy, there must be something that makes us say, *"Enough is enough devil!!"*

For much too long the Philistines have oppressed God's people. The giants of our world have paraded their intimidating sizes before the armies of the Lord; daring the believer to meet their 'new age' challenges. Like the armies of Israel, the Church is challenged by the giants of witchcraft and occultism, heresies and doctrines of devils, liberal theology and scripture twisting; deceptions, pride, weakness, selfishness, fear, greed, bigotry and indifference, etc.

A list of weapons deployed

a. Abraham used **Obedience** to gain God's favor and blessings (Genesis 22:15-18).

b. Jacob selected the mental weapon of **Persistence**, and refused to let the angel go till he was blessed by him. Jacob's weapon prevailed over the angel of the Lord (Genesis 32:26-28).

c. Joseph deployed the weapon of **Temperance** when he was tempted by Potiphar's wife (Genesis 39:7-10).

d. When Israel reached the bitter waters of Marah, Moses cried unto the LORD; the LORD shewed him a **Tree**, which he cast into the waters, and the waters became sweet (Exodus 15:25).

e. The children of Israel **Shouted** as the priests blew the trumpets, and Jericho's walls came tumbling down (Joshua 6:20).

f. **Silence** was used as a weapon by the Israelites on the wall (2 Kings 18:27-36), when the Assyrian ambassador insulted them, their king Hezekiah, and their God.

g. The harlot used **Love** as a weapon which appealed to the **Wisdom** of Solomon and was rewarded with her son (1 Kings 3:23-28).

h. Joash, the royal seed was preserved **Secretly** from wicked queen Athaliah, who destroyed all the royal seed of David; except Joash (2 Kings ch.11-ch.12).

i. Elisha used **Prayer** as a weapon and smote the Syrian army with blindness (2Kings 6:18).

j. **Fasting** is chosen to loose the bands of wickedness, to undo the heavy burdens, and to let the oppressed go free, and that ye break every yoke (Isaiah 58:6).

k. **The Signed document** was the weapon God used to finish Zerubbabel's temple when they were ordered to stop building (Ezra 6:1-14).

l. Jesus used the **Word** of God to overcome his temptations from the devil (Luke 4:1-13).

m. The woman with the issue of blood used **Faith** to overcome religious bigotry and her issue (Luke 8:43-44).

An excellent case study of Identifying and selecting your weapons is provided in the story of David, against the Philistine giant, Goliath, so, let's conclude this chapter with a study of David (1 Samuel 17).

David, the sweet Psalmist, poet, and King of Israel, has always been an intriguing Bible character to me. Although he was an ardent worshipper of Jehovah, he was a man of as many weaknesses as his strengths. Many of the points and principles in this closing chapter of Armed and Extremely Dangerous, is taken from my book, *A Man After God's Own Heart.*

A Brief History

David's name means, beloved, and he was truly loved by God. In fact, he was the only man to earn the title given to him by God; *"A man after God's own heart" (1 Samuel 13:14; Acts 13:22).* He was the youngest of the eight sons of Jesse, the Bethlehemite; he was a shepherd over his father's flock from his youth and he was carefully chosen as Israel's second king by God Himself (1 Samuel 16:12-13).

I have found that when God sizes up a man for the picking, He puts the tape measure around his heart, not his head.

A brief description was given of David, the son of Jesse, in 1 Samuel, chapter sixteen, to King Saul, as his chamberlains and servants made recommendation for Saul to hear anointed music as a means of calming his troubled mind from an evil spirit.

*"Then answered one of the servants, and said, Behold, I have seen a son of Jesse the Bethlehemite, that is **cunning** in playing, and a mighty valiant man, and a man of war, and prudent in matters, and a comely person, and the LORD is with him" (1 Samuel 16:18).*

David was *'selected' as a weapon* for Saul, against the evil spirit which made Saul a manic depressant (1 Samuel 16:14). Although David's primary role in the palace was to 'play the music,' he appeared overqualified for the job. His resume gives a list of seven impressive things about him:

1. He was a skilful (cunning) musician (1 Samuel 16:18).

2. He was a mighty man (1 Samuel 16:18).

3. He was a valiant man (1 Samuel 16:18).

4. He was a man of war (1 Samuel 16:18).

5. He was a man prudent in matters (1 Samuel 16:18).

6. He was a comely (well groomed, handsome) man (1 Samuel 16:18).

7. The Lord was with him (1 Samuel 16:18).

David remained in the palace of King Saul for some time, as a skilled anointed musician; playing the harp with his hands whenever the evil spirit came upon Saul. King Saul came to love David, and made him his armor bearer (1 Samuel 16:21).

"And it came to pass, when the evil spirit from God was upon Saul, that David took an harp, and played with his hand: so Saul was refreshed, and was well, and the evil spirit departed from him" (1 Sam 16:23). There are times when God will select and use unconventional

weapons to bring about our deliverance. In this case, the "selected" weapon of Saul's mental war was an anointed musician named, David. David became the instrument through which Saul became refreshed, and was able to resume his role as commander and chief. Afterwards, David returned home again to his father's house; to resume *his* role as a shepherd over the flock.

It appears that during the time of Saul's sickness, the enemies of Israel heard that the King of Israel was depressed and demonized; they saw this low period of Saul's life as an opportunity to regroup and come again. Twenty seven years after their overthrow in Micmach (1 Samuel chap.14), they returned again to possess themselves in Israelite country to fight with Israel. Isn't that like the devil? You would think that when Satan loses a battle with a child of God, he would learn his lesson and not bring it to them again, but not Satan, nor those that do his bidding; they often regroup and return, with evil intentions.

The Philistines returned and gathered their armies for battle near the Valley of Elah, southeast of Jerusalem, in territories belonging to Judah, not far from Gath. Saul and the armies of Israel assembled nearby, with the valley of Elah between them. This time a champion came out of the camp of the Philistines; a man of enormous size, over nine feet tall. He not only looked big, but he talked big too. The challenge of the Philistine giant was, *"We don't need a whole army to settle the dispute between our two nations, choose ye a man and let him come down to me" (1 Samuel 17:8)*. The conditions were, if your man defeats me, we will serve you and your king, but if I defeat your best man, your nation will serve the Philistines.

Goliath's challenge totally demoralized the nation of Israel, because he was big, bold, and strong.

"And he stood and cried unto the armies of Israel, and said unto them, Why are ye come out to set your battle in array? am not I a Philistine, and ye servants to Saul? choose you a man for you, and let him come down to me. If he be able to fight with me, and to kill me, then will we be your servants: but if I prevail against him, and kill him, then shall ye be our servants, and serve us. And the Philistine said, I defy the armies of Israel this day; give me a man, that we may fight together. When Saul and all Israel heard those words of the Philistine, they were dismayed, and greatly afraid" (1 Samuel 17:8-11).

For forty days, Goliath strutted back and forth in front of the armies of Israel, issuing the challenge and insulting them. King Saul searched in vain for someone with the courage, faith, tenacity or reckless abandonment to take on such a giant of a problem.

I want to make an observation here, the fate of a nation would rest upon 'one man,' and the future of every Israelite would be on one man's shoulder. If this man is not a proven, seasoned, accomplished fighter and a man of war, then he'd better be an anointed *Man After God's Own Heart;* one full of faith and power!

During the time when the Israelites gathered together against the Philistines at Shochoh, Jesse grew concerned about three of his sons in Saul's army. Jesse called David and sent him with food to the camp of the Israelites (1 Samuel 17:17). King Saul, no doubt, spent sleepless nights trying to figure a way out of his dilemma, while his generals remained divided and confused with respect to strategy.

David arrived on the scene of battle as an errand boy, dressed like a poor country shepherd, but spoke with courage and confidence, like a seasoned soldier. He may have been young, but he showed uncommon courage and the heart of a warrior. He had not reached the years of manhood, yet he possessed the kind of stuff every soldier of the

Lord needs. When he saw and heard the brashness and arrogance of Goliath, he was moved with righteous indignation against Goliath.

"And as he talked with them, behold, there came up the champion, the Philistine of Gath, Goliath by name, out of the armies of the Philistines, and spake according to the same words: and David heard them. And all the men of Israel, when they saw the man, fled from him, and were sore afraid" (Verse 23)

And the men of Israel said, Have ye seen this man that is come up? surely to defy Israel is he come up: and it shall be, that the man who killeth him, the king will enrich him with great riches, and will give him his daughter, and make his father's house free in Israel. And David spake to the men that stood by him, saying, What shall be done to the man that killeth this Philistine, and taketh away the reproach from Israel? for who is this uncircumcised Philistine, that he should defy the armies of the living God?" (1 Samuel 17:25-26).

David had no conventional weapons, except for the five pieces of items he took with him into the battle vs.40. He had (1) His shepherd's staff or club, (2) five smooth stones, (3) a shepherd's bag, (4) his sling was in his hand, and (5) His faith in God (vs.40).

The language of David expresses principles of faith, confidence, and complete trust in God"...*Who is this uncircumcised Philistine, that he should defy the armies of the living God?" (1Samuel 17:26c).*

"And David said to Saul, Let no man's heart fail because of him; thy servant will go and fight with this Philistine. And Saul said to David, Thou art not able to go against this Philistine to fight with him: for thou art but a youth, and he a man of war from his youth. And David said unto Saul, Thy servant kept his father's sheep, and there came a lion, and a bear, and took a lamb out of the flock: And I went out after him, and smote him, and delivered it out of his mouth: and when he arose against me, I caught him by his beard, and smote him, and slew

him. Thy servant slew both the lion and the bear: and this uncircumcised Philistine shall be as one of them, seeing he hath defied the armies of the living God" (1 Samuel 17:32-36).

A close examination of David's statements from the moment he entered the arena of challenge gives a hint to the undaunted progressive mindset of the Man after God's own heart. Faith in itself is a formidable weapon against the enemy, however there are some principles of faith that are weapons within the arsenal of creativity. We must be ever mindful that whatsoever things were written before in the Scriptures, were written for our learning, therefore, when we approach the sacred book, we should be ready to extract from its contents, principles to live by.

Like David, you may be facing a giant in your life, or maybe you will be called on to fight someone else's giant. The principles that you will glean from this battle between David and Goliath, could very well be the art of war you need for victory in your next battle.   You may ask, "What do I do if I have limited training and very little resources?" or, "How can I take on a problem that is much bigger than I am?" Well, let me show you five key principles to being "Armed and Extremely Dangerous."

Principles of War

The First action principle of faith for giant challenges is found in 1 Samuel 17:24-49; *"And all the men of Israel, when they saw the man, fled from him, and were sore afraid. And the men of Israel said, have you seen this man that is come up?"* In these passages you will notice that an attempt was made by the men of Israel to transfer their fears upon David, who **first** of all, *Minimized his fears*, by saying; *"...Who is this uncircumcised Philistine...?" (vs.26).* This is a very important part of engaging in spiritual warfare, you must minimize your fears. Even if you are somewhat fearful inside, never verbalize it!

What you say can and will be used against you in a spiritual battle; "Minimize your fears!"

The Second action: David *Maximized his faith.* Christians, who lack faith, disappoint themselves, discourage others, and defeat God's purpose. But not David, he was a purpose-driven man, he was a man Armed and Extremely Dangerous; A man after God's own heart, a man who desired the things that God required, and he tapped into the very heart of God. *He maximized his faith* (vs. 34-36). David proclaimed to Saul; *"Thy servant slew both the lion and the bear: and this uncircumcised Philistine shall be as one of them, seeing he hath defied the armies of the living God" (vs.36).* David used his past triumphs over the bear and lion as a spring-board to the present situation, he attributed his victories to the help of Almighty God; and today this was just another occasion for God to work again on his behalf; *he minimized his fears, and maximized his faith in God.*

The Third action: He *Magnified his fervor.* We often meet people who desire to do exploits for God, but have no fervency in their spirit to serve; that is pipe dreaming! David employed the principle of 'not being slothful in business,' and 'being fervent in spirit while serving the Lord' (Romans 12:11). His fervency is seen in his eagerness to bring the fight to Goliath. His was a *right now* kind of faith. He said; *"...Thy servant will go and fight with this Philistine."* David was fervent; ardent in feeling, burning, very hot, he was eager to take the fight to the enemy; he did not walk towards Goliath, but rather hasted and ran toward the army to meet the Philistine (vs.48).

Your enthusiasm is fuel for your fight!

This confidence that David displayed was not in his natural abilities and skill with a sling, nor was his confidence in the weapons he selected, but David's most lethal weapon was the name of the Lord (1 Samuel 17:45). Too often, believers see the name of the Lord as a defensive tower into which the righteous runs and are safe, but David recognized and used the name of the Lord as an offensive weapon. In the name of Jesus, demons will have to flee!

David was anointed, and his anointing provided for him divine enabling. Whenever you are anointed of God, it enables you with supernatural boldness to go where the average Jo Blow dare not go.

Anointed folks are not easily intimidated at the size of a situation, but motivated by God's revelation; they don't run from things, they run things!

There are times when certain situations may come your way, and you may be tempted to ask, "Why me Lord?" It is important to remember that God does not give us more than we are able to handle (1 Corinthians 10:13), and the reason He allows those degree of challenges to come our way is not to break us, but to make us, the challenges are character and faith builders, and they come because we are anointed to deal with it. The wherewithal to accomplish a difficult task is already given by God, it's wrapped up in our anointing, and we can handle it!

The Fourth action: David *Manifested his Freedom*. There are times when we are tempted to be relevant at the expense of our covenant. David realized that although Saul was willing to clothe him with his armor, he would be more clothed in the invisible armor of God that he was more accustomed to wearing. David opposed the use of Saul's armor; he simply declined by saying *"... I cannot go with these; for I have not proved them"* and David manifested his freedom *by putting them off* (vs.39c). The Scripture says;

"And David girded his sword upon his armour, and he assayed to go;
for he had not proved it. And David said unto Saul, I cannot go with
these; for I have not proved them. And David put them off him
(1 Samuel 17:39).

Too often we attempt to undertake momentous tasks without adequate preparation, sometimes a prayerful study of the situation will give the spiritual demographics that provide the wisdom needed to gain the upper hand. It is easy to get caught up with what is popular and prestigious; but remember, what works for the other guy won't necessarily work for you; God has a battle plan for the challenges of *your* life.

Your purpose may be so different,
so extraordinary, no one before
you have ever attempted it.

No doubt, David was unaccustomed to the cumbersome feelings of Saul's amour and the restriction and additional weight it carried, and not having proven it experientially, felt that it would have prevented his maneuvering ability. There are times when we must not be quick to try new things in new situations, but in such times use what you know. Whereas it might be true that 'new broom sweeps clean,' remember that the 'old broom knows the corners.'

David put off Saul's armour; it is important to recognize the selfless actions of the *Man After God's Own Heart*. How many servants of God would take pride in entering into a battle with the general's armor or uniform, thinking it would gain him an advantage or intimidate the opponent? But David was not in this thing for a show. One can be armed and only look dangerous, while another could appear unarmed and yet be extremely dangerous. David refused to wear the King's (General) uniform into battle, he was not into style and fashion, he just, "put them off!"

In like manner, there are some things that we are clothed with that are not conducive for victory in the arena of spiritual warfare. David was not afraid to 'lay aside the weight.' Sometimes the *weight* is not physical, but spiritual or ideological. Some of the things Paul admonishes us to put off are found in Colossians 3:8;

> *"But now put of all these; anger, wrath, malice, blasphemy, filthy communication out of your mouth." In order to achieve victory, we must lay aside the weight, and the sin that doth so easily beset us (Hebrews 12:1).*

Quite often, the thing that we are told to put off is not obvious in the sight of man, but in the eyes of God. It separates us from His grace and favor, and prevents us from obtaining victory over the enemy. When we exercise our free wills to sanctify ourselves for the glory of God, we will find that God rises to our aide and defense. He is quick to honor those who endeavor to honor Him.

The Fifth action: David *Mobilized His forces*. *"…David hasted and ran toward the army to meet the Philistine" (vs.48)* Notice also that before David disclosed the contents of his bag, he mobilized himself first. Unless you take action and get into the proximity of the expected miracle zone, you are only shooting the breeze, he mobilized himself!

From the moment David opened his mouth, he never ceased to speak forth words of faith and deliverance. David spoke prophetically to his challenge; he declared the outcome of the battle, before the battle began. Notice his speech from the moment he came on the scene, *"And David spake to the men that stood by him, saying, what shall be done to the man that killeth this Philistine?" (Samuel 17:26).*

"And David said to Saul, let no man's heart fail because of him; thy servant will go and fight with the Philistine" vs. 32.

Prophesy your outcome, declare it!

David proceeded to predict the fate of Goliath; vs.36 *"Thy servant slew both the lion and the bear: and **this uncircumcised Philistine shall be as one of them**..."* You will notice that the weapon of the spoken word of faith advances more and more with confidence toward its target. David knew that faith activates the invisible power of God. He took it to another level and said: *"...Moreover, the Lord that delivered me out of the paw of the lion; and out of the paw of the bear, he will deliver me out of the hand of this Philistine" (vs. 37).*

Observe how David attributed his previous successes to the Lord. His God honoring testimony of faith used his former challenges as a stepping stone to improve his faith in God to count upon Him for further victory. *"David said moreover..., he will deliver me out of the hand of this Philistine" (1Samuel 17:37).*

David was *'Armed and Extremely Dangerous,'* he was not just filled with talk, but he had faith-packed actions to back it up. He used five action principles. He; (1) Minimized his fears, (2) Maximized his faith, (3) Magnified his fervor, (4) Manifested his freedom, and (5) Mobilized his forces. David had a *five* piece armor that he took with him into battle, vs.40. He had (1) His shepherd's staff or club, (2) *five* smooth stones, (3) a shepherd's bag; (4) his sling was in his hand, and (5) His faith in God (vs. 36-37).

What I have found in many a conflict, is two opponents can have the same weapons, but it's the spirit of the man that makes the decisive difference. It is the man that makes the invisible weapon lethal. It is a very sad thing to see when someone with full gear and modern equipment get himself whipped by an opponent with inferior stuff. It is not so much what you have, but how you use it! Notice the frequent occurrence of the number five in the battle of David versus Goliath. David employed five faith-principles, carried five pieces of armor, and chose five smooth stones as offensive weapons of deployment. You will notice that throughout the Scriptures, the number five is often used to signify grace; David relied heavily on the unmerited favor of God.

Goliath was a type of anti-Christ who cursed David by his gods (vs.43). His name means, soothsayer, connecting him to the source of evil. He is linked to the number 666, (a) He was six cubits high (1 Samuel 17:4), (b) He had six pieces of armor enumerated; helmet, coat of mail, greaves, target, staff, and shield, (1 Samuel 17:5-7), and(c) His spear's head weighed six hundred shekels of iron (1 Samuel 17:7). Goliath's armaments were three sixes. He represents the end time satanic trinity of false prophet, beast, and anti-Christ. Not only did Goliath look big, but he talked big, and he used words also as a weapon. As though his intimidating size was not enough; he spoke with arrogance and displayed undaunted confidence.

It was not Goliath's enormous size that caused Israel to shrink into retreat, but his trash talk. It was emotionally and mentally over-powering. Isn't that like the devil? He uses the same intimidating talk today; belittling, defaming, maligning, reviling, smearing, swearing and talking mess.

"Meanwhile, the Philistine, with his shield bearer in front of him, kept coming closer to David. He looked David over and saw that he was only a boy, ruddy and handsome, and he despised him. He said to David, "Am I a dog, that you come at me with sticks?" And the Philistine cursed David by his gods. "Come here," he said, "and I'll give your flesh to the birds of the air and the beasts of the field!"
(1 Samuel 17:41-44 New International Ver.).

He was saying; *"I'll show you who the tough guy really is...I'll beat the living daylights out of you..." I'll beat you down so hard; you won't even know what hit you, come to me little fellow!"*

What we must understand here is that the battle was already raging in the verbal arena, because Goliath had released verbal curses at David by his gods (demons) vs.43. We must know how to reverse the curse! It was a spiritual battle of words before it became a physical battle of weapons. David identified the weapons of Goliath as carnal, and employed the name of the Lord as a defense against the curses Goliath had spoken over his life. "Then said David to the Philistine, *"Thou comest to me with a sword, and with a spear, and with a shield:* **but I come to thee in the name of the Lord of hosts..."** *(Verse 45).*

There is protection and deliverance in the name of Jesus, and David understood that. *"The name of the LORD is a strong tower: the righteous runneth into it, and is safe" (Proverbs 18:10).* David found safety and protection in the Lord; from every curse Goliath hurled against him. He selected weapons that were pertinent and relevant to the challenges that he faced, he understood the importance of relativity, and released words of faith, like a spear against Goliath.

There are times when a warrior cannot be satisfied just to break the enemy, but he must grind him to powder. David was not content to engage in physical battle until he had fully mobilized his forces, and one of his main mobilizing forces was *his word.*

The Bible says, *"Through faith we understand that the worlds were framed by the Word of God, so that the things which are seen were not made of things which do appear" (Hebrews 11:3).*

David mobilized six predictions that framed the outcome of what he hoped for, by declaring them. In verses 46-47 He said:

(1) This day will Jehovah deliver thee into my hand

(2) I will smite thee

(3) I will take off your head

(4) I will give the carcasses of the host of the Philistines this day unto the fowls of the air, and to the wild beasts of the earth that all the earth may know that there is a God in Israel

(5) And all the assembly shall know that the Lord saveth not with sword and spear: for the battle is the Lord's, and

(6) He will give you into our hands.

David promised to take off Goliath's head, and that was not trash talk. There is nothing like a soldier whose heart is bigger than his mouth.

Now the hype was peaked, and enough was enough, this was the moment of reckoning; now he will face off with Goliath one on one. Now, who will be man enough to bring it on?

What's in the bag? That is probably the question most frequently asked concerning you in the day of *your* battle. Whatever it is that you have at your disposal, whatever your resources are, or your arsenal holds, whatever that trump card is that you hold, be sure that it is a prayerfully selected, tried, and proven weapon of war. God has a host of weapons in His arsenal that are available to the believer, such as: His Word, Warfare prayer, Binding, Loosing, Praises, Marching, Shouting, Dancing, Singing, Keeping Silent, Written Documents, Standing still before God, and many more. Choose your weapon prayerfully!

David chose five smooth stones out of the brook, and put them in his bag (vs. 40). The selection of your weapons is a critical part of your warfare. Notice, the bible says; *"David chose him five smooth stones."* **There comes a time when you will have to do it for yourself.**

There are some things that neither your spouse, your staff, your armor bearer, nor your prayer partner will be able to do for you; you have got to do it for yourself, select your own stone!

In my early, youthful days of growing up in the island of Jamaica, we used to make our sling-shots from a "Y" shaped branch of the Lignum Vitae tree. It was a very durable tree, whose branches were flexible for extreme bending without easily breaking. We used the red tubes from the wheels of our bicycles, because unlike the black tubes it had more elasticity and greater thrust. We used these weapons to hunt birds in the bushes of Vineyard Town, Kingston 3. As a child, I had enough sense to know that while hunting from a long distance, I needed a smooth heavy object to shoot at my prey from a long distance, such as; iron marbles or smooth round stones, which were more aerodynamic than the objects which had jagged edges, and were not stable against the wind. In like manner, the child of God should be deliberate to deploy God's mighty weapons of war, for they are the most effective in waging a campaign against the enemy; we must choose our weapons wisely!

David used what he had at his disposal and what he was familiar with; his sling, a club, and some smooth stones. He came to the battle front Armed and Extremely Dangerous.

"When the Philistine arose and came and drew near to meet David, David ran quickly toward the battle line to meet the Philistine. And David put his hand in his bag and took out a stone, and slung it, and struck the Philistine on his forehead; the stone sank into his forehead, and he fell on his face to the ground. So David prevailed over the Philistine with a sling and with a stone, and struck the Philistine, and killed him; there was no sword in the hand of David. Then David ran and stood over the Philistine, and took his sword and drew it out of its sheath, and killed him, and cut off his head with it. When the

Philistines saw that their champion was dead, they fled"
(1Samuel 17:48-52 RSV).

It's not enough to stand triumphantly
upon your opponent; unless you beheaded
him you cannot enjoy total victory.

David took off the head of Goliath as he promised, Glory to God! He understood that the serpent stores his venom in his head, and that the head is the central computer; so he disabled the beast! David took the head of Goliath to Jerusalem (1 Samuel 17:54), hence, the place is called "Golgotha," the place of the skull.

It was upon Golgotha's hill that Jesus was crucified. He was elevated from the earth upon the cross; He crushed the 'skull' of every serpent and spiritual Goliath so that we might be free to serve Him. Never forget, that whenever you prayerfully Identify and Select Your Weapon for the battle at hand, you will be Armed and Extremely Dangerous. God will give you the head of your enemies!

It is my sincere prayer for you that you would come into a personal knowledge of the awesome *Power of Intercession.* May the Lord make known to you the *Reality of our Warfare*, taking you *Through the Open Doors* of His uncommon favor. I pray that you obtain the victory in *The Territorial War* we fight; for our community, our nation, and our world. Take what you have learned from these writings and be found *Dismantling the Strongholds* of the enemies of the cross.

Remember to survey your thoughts prayerfully, being sure you have the mind of Christ, that you may stand victorious in the *Battlefield of the Mind. A change of Mind* is not an option, but an absolute necessity in order to *Recognize Who the Real Enemy Is*. I pray that yours battles will go beyond *Shallow Victories*, and be lasting ones.

May the Lord give you the fortitude of *Winning the War Within*. I thank God that the *Faith Charged Word*, which is in you, will enable you to win *The Psychological War*. Put on the whole armor of God, because when you are *Fully Dressed for Battle* you will be furnished completely to engage the unseen forces and win. I pray that your discernment will be sharpened by the Holy Spirit, and like David, you too, will *Identify and Select Your Weapon of War*. May the Lord of heaven bless and keep you, and may you be victorious in all your undertakings, having done all to stand, stand triumphantly in Jesus name, Armed, and Extremely Dangerous!

READER'S DIGEST

My Personal Reflection

_____

_____

_____

_____

_____

_____

_____

_____

_____

_____

_____

_____

_____

_____

_____

_____

_____